LUTHER
An Introduction to his Thought

LUTHER

An Introduction to his Thought

GERHARD EBELING

TRANSLATED BY R. A. WILSON

COLLINS

ST JAMES'S PLACE, LONDON

1970

First published by J. C. B. Mohr (Paul Siebeck), Tübingen, 1964
as *Luther: Einführung in sein Denken*

S.B.N. 00 215458 7

Printed in Great Britain
Collins Clear-Type Press
London and Glasgow

CONTENTS

ACKNOWLEDGEMENTS

The author, translator and publishers wish to acknowledge their indebtedness for permission to reproduce copyright material from *Reformation Writings of Martin Luther*, volume I, by Bertram Lee Woolf, published by Lutterworth Press, London, 1952.

REFERENCES

References to the Weimar Edition of Luther's works (*Kritische Gesamtausgabe der Werke D. Martin Luthers*, Weimar, 1883 ff.) are given only by volume, page and line number. References to the selected edition published in Bonn, to the Weimar editions of the German Bible, Luther's Table Talk and his correspondence, and to the English translation of a selection of Luther's works by Bertram Lee Woolf are given as below. The year of each quotation is given in parentheses, and in the case of the letters, the exact date.

Bonn Ed.   *Luthers Werke in Auswahl*, ed. by O. Clemen.

WA, TR   *Kritische Gesamtausgabe*, etc. (*Tischreden*), Weimar Ed. (Table Talk).

WA, Br   *Kritische Gesamtausgabe*, etc. (*Briefwechsel*), Weimar Ed. (Correspondence).

WA, DB   *Kritische Gesamtausgabe*, etc. (*Deutsche Bibel*), Weimar Ed. (German Bible).

Woolf   *Reformation Writings of Martin Luther*, trans. and annot. by Bertram Lee Woolf (Lutterworth, 1952).

PREFACE

THE attempt made in this book to provide an introduction to the thought of Luther does not assume any specialist knowledge on the part of the reader, but only that he is prepared to think along with and through what is presented here. Instead of producing a popular work, and making extensive use of the more striking elements of Luther's biography—such portraits of Luther are perhaps partly responsible for the ignorance of Luther on the part of educated persons in our day—I have taken on the task, the most difficult from the theological point of view, of examining the tension that runs through the whole of Luther's thought, the play between the harsh opposition of opposing theses and the spirit of compromise which reconciles both sides of an issue. But I have tried to do this not by compiling a list of individual ideas to illustrate this theme, or by giving an account of Luther's theology as a whole, but by concentrating as it were on the inner dynamic of his thought; this seemed the best way to make clear its contemporary validity.

The chapters that follow were first given as lectures to members of all faculties of the University of Zürich in the winter term 1962/63, and a selection also as public lectures at Drew University, Madison, New Jersey, in the autumn term of 1963. I have also included a lecture first given on 10th December 1963, as one of a series of lectures on the subject 'The Idea of

God in the West', sponsored by the *Goethe-Gesellschaft* in Wiesbaden, and published with the rest of the series under that title by Kohlhammer of Stuttgart. I wish to thank the publishers for permitting its republication here.

The lectures are reproduced as they were given. This explains why there are lengthy quotations in certain places, but far too few as a whole. I have added no further quotations. References are given to the complete critical edition of the works of Luther published at Weimar from 1883 onwards, and also to the selected edition published in Bonn by O. Clemen. The student is referred to the useful key to the editions of the works of Luther in Kurt Aland, *Hilfsbuch zum Luther-studium*, 1957. The year in which each statement was made is given in brackets, and in the case of the letters, the exact date.

Where I have made use of the suggestions of others, it has not been possible to acknowledge this explicitly, and I have had to exclude almost all references to other literature. I must leave it to the experts to find out where I agree and where I differ from other Luther scholars; I can only say in general how very much I am indebted to them. Bibliographies can be found in the articles: 'Luther, Martin, I, Leben und Schriften' by Heinrich Bornkamm, and 'II, Theologie' by Gerhard Ebeling, in *Die Religion in Geschichte und Gegenwart*, 3rd ed., vol. IV, 1960. The reader who wishes orientation in Luther's biography and a summary of the sources will find them in Franz Lau, *Luther* (trans. by R. H. Fischer, S.C.M. Press, London, 1963) and in Heinrich Fausel, *D. Martin Luther. Der Reformator im Kampf um Evangelium und Kirche. Sein Werden und Wirken im Spiegel eigener Zeugnisse* (Calwer Verlag, Stuttgart, 1955).

GERHARD EBELING

Zürich, July, 1964

CHAPTER I

LUTHER'S LINGUISTIC INNOVATION

LECTURES for all faculties are a test both of the university and of our role in it. We may think of the 'university' in the original personal sense of the term, the *universitas magistrorum et scholarium*, as an association of teachers and students with no social or national restrictions, gathered in one place to carry out the *studium litterarum*. Or we may think of it in the new modern sense of the *universitas litterarum*, where the essential point is the association of the different branches of knowledge. In either case, lectures intended for all faculties offer an opportunity for the *universitas* to be manifested in something not conditioned by the limits imposed by separate faculties, or arranged for convenience of organization or for ceremonial reasons. Instead they can form part of its everyday task of study, because their subject genuinely concerns everyone.

No course of lectures can claim to be of interest to every faculty on the grounds that it deals with a general theme that lies beyond the competence of every individual faculty; for, of course, it represents one particular faculty which is speaking to the others. Nor is it sufficient for the lectures to be given in a popularized form comprehensible to everyone. (Naturally, the lecturer ought to avoid his own technical terminology as far as possible; to do so is a wholesome test of his understanding of his own subject.) The real justification for a course of lectures for all faculties is this. It demonstrates that what is studied by one faculty is of interest to all. Of course it is usual to look carefully for a theme appropriate to this purpose, but only so that the theme may suitably show how the work of a particular faculty concerns everyone. And it is a test of the university in two senses. First, are we prepared to take an interest in something that concerns us, although not in the area of our own faculty? Second, and even more important, are we able to claim that our own work is relevant to the university and to subject our work to the judgement of the university?

There are branches of study which require such a high degree of specialist knowledge and familiarity with a technical language that, even though non-specialists are necessarily affected by these studies, it is very difficult to explain the technical language to them. The exact contrary seems to be the case with *theology*. Of course to a certain extent theology also has its specialist terminology. But on the whole, at least with regard to its vocabulary, theology does not use a language that is unknown to non-theologians. What makes the language of theology seem to be so difficult or even incomprehensible is the feeling which so many people share that the *subject-matter* of theology is inaccessible to them. They cannot perceive anything in it which impresses itself upon everyone as a reality. This makes it seem doubtful whether theology is a true branch of knowledge, and so calls into question not only theology's place in the university, but also the claim of a theological lecture to be of interest to students of every faculty.

As an institution, the university originated in a period in which the primacy of theology, embracing and dominating every other faculty, was taken for granted. The theological faculty still possesses a primacy of honour in many universities, but for historical reasons, not because its subject-matter is generally accepted. Moreover, it is doubtful whether a universal system of knowledge can be constructed in our day, with or without the inclusion of theology. What does this mean for the university as a whole, and especially for the way in which the theological faculty regards itself? We can only hint at the answer here by saying that the existence of different faculties, including the faculty of theology, in the same university is justified only as a challenge to them to demonstrate their mutual responsibility. If the deepest urge which drives us to seek knowledge is the kind of thinking which recognizes its wider responsibility, a lecture for students of all faculties signifies not the abandonment by one faculty of its rigorous scientific method, but a determination to see the task of scientific study in a profound sense, as a readiness to accept this responsibility.

These introductory reflections on the nature of the present lectures are by no means incidental to our theme. In the case of Martin Luther there are special reasons for bearing in mind that the university was the primary place in which his life and work was conducted. The various pictures that we have of him: the former monk, the preacher, the writer, the reformer of the Church, the spiritual leader of a popular movement which spread throughout Europe, make it very easy to forget that his work as a university professor was not just incidental to his other work. In fact, the rest of his work was intimately related to his university post, and the obligation this imposed was expressed in his doctorate, a degree which at that time was still rare, and one which was held by few professors.

Luther was a promising student, who had already successfully completed the general basic course in the faculty of arts, and had taken the degree of Master of Arts. In accordance with his father's wish he had gone on to the study of law, when he suddenly left the university. But his entry into the monastery was only a transitory interruption in his academic career, though this he had not planned in advance. His superiors assigned him to the study of theology. Finally, against his strong opposition, he was appointed as the biblical lecturer at Wittenberg, a chair held by the Augustinian Hermits. 'I . . ., Dr. Martin, was called and forced to become a doctor, against my will, from pure obedience, and had to accept a doctor's teaching post, and promise and vow on my beloved holy scriptures to preach and teach them faithfully and sincerely.'[1] This reminiscence, uttered precisely twenty years after he assumed his professorship, is no exaggeration of the pressure placed upon him. Indeed, it illuminates the gloomy foreboding he had at the time of an inescapable weight of responsibility, by its reference to the overwhelming experience he had undergone in the meantime: 'In the course of this teaching', he continued, 'the papacy slipped away from me.'[2] In other words, his whole world fell apart.

We cannot at this point go into the profound meaning of this affirmation. Nevertheless, it is clear that this academic post, with its close associations with the preaching ministry, was Luther's starting-point and remained the firm foundation which compelled and enabled him to undertake the revolutionary activity which is customarily and inadequately known as the 'Reformation'. Unless this close connection with Luther's calling as a university professor is taken into account, the true essence and meaning of the Reformation is bound to be misinterpreted, the figure of the reformer himself distorted. All Luther's most characteristic actions, his struggle and his testimony, his work as a publicist and his bitter polemics, his activities as a churchman and popular teacher, can only be seen in their true light when we recognize in them the work of the professor of holy scripture, whose teaching was the product of rigorous intellectual concentration—clearly to be recognized in his scholarly handwriting—and whose actions were no more than the persevering, conscientious and responsible putting into practice of his teaching. His teaching post drove him to take a course that made him the focus of the history of his age. At the same time it provided his most reliable support when he was plagued by the question of the legitimacy of his revolutionary activity and of the way in which he could exercise his responsibility for the consequences of his teaching. For 'if God does not summon you to do a work, who are you, you fool, that you dare to take it upon yourself? ... A certainty of divine calling is necessary for a good work ...'[3] Luther received this certainty of vocation from the sober fact of his academic calling, which gave him the right and the duty to speak, even against his monastic vows and his duty of obedience to the hierarchy and the Church: 'I have often said, and say again: I would not exchange my professorship for anything in the world; for in truth I should have been bound in the end to sink into despair at the weary and heavy task that was laid upon me, if I had begun it surreptitiously, without a calling and a command. But God and the whole world must bear witness that I began my teaching and preaching office publicly, and have conducted it publicly up to the present, by God's grace and help.'[4]

We must look a little closer at Luther's relationship with the university. It is no exaggeration to say that never in the history of the university has the work of a scholar, in the study and in the lecture-room, had so direct and so extensive an influence upon the world, and changed it so much. If we ask what is the utmost that can be expected from a university, Luther provides the answer. Even a brief glance at his career reveals certain remarkable facts, usually overlooked in the upheaval of the Reformation, which are perhaps not unique but are very unusual.

When Luther took up his professorial post, Wittenberg was still a new and unimportant university. It had been founded ten years previously by the Elector of Saxony, Frederick the Wise, principally because of dynastic rivalries, in a town which, with its limited material provisions, could not compete with the long tradition of the great universities of the Empire, such as Vienna, Heidelberg, Cologne, Erfurt, Leipzig, and others. A few years after Luther began to teach, however, the number of students went up by leaps and bounds—a dramatic process which we can follow from comments in Luther's letters.[5] In 1519, he noted that the number of students was rising like a flood, and that the town was quite unable to accommodate them. Many had to return home, he tells us in 1520. We also have a number of figures. Spalatin, the Elector's chaplain, records that as early as the end of 1518 Melanchthon's Greek lectures were regularly attended by four hundred students, while he estimated that two years later the number had risen to five or six hundred. It was an international concourse; there were representatives not only from every part of Germany, but also from Switzerland, Poland and Bohemia, and later on from almost every European nation. By 1520 Wittenberg far surpassed every other German university. For several decades it was far and away the leading one.

There is a further point. The opening stages of the movement initiated by Luther were regarded by those who took part in it as a university reform, a reorganization of academic instruction and the awakening of a new academic spirit. In the spring of 1517, that is, before the dispute over indulgences let loose the flood of events which formed the outward course of the

Reformation, Luther wrote: 'Our theology and St. Augustine are making good progress, and are dominant in our university, thanks to what God has done. Aristotle is gradually declining, and is approaching his imminent and final demise. To an astonishing extent, lectures on the *Sententiae* are disdained, and the only people who can expect anyone to attend their lectures are those who have resolved to deal with this theology, that is, the Bible or St. Augustine, or one of the other neglected Fathers of the Church.'[6] A year later Luther wrote to his former teacher in Erfurt, Professor Jodokus Trutfetter: 'I am firmly convinced that it is impossible to reform the Church unless the canons, the decretals, scholastic theology, philosophy and logic, as they are now taught, are completely uprooted, and other subjects are taught. And I go so far in this conviction, as to beg the Lord every day that the study of the Bible and the holy Fathers may at once be restored in all its purity.'[7] The whole subsequent course of the Reformation was accompanied by extremely significant educational and university reforms. We are looking at only a part of the Reformation, but a very important part, when we consider it as a decisive turning-point in the history of the university, and hence in the history of education as a whole.

Thus from many points of view one can claim that the whole university has an interest in Luther, particularly as not only theologians, but also historians, philologists, philosophers and legal historians are also involved in the study of Luther. But we shall deal not with these numerous subsidiary issues, but with the fundamental point which underlies them all.

Though it is indisputable that a knowledge of Luther forms part of a general education, most people's knowledge of him is restricted to a few set clichés, formed without a real understanding of the structure of his thought. Considering the change Luther wrought in the world and the fact that the hidden effects of his work influence us perhaps even more than those of which we are aware, the degree of ignorance concerning Luther amongst educated people at the present day, their indifference to him and their failure to come to terms with him, is shameful. One might go so far as to say that Luther has been forgotten. Even theology has not benefited as much as one might have expected from the recent upsurge in research on Luther. Furthermore, amongst Church people as a whole a handful of slogans, no longer understood in their proper sense, such as 'justification by faith alone' or 'the priesthood of all believers', and conventional romantic ideas such as that of the 'hammer-blows on the church door at Wittenberg', the burning of the bull of excommunication, and so forth, have hindered rather than promoted a true knowledge of Luther. The question which we have to answer, as we stand here before the university, is this: why has more attention been paid, in the intellectual conflicts of the present day, particularly those which take place in the field of philosophy, to Augustine, Thomas Aquinas and Kierkegaard amongst thinkers of the past, than to Luther?

Evidently this has not always been the case. The attempt to obtain an intellectual understanding of the life and work of Luther has gone on continuously throughout the centuries since the Reformation. Selections from numerous writers in this field are available with commentaries in many recent studies.[8] The history of the understanding of Luther—including the history of the portrayal of his personality, which forms a parallel to it—is a reflection of the whole history of thought. The men of the Reformation century, with the exception of his opponents, regarded Luther as an extraordinary occurrence, part of the history of salvation itself, and the attempt was made to express this view by applying the category of 'prophet'. No less a person than Huldrych Zwingli was responsible for this view of Luther. He calls him 'Elijah' in a letter, written in the autumn of 1519, to the humanist jurist Ulrich Zasius in Freiburg im Breisgau.[9] The period of Protestant orthodoxy modified the view of him as a prophet, emphasizing more his restoration of pure doctrine. A section *de vocatione Lutheri* actually occurs as a part of dogmatic theology in some works of early Protestant orthodoxy. Pietism made a similar appeal to Luther, but distinguished between Luther in his early and in his later years. A contrast was drawn between the period when he was supposed to have become embittered by his opposition to the enthusiastic sects and by disputes within Protestantism, if not actually inclined to a certain extent to a return to Catholicism, and the early period in which, it was felt, the gospel of repentance and grace, still pure and still close to the devotional literature of German mysticism which was so highly regarded by pietism, remained clearly visible. The Enlightenment also saw Luther as its pattern and example, emphasizing the freedom of conscience which he had made possible. A more profound version of this view of Luther, associated with the appreciation by the writers of the *Sturm und Drang* period of Luther's linguistic genius, dominated the view of Luther held by the thinkers of the German classical period and of idealism; then romanticism, together with a growing historical understanding, began to ask what Luther's true place was in the transition from the Middle Ages to the modern period. The dominant view, inspired by denominational and idealist motives, regarded Luther as the forerunner of the modern period. It was Ernst Troeltsch who first showed the considerable extent to which the orientation of Luther's thought depended upon the questions posed by the Middle Ages, and the part it played in retarding the process of secularization which took place from the Renaissance to the modern period.

We have given only a rough outline of the kaleidoscopic variety of views of Luther. But we must not jump to the conclusion that every interpretation of Luther is arbitrary and capricious. We must rather lay special emphasis on the necessary mutual relationship between one's understanding of history and one's understanding of one's self. The effect of this relationship is greater, the more what we find expressed in history touches the basic problems of our own existence. Thus it is perfectly proper for each age to put forward a fresh understanding and reinterpretation of so epoch-making a linguistic innovation[10] as is represented by Luther, and that different issues should be in dispute in every period. Nevertheless, it is not difficult to see that the changes in the understanding of Luther which we have outlined were not based as a whole on an intensive study of the sources, but were derived essentially from sweeping value judgements.

That our own time has not produced a comparable summary judgement upon Luther is due, amongst other important reasons, to the caution induced by an understanding of the nature of historical change. While the question whether Luther belonged to the Middle Ages or to the modern period must not be reduced to a straightforward alternative, and cannot be elucidated with the aid of conventional intellectual clichés, it nevertheless provides a sound methodological guide to the study of Luther. Scholars have learned—some only recently, and some, indeed, not at all—that the careful evaluation of the traditions which Luther inherited is indispensable to any profound interpretation, as this is the only means of distinguishing what it was in fact which first came to utterance in his work. Moreover, this problem of the transition between one period and another leads us to the heart of the historical phenomenon of Luther himself. Conrad Ferdinand Meyer, in his poem *Huttens letzte Tage*, gave incomparable expression to this:

> The more grievously a son of earth struggles to be free, the more powerfully he stirs our humanity.
>
> I, who early escaped from the cell, shudder, at the time Luther struggled within it.
>
> He kept concealed within his breast the battle which now rages over half the earth.
>
> With the courage of death he broke the barrier of the cloister—the greatest things are achieved by him who can do no other.
>
> He perceived the immense catastrophe of the times, and firmly grasped his Bible.
>
> Within his soul the future fought with the past—two wrestlers, gasping and locked together.
>
> His mind was the battle-ground of two ages—I do not wonder that he saw demons!

Has this struggle been resolved for us? Is the explanation of the way Luther is forgotten at the present day that those who have resolutely turned to what is new regard Luther, who belonged to a period of transition, as superseded, while those who cling fiercely to the old do not wish to be drawn into the struggle which awaits them in Luther? This disregard for Luther unquestionably contains an element of the fear of something uncanny, of which no one wishes to be reminded. So long as the 'two ages', the old and the new, which are locked in conflict, are seen merely as two successive periods in the course of the history of thought, our understanding will be purely superficial, and we shall not have found the key to the real substance of what concerns us here. Luther also realized that he was under the influence of the struggle between the old and the new, a conflict between two ages—but in a quite different sense, that of the antithesis between the old and the new man, the 'age of the law' and the 'age of grace'.[11] This conflict, most pointedly expressed in the paradoxical formula *simul iustus—simul peccator*—'righteous and a sinner at one and the same time'— is the fundamental and typical characteristic of Luther's thought. And we are perhaps not far wrong if we suspect that there may be a profound and hidden relationship between this new definition of the field of conflict between two ages in the theological sense, and the ultimate bone of contention in the battle between one age and the next.

This points to the method which we shall follow. Our method is quite different from the conventional and well-worn pattern of works on Luther. We shall not follow the obvious course of giving a chronological and biographical account, though we have no intention of departing from strict historical accuracy. Nor shall we attempt to portray his personality, either in psychological terms, or in symbolical form, as for example (an aberration which ought not to go unmentioned) the 'eternal German', a concept applied to Luther not merely in the recent past, but as early as the period of idealism. Nor shall we attempt to give a systematic description of his most important ideas, ordered according to the principal subjects of dogmatic theology: the scriptures, faith, the sacraments, the Church, civil authority, etc. In one sense what we propose is more modest: we are only attempting an *introduction* to the thought of Luther. Consequently, we renounce from the start any attempt to be comprehensive. We seek no more than to give an introduction to Luther, leading to an encounter that may be a basis for further study. In another sense, what is proposed is more ambitious than other alternatives. We do not intend to be satisfied merely with the presentation of individual facts or ideas, but to attempt to penetrate to the cause which gave rise to them. We must be drawn into the *thought* of Luther, into a process in which we ourselves must share if we intend not merely to say what his ideas are, but to understand them; not merely to repeat his words, but to respond to them.

In order to carry out this intention, we must first map out the path to be followed. The clue to this seems to lie in the observation that Luther's thought always contains an antithesis, tension between strongly opposed but related polarities: theology and philosophy, the letter and the Spirit, the law and the gospel, the double use of the law, person and works, faith and love, the kingdom of Christ and the kingdom of the world, man as a Christian and man in the world, freedom and bondage, God hidden and God revealed—to mention only the most important examples. These will be the guides which will lead us into the process of Luther's thinking.

Thus it can be seen at once that the question of the nature of his thinking cannot be answered by reference to general forms or structures of thought. His thinking, and the substance of what he thought, can only be understood together as a unity. Perhaps this is why Luther is so much a closed book to the thought of our time. We, like Erasmus, find Luther's thought too assertive, too much a confession of faith, and his mode of thought, in consequence, too little humanist and too barbaric.

We need not discuss what truth there is in this impression. As we inquire into Luther's thought, we are also ready to encounter Luther as a linguistic innovator. For he had no other concern than to give proper utterance to the word.

First of all, however, we must discuss his person, his acts and his words by way of introduction.

CHAPTER 2

LUTHER'S PERSON

THE expression 'Luther's linguistic innovation' (*Luther als Sprachereignis*) has shown the direction we must follow in our whole attempt to come to grips with Luther. The expression is one which has been formed as a result of the constant concern of present-day theology with hermeneutics, with the right interpretation of texts and sources.[1] It implies a particular understanding of what is the real concern of historical study. It is no accident that an historical event of such extraordinary profundity and far-reaching effect as the career of Luther, which overtook and transformed the West like an earthquake, should provoke a consideration of the nature of history, and the right way to conduct an historical inquiry. We cannot enter here into a full discussion of this problem. We shall do no more than elucidate the direction given to our own inquiry by the expression 'linguistic innovation' by defining it in certain respects.

It is immediately obvious that it leads us to consider the substance of what Luther expressed in his words and writings, rather than to concentrate upon his personality. Thus the subject of our inquiry is not that which Goethe, writing in 1817 about the third centenary of the beginning of the Reformation, regarded as the only matter worthy of consideration: 'Between ourselves, there is nothing of interest in the whole matter except the character of Luther, and this is also the only thing which makes any real impression upon the mass of the people. Everything else is confused rubbish, with which we are still daily burdened.'[2] But it would likewise be a misunderstanding to describe the subject of our inquiry as 'Luther's teaching', in so far as this simply means a dogmatic system which has to be accepted as such. A major 'linguistic innovation' is obviously more than a 'dogmatic construction'. Whereas the latter at least tends to become something final and conclusive, the expression 'linguistic innovation' implies a process of opening up, of revelation and disclosure. Whereas someone else's dogmatic construction offers at best a dwelling-place in which one can find shelter as a guest and a stranger, a 'linguistic innovation' provides a place to live and make one's own home.

To come to grips with Luther as linguistic innovation does not mean abandoning the theological consideration of his work in favour of the general cultural point of view, through which Luther's achievement has rightly become so famous, regardless of denominational views. Klopstock considered that 'no one who knows what a language is can come face to face with Luther without venerating him. There is no nation in which one man has done so much to form its language.'[3] Herder affirms: 'It is he who awoke and set free the sleeping giant of the German language; it is he who cast out the trade in mere words of scholasticism like the tables of the money-changers; through his Reformation, he made a whole nation able to think and to feel. It is of no account that Erasmus, perhaps the most precise scholar the world has ever known, accused him of having brought Latin literature to an end. This reproach is no disgrace to him, and it should not be denied in the face of all the historical facts. For Latin religion, scholastic learning and the Roman language were far too closely bound together.'[4] Friedrich Schlegel, who became a convert to

Catholicism, made this judgement on Luther's translation of the Bible: 'Equally, we owe an unmistakable debt to him personally for his forceful language and the spirit of his writing, his lofty and powerful mode of expression in German. For even in his own writings there is an eloquence such as has rarely appeared with such a force in any country throughout the centuries. Of course, his style also possesses all the attributes which one expects to find in a completely revolutionary eloquence. But this revolutionary style, with a force peculiar to Luther, is not found merely in his semi-political writings, his violent interventions in public life which shook it to the very depths, such as the address "To the Nobility of the German Nation", but also in all his other works. For in almost all his writings we find ourselves face to face with his great inward struggle. It is as though within this human soul, so powerful and so richly endowed by God and by nature, two worlds were in conflict, both seeking to tear at each other. Everywhere in his writings there is a struggle between light and darkness, between a firm and unshakable faith and his equally wild and unrestrained passion, between God and himself.'[5]

These classical utterances on Luther's linguistic genius of course make it clear that such a creative effect on the German language cannot be reduced to formal categories. And in fact the service he performed for the German language is a noteworthy manifestation of what we are referring to, in a wider sense, as a 'linguistic innovation'. Luther describes the way in which the fundamental relationship between language and theology operates in the address 'To the Councilmen of All Cities in Germany, That They Establish and Maintain Christian Schools' (1524): 'Although the gospel came and comes every day through the Holy Spirit alone, nevertheless it came by means of languages, spread through them, and must also be maintained through them. . . . Thus if the gospel is dear to us, we must pay great attention to the languages in which it comes. For it was not without purpose that God let the scripture be written in two languages alone, the Old Testament in Hebrew and the New in Greek. . . . And let us realize that we shall scarcely be able to maintain the gospel without languages. Languages are the sheaths in which the knife of the Spirit is contained. They are the case in which this jewel is borne. They are the vessel in which the drink is held. They are the room in which this food is stored. And as the gospel itself tells us [Matt. 14: 20], they are the baskets in which the bread and fish and fragments are gathered up. In fact wherever we allow languages to be neglected, we shall lose not only the gospel, but will also finally come to the point where we can speak or write neither Latin nor German properly.'[6]

But at this point a real issue, which concerns Christianity and in fact the whole world, seems to have been confused to a damaging extent with the personality of an individual. The urgent question arises, whether the events of the Reformation may not amount to problematical consequences provoked by an extremely wilful personality, whose influence ought not to be increased by paying too much attention to him. And in fact anyone who is concerned for the spread of the gospel is bound to become suspicious when it is so closely associated with a single person, whose own experience and individual interpretation ought not to become the rule of faith. In the Catholic interpretation of Luther in particular, it has been alleged that subjectivism is the dominant characteristic of Luther himself and of his work.

However, it is quite certain that Luther rejected with great vehemence—'that we may be sure that the Church is not founded upon a bog or a dunghill'[7]—any submission to the authority of a human being in matters of faith and any reliance on human ordinances of one's own choosing instead of the liberating word of God. He made it quite clear that the same was true of anyone's attitude to his own person. In the 'Sincere Admonition to all Christians to Guard Against Insurrection and Rebellion' of 1522 he says: 'The first thing I ask is that people should not make use of my name, and should not call themselves Lutherans, but Christians. What is Luther? The teaching is not mine. Nor was I crucified for anyone. St. Paul, in 1 Cor. 3, would not tolerate Christians calling themselves Paul's or Peter's, but only Christians. How did I, poor stinking bag of maggots that I am, come to the point where people call the children of Christ by my evil name? Not so, dear friends, let us do away with party names, and be called Christians, for it is his teaching that we have. The papists are rightly called by a party name as long as they are not satisfied with the doctrine and the name of Christ, and want to be papists as well; let them be papists; for the Pope is their master. I am no one's master, nor do I wish to be. I share with all men the one common teaching of Christ, who alone is our master [Matt. 23: 8].'[8]

But even such a protest against dependence on human beings is at the same time a striking example of the way personality and teaching are closely involved with one another. Fundamentally, this is something which can be taken for granted in all intellectual activity, and has only to be understood in the proper sense. Admittedly, not every sphere of intellectual activity tolerates or demands in the same way or to the same degree the involvement and intervention of the historically unique and distinct personality of the creative mind. But in theology, as elsewhere, there is a connection between personality and works, and because of the subject of theology, it is particularly close. Thus theology does not demand that the personality be as far as possible secluded, but that it be drawn in as intensively as possible, provided this process is rightly understood. What is most significant in theology does not occur when the theologian adopts an indifferent and neutral personal attitude to the word, but when he responds to it, so that his utterances display the unmistakable hand of their author, and when even the circumstances of his life, that is, the situation in which he responds to the word, belong inseparably to his theological utterance.

And it is simply a fact that the study of Luther's theology involves us to a greater degree than in the case of almost any other theologian with his person. Luther's statement '*Sola . . . experientia facit theologum*'[9] is as it were a motto interpreting the whole of his life. If we turn to his theology, we cannot overlook his life and his experience. Even the question of the origin of his theology faces us with the difficult task of understanding the way he came to perceive the basic Reformation principle, that of justification by faith alone, which was involved on the one hand with a personal experience of crushing temptation and liberating certainty, and on the other hand with particular theological problems. Following on from this, we come to the breath-taking process by which, step by step, in a compelling association of bold temerity and sheer inevitability, a theology came into being which was not merely new by normal standards, but overwhelmed the force of fifteen hundred years of tradition. Luther's new understanding of the word of God, the sacraments, the Church, moral action and secular authority left no part of life untouched. An upheaval of this nature cannot be the product of uncommitted theoretical speculation; nor of course can it be the product of revolutionary activity, as is implied by the popular picture of Luther as an imperious and violent figure, deeply emotional in his behaviour. Rather, it is the putting into effect of a theological thinking so involved in its subject that to carry it out means the endurance of struggles of conscience, the risking and accepting of unavoidable decisions, and the total commitment of one's personal existence in the form of a theology which is lived existentially.

Naturally, this process brings with it great dangers of misunderstanding Luther or of being hypnotized by him. He is like an instrument which contains the most melodious and the most thunderous stops. Only a practised ear can appreciate all its harmonies. And unless we understand what it was that preoccupied his mind, we may be taken aback by the discovery that he was no 'saint', and sometimes flew out at his opponents with an unrestrained ferocity which cannot be adequately explained as the outburst of his own temperament, until one takes into account the force of his inner and outward struggles, and the overpowering burden of historical responsibility he had to bear. Furthermore, the realization of Luther's weaknesses is a guard against the danger, when person and works are so closely linked, of failing to distinguish between them. Lessing formulated this very precisely: 'I have such a veneration for Luther, that when everything has been considered, I am most pleased to have discovered a few small deficiencies in him, for in truth I would otherwise have been in danger of deifying him. The traces of humanity that I find in him are as precious to me as the most dazzling of his perfections. In fact I learn more from them, than from all the latter put together; and I regard it as a worthwhile thing to show them.'[10]

We turn now to the delineation of certain traits of Luther's personality. A psychological analysis would be inadequate to this task. That is not to say that such an analysis is not justified within its limits. Much, of course, can be said about his tendencies, abilities and character. The conclusion of one psychological analysis is that 'Luther appears to have been a personality showing dominant signs of cyclothymia, of a pyknic physique, with a scale of emotions alternating between hyperthymia and hypothymia, together with sthenic motivation.'[11] But what makes someone a person is not what is present in him and what proceeds from himself, but, if I may so phrase it, what goes on in and about him. Thus the decisive element in our picture of the intellectual features of a person is supplied by the linguistic process in which he encounters the traditions which press upon him, deals with them, comes into conflict with them, and in some cases changes them into something that is his own, which it is his task to utter. There are good reasons, therefore, why the question of someone's personality is identical with that of his office, his calling and his mission.

In the light of Luther's historical role, the question of his person falls in the main into two parts, which are, if I may be allowed a very summary expression: 'How did he become a Catholic theologian?' and 'How did he become a Protestant theologian?' Or, to phrase the questions in such a way as to make their historical implications more clear: 'How did he become a late medieval scholastic?' and 'How did he become a reformer?' It is also possible to ask a third question: 'How did the Luther of the early Reformation become the so-called "later" Luther?' While the latter question refers to what was only a gradual change, a mere shift of emphasis, the consideration of the first two processes is associated with the idea of a sudden reversal, an upheaval in his development in the nature of a conversion.

The sudden change which drove the young Master of Arts and student of jurisprudence into the monastery raises no particularly difficult problem. In every respect it displays typical medieval features. His lower-middle-class upbringing amongst a section of the community which was climbing socially was strict, but not excessively severe; he was religiously inclined by temperament, but also cheerful and companionable. In no sense was he the type of person who seeks gratification in an exaggerated devotion, despising the world. Against his natural inclination, he was driven by the experience of the imminence of death during a thunderstorm in open country, on to a course which he had not sought. Naturally, this step was not taken entirely without preparation. The problem of the salvation of his soul had obviously preoccupied him previously. A direct confrontation with death and imminent judgement aroused in him the desire to make a radical and determined attempt to arm himself, if he were given time, for this eventuality, so that when the time came he could face the inescapable reality of God under different conditions. He later summed up his purpose, no doubt accurately, in these words: 'I want to escape hell by being a monk.'[12] 'What we were trying to do was to deserve God and win God with works of this kind and to acquire the forgiveness of sins.'[13] The vows he had made in a moment of danger he fulfilled with sober resolution, after two weeks of consideration, by entering the monastery in Erfurt of the Augustinian Hermits, a mendicant order. Although he felt himself to be under compulsion, he adhered to this resolution as to a calling from God, even in the face of a suggestion, by his disappointed father, that it might perhaps be a delusion of Satan, and that God's commandment to obey one's parents ought to be weighed against it.[14]

Thus there was no question of a resolution to change his course of study and his vocation. It would naturally have been open to him to study theology without becoming a monk,

Rather, he was choosing to renounce every secular calling, and on principle at least to give up further study. Although his education destined him from the first to become a choir monk, the specific instruction of his superiors was necessary for him to undertake the study of theology. Preparation for the priesthood did not require the study of theology. Luther did not begin this until after his ordination, although in accordance with the scholastic syllabus it formed a continuity with the studies he had already completed in the faculty of arts.

There were external reasons for the choice of Erfurt as the place of his studies, but this choice had important consequences. Academic instruction in late medieval universities was dominated by two methods, which made their mark not merely on the theological faculty, but on all faculties. The distinction between these two methods was philosophical, and even in the faculty of arts had a decisive effect in forming the thinking of the students. These methods were distinguished as the 'two ways'. The *via antiqua* followed the thinkers of the golden age of scholasticism, sometimes Thomas Aquinas and sometimes Duns Scotus, the two leading representatives of the Dominican and Franciscan schools. The *via moderna* originated at the beginning of the final period of the Middle Ages with William of Ockham, and its main features were laid down by him. At many universities, only one method was taught, while at others both were in use. If Luther had gone to Leipzig, he would have become a Thomist, for there the dominant method was the *via antiqua* in its Thomist form. At Erfurt, where only the *via moderna* was practised, he inevitably became an Ockhamist, or a nominalist, to use the term which reflects the attitude of this school of thought to the ontological and epistemological problem of universals, over which the two schools were in disagreement. The so-called *via moderna* was not 'modern' in the sense that it had any time for the humanism which at that time was beginning to come to the fore in the universities. During his studies in the faculty of arts, Luther would have come in contact with humanism at best to a very limited extent; he differs in this from Zwingli, for whom from the very first humanism was the main formative influence in his education.

Luther's Ockhamist training continued to be the decisive influence upon his theological studies. At the same time, one must not overlook other factors that were at work. From the time of his entry into the monastery he had the opportunity to become familiar with the texts of the holy scriptures, naturally in the Latin Vulgate. In particular, he soon came to know the Psalter by heart, in the course of the choir office. Apart from this, however, Luther soon laid the basis of an impressive knowledge of the Bible. In addition, he became familiar with the greater part of the works of Augustine, as well as with mystical devotional literature, to mention only two of the main elements in the tradition which he received. To a considerable extent we can reconstruct the long list of books which Luther had studied thoroughly before he took up his professorial post.

The usual conception of Luther's so-called struggles in the monastery is difficult to reconcile with the strenuous intellectual activity which he carried out. After a few years, however, and while he was still studying theology, he also took on certain teaching duties and administrative responsibilities in his own order. This was a programme of work of which someone who was mentally disturbed would have been incapable. Thus a superficial explanation should not be sought for his temptations, which only began to beset him after some time. His distress was caused not by the discipline of the monastery, but by the very progress he had made there. The holier his way of life was in outward appearance, the more he despaired within himself. Instead of finding peace of mind, he was increasingly tormented by the uncertainty of salvation. Neither the usual spiritual direction available in the monastery nor the intensive use of the sacramental means of grace were of any help to him. He found no reason in himself not to despair at the thought of judgement. But the Church teaching and theological doctrine that was dominant at that time understood grace as a possession imparted to the believer. This drove him even more into a despair which seemed to him to be a symptom of God's just judgement on him, and of his exclusion from predestination to salvation.

From the year 1518 we possess a description of such a temptation, reminiscent in its wording of 2 Cor. 12: 2: 'I too know a man, who, as he has affirmed, has frequently suffered such punishments, admittedly for only a short time, but so monstrous and hellish that no tongue could tell, no pen write and no one believe who had not experienced them himself; they were such that if these pains had been borne to the end, or had lasted for only half an hour, or for no more than the tenth part of an hour, he would have been completely overcome, and all his bones would have become ashes. In them God appears terrible in his anger, and so, in the same way, does the whole creation. There is no refuge, no comfort, neither within nor without, but everything accuses. Then he screams this verse, "I am driven far from thy sight" [Ps. 31: 22]. And he does not even dare to say, "O Lord, rebuke me not in thy anger" [Ps. 6: 1]. At such a moment, strange to say, the soul is not able to believe that it can ever be redeemed, but merely feels that the punishment is not yet at an end. This punishment is in fact eternal, and the soul cannot regard it as merely temporary.

All that remains is a naked desire for help and a dreadful sighing, but the soul does not know where to cry out for help. The soul is stretched out with [the crucified] Christ, so that all its bones can be counted, and there is not a single corner in it which is not full of the bitterest bitterness, of terror, of fear, and of sadness, but in such a way as though everything without exception were eternal. To give an approximate illustration: roll a ball along a straight line, and any point that touches it bears the weight of the whole ball, and yet does not include it all. So, when the soul, in its momentary existence, is touched by the eternal flood that goes far beyond this existence, it feels and drinks only eternal punishment. But it does not remain, because it passes on. Thus if living persons can be overtaken by this punishment of hell, that is, this unbearable, comfortless terror, then it seems this must be even more true of the punishment in purgatory, though it is more restrained. And this inner fire is far more terrible than the outward fire.'[15]

We shall first simply compare this with the testimony in which shortly before his death, in the year 1545, Luther described, long after the event, his decisive conversion, the fundamental theological perception of the Reformation: 'A strange burning desire had seized me to understand Paul in the Epistle to the Romans; it was not coldness of heart which had stood in my way until then, but a single phrase in chapter 1: "For in it the righteousness of God is revealed" [Rom. 1: 17]. For I hated this phrase, "the righteousness of God", which I had been taught to understand philosophically, from its normal usage by all who teach doctrine, as referring to the so-called formal or active righteousness, by means of which God is righteous and punishes sinners and the unrighteous. But I, who, however blamelessly I lived as a monk, felt myself to be a sinner before God, with a deeply troubled conscience, and could not rely on being reconciled through the satisfaction I could carry out myself, did not love—no, hated—the just God who punishes sinners; and I silently rebelled against God, if not with blasphemy, at least with dreadful murmuring: Was it not enough that poor sinners, eternally lost as the result of original sin, should be cast down in pure wickedness through the law of the Decalogue, but that God should add one torment to another through the gospel, and even through the gospel should threaten us with his righteousness and his anger? So I raved on with a wild and confused conscience; and yet I returned time and again to this very passage in Paul, burning with thirst to know what St. Paul meant. Finally, thanks to the mercy of God, and thinking ceaselessly of this matter one night, I recalled the context in which the words occur, namely: "In it the righteousness of God is revealed . . . as it is written, 'The righteous shall live by faith'." Then I began to understand the righteousness of God as that through which by God's gift the righteous lives, that is by faith, and that this is the meaning of the passage: through the gospel the righteousness of God is revealed, that is, passive righteousness, through which the merciful God makes us righteous through faith, as it is written: "The righteous shall live by faith". Then I had the feeling that straight away I was born again, and had entered through open doors into paradise itself. The whole scripture revealed a different countenance to me. I then went through the whole scripture in my memory and compared analogies in other expressions: for example, the work of God, that is, what God works in us; the power of God, through which he makes us powerful, the wisdom of God, through which he makes us wise, the strength of God, the salvation of God, the glory of God. As I had hated the phrase "the righteousness of God" before, I now valued it with equal love, as the word which was sweetest to me. Thus in truth this passage of Paul was the gate of paradise for me . . .'[16]

This account is impressive in its simplicity, but it has given rise to difficult problems, with which the study of Luther has been concerned for many years. The main difficulties are as follows: we first hear of such a sudden experience of the revelation of the basic Reformation principle from a number of later reminiscences of Luther after the beginning of the 1530s, that is, many years later. And it is the last which is the most detailed. We learn nothing of any such experience in direct sources from Luther's early period. This of course does not mean that the later accounts are not reliable. In fact, from the point of view of their content, and apart from a certain change in terminology, they are entirely in accord with the theological material in testimonies from Luther's early period. The dating of this experience has given rise to many different suggestions, because the indications of the date in the context of the reminiscence of 1545 are ambiguous, and their verification in earlier testimonies, depending upon the standard one applies, is doubtful. Attempts to fix the date have varied between the extremes of 1512 and 1519, although the majority of scholars tend to place it in the year 1514.

But it is questionable whether it is worthwhile at all to attempt to fix the date of the so-called Reformation experience. For although such an illumination may well have taken place, if it is considered in isolation it gives a completely false picture of Reformation theology. This was not based upon a sudden isolated illumination, but, as we can see by carefully comparing Luther's earlier extant theological testimonies with the tradition, was prepared and anticipated over a wide field. Only in this way can we obtain a reliable insight into the way in which Luther became a Reformation theologian, and tell at what point in this process the turning-point occurred which he describes in his later reminiscences. To obtain real insight into what it was that formed Luther's personality, it is not enough to have this picture of a kind of second conversion experience; it is also necessary to make a profound study of his words, which have been preserved for us in unusual fullness.

CHAPTER 3

LUTHER'S WORDS

LUTHER's works were worthy of his words. To be concerned with words alone, whether as a teacher or a writer, a lawyer or a preacher, may appear a comfortable activity, while 'to ride in armour, to suffer heat, frost, dust, thirst and other discomforts, would be real work'. 'It is true', says Luther, 'it would be difficult for me to ride in armour. All the same, I would like to see the horseman that could sit still for a whole day looking at a book, even if he did not have to compose, think or read or worry about anything else. Ask a clerk, a preacher or a speaker what kind of work writing and speaking is; ask a schoolmaster what kind of work the teaching and education of boys is. A pen is light, certainly . . . but at the same time the best part (the head), the noblest member (the tongue), and the loftiest activity (speech) of the human body have to bear the brunt and do the most work, while with others it is the hand, the foot and the back or some similar limb which does all the work, while at the same time they can sing merrily and joke as they please, which a writer cannot do. Three fingers do everything (so they say of writers), but the whole body and soul take part in the work.'[1] Thus speech, the word, is the highest activity of man, and also the work which demands most of him: 'The body and soul take part in the work'; this is more accurate than our expression 'brain-work'.

In Luther's case, this work grew to an unimaginable extent.

43

As early as 1516—a year before the violent struggle broke out —we hear in a letter to a fellow-member of his order, who was a friend of his, the complaint that he was utterly overburdened: 'I almost need to have two secretaries or clerks. The whole day long I do virtually nothing but write letters . . . I preach in the monastery and at table; every day I am also asked to preach in the parish church, I am Director of Studies and Vicar-General of the Order, that is, prior eleven times over, administrator of the fisheries in Leitzkau and steward of the Herzberg affairs in Torgau; I lecture on Paul, and am gathering material for lectures on the Psalms; besides this there is correspondence, which as I have said claims the major part of my time. It is very rarely that no inroads are made on my time for the breviary and for celebrating mass; not to speak of my personal struggle against the temptations of the flesh, the world and the Devil. See what an idler I am!'[2] But we do not have to rely on these personal testimonies. Our knowledge of the work Luther in fact achieved confirms them in full. Two individual examples we happen to possess illustrate this. From Palm Sunday to the Wednesday in Easter Week of 1529, that is, in eleven days, Luther preached eighteen sermons in Wittenberg, in addition to everything else. Or consider the extent, and most of all the profundity and significance, of the literary production of a year such as 1520, which shows an unparalleled intensity of intellectual creation. Several printing works were occupied simultaneously to keep pace with him.

At the same time, he was not concerned with *his own* word. The certainty that he was dealing with the word of God, and that this was his duty to the world, gave him courage to make the boldest utterances, but also brought him moments of bitter disappointment, such as in 1530, when for a time he refused to preach to the ungrateful congregation of Wittenberg.[3] This feeling can be perceived in his 'Exhortation to All Clergy Assembled at Augsburg', written in the same year: 'Not that we have any great pleasure in preaching. For speaking for myself, there is no message I would rather receive than that which would relieve me of the duty of preaching. I am so weary of it because of the intolerable burden the Devil and the world place upon me. But the poor souls will not have it. There is also a man, who is called Jesus Christ, who says no. I am ready to follow him, since I am even more beholden to him.'[4] We who preach the gospel, say the startling words of one sermon, 'are a highway over which Satan rides'.[5]

This task was carried out by means and for the sake of the word, which did not spring from his own mind and heart, but was drawn from the text of holy scripture and came to utterance as a result of constant attention and strenuous study. It was also a liberation from his own literary works. This is expressed at the conclusion of the Christmas sermon of 1522: 'O that God should desire that my interpretation and that of all teachers should disappear, and each Christian should come straight to the scripture alone and to the pure word of God! You see from this babbling of mine the immeasurable difference between the word of God and all human words, and how no man can adequately reach and explain a single word of God with all his words. It is an eternal word, and must be understood and contemplated with a quiet mind, as the 83rd Psalm says: "I will hear what God himself speaks in me" [Vulgate, Ps. 84: 9: R.S.V., Ps. 85:8]. No one else can understand except a mind that contemplates in silence. For anyone who could achieve this without commentary or interpretation, my commentaries and those of everyone else would not only be of no use, but merely a hindrance. Go to the Bible itself, dear Christians, and let my expositions and those of all scholars be no more than a tool with which to build aright, so that we can understand, taste and abide in the simple and pure word of God; for God dwells alone in Zion.'[6] After resisting for a long time the project of a complete edition of his works, he finally consented, but in 1539 and 1545, in the prefaces to the first volumes of the German and Latin writings respectively, he emphasizes that he would gladly have seen all his books destroyed, and buried in oblivion.[7] Moreover, he expected this: 'I comfort myself with the thought that with time my books will remain covered in dust, except where I have written something good (through God's grace).'[8]

To obtain a concrete conception of Luther's word, we must glance briefly at his extant writings and classify them according to their nature and origin. To undertake the study of his writings is to set sail upon an ocean. More than eighty years have already been spent upon what is at the present time the standard edition of his works, the Weimar edition. Although almost all his writings are available in this edition, the end is scarcely in sight, since, besides additions, its deficient quality in some parts makes a revision in the form of supplements and corrections necessary, while the preparation of an index in particular presents great difficulties. The Weimar edition consists at the present time of a hundred folio volumes of approximately seven hundred pages each.

In spite of its evident deficiencies, this edition is of great importance for our knowledge of Luther by comparison with earlier editions, not merely with regard to the text, dating and commentary, but also because it includes extensive material that literally 'lay forgotten in the dust'. There are two great complexes of such material. The first consists of transcriptions from the period of Luther's maturity. The many volumes of transcriptions of sermons, which cover much previously unknown material, are of particular importance. The transcriptions of disputations and lectures from this later period in the main enlarge what we already possess, and to some extent bring us nearer to the original wording. Of incomparably greater importance, however, is the material from Luther's early period, about which previous centuries had no authentic knowledge apart from a handful of dates. When one considers that the first work which Luther himself had printed[9] takes us back only to the spring of 1517, and that up to the second half of the nineteenth century this formed for practical purposes the limit before which no insight into his intellectual activity was possible, it can be seen how much the situation in research on Luther has changed. For beginning with the year 1509, though to a limited extent at first, Luther's marginal notes in numerous text-books[10] give us the first direct evidence of his thinking, while from 1513 we suddenly have a stream of works, some of them in an excellent manuscript tradition. There is the virgin forest, filling twelve hundred pages of the Weimar edition, of his preparatory work for the first course of lectures, that on the Psalms from the years 1513 to 1515.[11] Then there are his lectures on the Epistles to the Romans,[12] Galatians and Hebrews.[13] Thus from the beginning of his professorship to the struggle over indulgences we possess an unbroken documentary record of his theological development, texts which were never intended for publication and which were not even known in their entirety to those who heard his lectures at that time. They are merely preparatory notes, serving to clarify his own mind, and consequently to be dated at the very moment of his spiritual and intellectual struggle. It is only by means of this material, which is far from being exhausted, that we have been able to study in detail Luther's conversion from scholasticism to Reformation theology in constant comparison with the tradition from which he came and the literature on which he was working—a laborious but stimulating subject for research. I know of no parallel in the whole of history, in which a spiritual upheaval of such proportions can be studied with anything approaching the same fullness of original sources.

Three general observations must be made on what we possess of Luther's words.

First, it is already obvious that the state of the tradition varies greatly. In some cases we still possess his original manuscripts, and in others only the earliest printed version. Sometimes we must make do with the transcriptions made by his hearers, or even with mere copies of transcriptions, and sometimes again with printed versions prepared by others with or without Luther's authority. Thus in handling the texts one must obviously be aware of this, in order not to be misled by a watering down of the language or a shift of theological emphasis on the part of an unsympathetic student. On the whole, however, a first-class tradition exists for the bulk of his work, which serves as a guide for the profitable use of the secondary material.

Secondly, when considering the importance of Luther for the German language, it is easy to forget that a large part of his work is in Latin. This is naturally true of all his lectures, in which only an occasional, usually emotional, German expression occurs. Thus for example in 1515, in a controversial anti-scholastic discussion of Romans 4: 7, he exclaims 'O *Sautheologen!*' ('pigs of theologians')[14] Similarly, it is Latin which is predominant in all works which are meant for those with a theological education, though again there are occasional German interjections such as '*Das ist zu viel!*' ('That is too much!') in *De servo arbitrio*;[15] and Latin is also used in the vast majority of the letters. The Church usage, scholasticism and humanism combined to give Latin this unique position, and one cannot overestimate its importance for Luther's thought. On the whole, it is his Latin writings which provide our real access to his theological thought.

Finally, for reasons which we have still to consider, Luther's work was influenced to an extraordinary degree by the situation for which it was written. In order to be aware of any changes that may have occurred in his thought, and above all to understand his every utterance in the concrete circumstances of its origin and purpose, the situation that gave rise to it and the aim it was intended to achieve, the circumstances that surrounded it, and the persons to whom it was addressed, its necessity and the specific issues that placed a limitation on it or liberated its ideas—that is, to understand it as words spoken to others—one must always take into account the time at which it was written. That is why the first concern of an adequate edition and interpretation of Luther's works must necessarily be that of chronology. A summary view of the mass of available material is naturally best obtained by classifying it according to the basic situations in which Luther spoke, and the literary forms that corresponded to them.

The first of these categories includes everything that belongs directly to his academic work, that is, his lectures and disputations. The lectures extend, with brief interruptions occasioned by external circumstances, from 1513 to 1546. They are exclusively concerned with biblical exegesis. This, of course, was an obligatory task from the end of 1512, as a result of his appointment to the *lectura in Bibliam*, as successor to Johannes von Staupitz. But it was unusual for a scholastic theologian to rest content with the exposition of scripture, and not to pass on to dogmatic teaching, normally in the form of a commentary on the *Sententiae* of Peter Lombard. Luther made a decision here which was closely associated with his conversion to Reformation principles, though it is not possible to give an accurate date, since there was no longer any possibility of Luther's transferring from biblical exegesis. His exclusive concern with the scriptures should also be contrasted not merely with scholasticism, but also with the humanist form of instruction adopted by Melanchthon, based on *loci theologici* and a continuous exegesis. Luther mainly dealt with Old Testament books, especially—I list them in the order of the canon— Genesis, Deuteronomy, the Psalms, Ecclesiastes, the Song of Solomon, Isaiah and the minor prophets. The only New Testament writings on which he lectured were epistles: Romans, Galatians, 1 Timothy, Titus, Philemon, 1 John and Hebrews. This choice was partly due to outward circumstances. The exposition of the gospels was the responsibility of other professors; Luther handed over that of the Epistle to the Romans to Melanchthon, who in the course of the years lectured five times on it, while Luther did so only once, during his early period. It is of great practical significance that Luther began his teaching with the exposition of the Psalms (1513/15), the book of the Bible with which he was most familiar through his monastic office, and which spoke to him most directly, pregnant as it is with religious emotion; and that he then proceeded methodically to the study of St. Paul, lecturing on Romans (1515/16), Galatians (1516/17) and Hebrews (1517/18), which was also traditionally regarded as Pauline, and finally returning, a proof as it were of his theological progress, to the Psalter (1518/19). In 1519 the first commentary on Galatians[16] was printed, and (between then and 1521) the *Operationes in Psalmos*.[17] He later lectured again on these texts, It is also characteristic that the emphasis is on the Old Testament. Among other reasons for this was the fact that Luther felt himself more of an expert in Hebrew than in Greek, by comparison with the Greek scholar Melanchthon. The form of exegesis he used is also important. In the early lectures, up to and including the lectures on Hebrews, he still held to the scholastic division into interlinear and marginal glosses (that is, brief explanations, which were written between the lines and on the edges of a text of the Bible printed with wide spacing for the purpose of lecturing) and *scholia* (that is, longer explanations of chosen passages, written on a separate sheet). When he returned to the beginning of his course, and at the same time began the publication of printed works with his commentaries on the Psalms and Galatians, his theological maturity had also brought a liberation from scholastic forms, and he turned to continuous exegesis of the whole context.

In addition to lectures, an important part was played in the university teaching of that time by disputations—something similar to the modern seminar, although following a quite different method. In the precise formulation of theses, which was the professor's task even in the disputations on which the awarding of degrees depended, and in those that were held merely for the sake of practice, Luther was an expert. He showed great patience in correcting the mistakes of his students, and in the contributions which he made himself he argued with telling force. The scholastic form of disputation disappeared with the beginning of the university reforms in Wittenberg, but was readopted in a modified form in 1535. It became an essential instrument in inculcating Reformation theology in the university, and in resisting false developments within the Reformation; the great disputations with the antinomians[18] are a notable example of this.

The translations of the Bible must also be regarded as part of his academic work. In the case of the Old Testament it was a task carried out in partnership with others, while the revision of the whole of the scripture was placed in the hands of a commission, whose minutes are still extant.[19] One can see in practice what Luther describes in his 'On Translation: an Open Letter': 'And it often happened that for a fortnight, or three or four weeks, we sought and inquired for a single word, and yet sometimes did not find it. We worked in this way on the book of Job, Master Philip, Aurogallus and myself, so that sometimes we scarcely succeeded in finishing three lines in four days.'[20]

Luther constantly moved between the lecture-room and the pulpit. In both he was concerned with the same issues, although he was carrying out different tasks, in part, though not solely, because he was addressing what was to some extent a different audience. But because the issues were the same, the two forms of the word, theological teaching and preaching, were very close to each other. *Doctrina*, in Reformation usage, can refer to both, without prejudice to either aspect. Another similarity is that he saw both entirely as the spoken word, temporal in the strictest sense, uttered here and now; and he did not concern himself a great deal about the preservation of the spoken word in writing. He completed in literary form himself only the first part of the Commentary on the Psalms (Ps. 1-22) and an early version of the Commentary on Galatians.[21] Similarly, Luther prepared for publication himself only a small number of the *Postillen* (homilies), and of the sermons, in so far as they appeared in print at all. This was partly due to shortage of time, and partly to the co-operation of willing helpers. The greatest service was rendered by Georg Rörer, who from 1522 up to the time of Luther's death transcribed both his lectures and his sermons. These are also of the utmost importance from the linguistic point of view, for they are the earliest direct transcriptions of spoken German. Of course we possess them only in a cryptic form, as a mixed German and Latin text in a telegraphic style; for the transcription was carried out using a system of abbreviation developed for Latin, and consequently involved a partial translation into Latin, with the inclusion of directly recorded German words. Thus a kind of paraphrase and retranslation is necessary in order to bring us back to the original. But this procedure has the advantage that it gives us a more accurate indication of the impression made by his words, whereas Luther's own German, which sounds old-fashioned to us, can produce, as a direct result of this patina of historical authenticity, the false impression that its original effect was similar. Well over two thousand sermons are still extant. Since for the most part they are on the traditional epistles and gospels of the Church, and therefore often comment on the same text year after year, they make it possible to study changes in his exegesis. And the series of sermons largely devoted to successive chapters from the gospels, which were delivered on weekdays, are a welcome supplement to the exegetical lectures, which are deficient with respect to the gospels.

Of course our view of Luther as a writer has been formed principally by his controversial works, in which he developed an uncanny talent for forceful polemic, sometimes going beyond tolerable limits. His much discussed coarseness must be regarded as a reflection of his times. But it cannot be denied that as Luther grew older he went far beyond what was normal in this respect, especially as his outbursts of empty insults are always associated with a deadly serious struggle about matters of ultimate importance, and at the same time with a sparkling wit that sprang from his vast ascendancy over his opponents. To give a fair picture, it is necessary to give a gross example of this, not exactly fit for the drawing-room. In a work written in 1541 against Duke Heinrich von Braunschweig-Wolfen-büttel, entitled *Wider Hans Worst* ('Against the Clown'), Luther intervened in an exchange of polemics that was already in progress, and that was full of violent abuse, between the Duke of Brunswick on the one hand, and the Elector of Saxony and the Landgrave of Hesse on the other. The already poisoned atmosphere was certainly not cleared by observations such as the following: 'You shouldn't have written a book, unless you had heard a fart from an old sow, when you should have opened your mouth wide to it and said, "Thank you very much, beautiful nightingale, that will make good text for me"!'[22] This sort of thing ought naturally not to be treated in isolation from the enormous inner strain under which he wrote, and we must also bear in mind its association with a cheerful calm on a much higher level, which is expressed, for example, in the introductory words of the same work with a triumphant freedom: 'Speaking for myself, I am very happy that books of this sort should be written against me; for it warms not only my heart, but my knees and my heels, when I see that through me, poor wretched man that I am, the Lord God so embitters and maddens both the princes of hell and princes of this world, so that they virtually explode and burst asunder from madness, while I sit in the shade of faith and the Our Father and laugh at the Devil and his hangers-on, bawling and writhing in their great anger. With all this they achieve nothing, except to make their own case worse every day, and advance and make better mine (that is, God's) ... for by this they make me young and fresh, strong and happy.'[23]

I have begun by commenting on this side of Luther's writings, in order to make clear by contrast that the real impulse which drove him to write lay elsewhere than in such extreme manifestations. Why was Luther not satisfied with lecturing and preaching? Why did he take up the pen? The primary reason was not the urge of the scholar nor the controversial zeal of a reformer, but the responsibility of a pastor for a pure, clear, comprehensible, convincing and liberating proclamation of the gospel. He had himself struggled to understand the righteousness of God, which, as the gospel reveals, means that the righteous live by faith. This struggle had to be proclaimed publicly to the people in the language which they spoke, that is, in German. In view of the fact that Luther was soon to become a controversialist, and was at the time a scholastic theologian, it is an astonishing fact that his first publication was a devotional work in German, an exposition of the seven Penitential Psalms, which appeared in the spring of 1517.[24] This provides a key to his entire theology, and so to his literary work as a whole. Then, in spite of the dispute over indulgences which began shortly afterwards, and developed with extreme rapidity into the great struggle with the Catholic Church, and in addition to the controversial writings and theological treatises which this demanded, there followed a constant and frequent succession of German devotional works, entirely non-polemical, and exclusively concerned with what makes a man a Christian: expositions of the Ten Commandments or the Lord's Prayer,[25] and brief, profound and yet universally comprehensible sermons on the contemplation of the passion of Christ,[26] on preparation for death,[27] on individual sacraments: the Eucharist,[28] baptism,[29] penance,[30] and also the 'Treatise concerning the Ban'.[31] There were also others on ethical subjects: on the married state[32] and usury,[33] and, the crown of this whole literature, the 'Treatise on Good Works'[34] and the treatise 'On the Freedom of a Christian'.[35] A large amount of devotional literature had already appeared previously in German. But Luther's word represented such an astonishing innovation, both in the fundamental understanding which inspired it, and also from the linguistic point of view, that it would inevitably have come to be regarded as epoch-making, even if it had never been associated with the mighty external upheaval of the Reformation. But the Reformation itself can no more be isolated from this quiet and unassuming literary work, than the inevitable consequences which Luther drew upon himself in the events of the Reformation can be disassociated from what he derived from the holy scriptures, *orans et laborans* in the concealment of the monastery.

The impulse that was at work in these early instructions in the Christian faith, written for general reading, was maintained in similar later works, including the catechisms[36] and the hymns.[37] These are the most impressive of their kind in the language, and through them the word of God became the nourishment and refuge of whole generations. The same basic impulse is also present both in numerous controversial writings, and also in strictly theological works (for which Luther in fact made time only because of the necessities of the struggle in which he was involved, and which were not the products of the leisure of a scholar with literary leanings).

The final group of the extant works of Luther consists of a complex of writings in which his word found its most personal form. This group includes in particular his letters, of which we possess about 2,800. They cover the whole range from everyday affairs to matters of national importance, from the most private utterances to letters written on the highest official level. Apart from the strictly theological statements they contain, they form as it were a compendium of theology which had been drawn from his immediate experience, and which provided one and the same person with the proper language for addressing princes and prelates, brothers and sisters in temptation, and not least, his own wife Käthe and his young son Hänschen. A distinctive mixture of intimacy and wide-ranging practicality marks the tradition of what is known as his 'Table Talk', which consists of notes which Luther's companions made during or after meals, from the beginning of the 1530s, on the numerous conversations which were conducted at table. They preserve for us, in fascinating variety and concrete detail, Luther's thought and judgements, appearing as it were in their everyday dress.

We shall be concerned from now on with the context and purpose of Luther's word, having only given a very sketchy outline here of the numerous forms in which it has been handed down. To conclude this brief summary, we shall anticipate the rest of our work by mentioning a few characteristics of his word.

To begin with its outward effect, his word, once it had been uttered, found a unique response. The wide public appeal which Luther achieved overnight was without question very complex in nature. All the religious longing and unrest, ecclesiastical problems and abuses, political tensions and upheavals, social discontent and ferment, changes in education and in the understanding of reality, which manifested themselves in a confused form at the end of the Middle Ages, were suddenly voiced and transformed into a unified movement (unified at least apparently and at first) by Luther's word. A new historical phenomenon appeared: there was suddenly something resembling a public opinion, more intensive and far-reaching than at almost any previous time. An objective symptom of this unique response is the wide circulation of Luther's writings, and especially of his devotional and religious works. One study on this subject has reached the following conclusion: 'Of about 30 works of this nature which Luther published between March 1517 and the summer of 1520, we know of 370 impressions by 1520.'

'Luther only needed to publish a new work in Wittenberg, for printers in Leipzig, Nuremberg, Augsburg, Strasbourg, Basle and other cities to fall upon it and reprint it, and this was usually done by two, three or four presses in the same city.' 'There is evidence extant that every popular devotional work which Luther published up to the summer of 1520, that is, until the appearance of the "Letter to the Nobility", was reprinted on average twelve times, sometimes less, sometimes more, and in some cases as often as twenty-four times.'[38]

As we have said, many factors combined to produce this effect. However cautious we are, we must not forget that these are the words of one who spoke to his own time what it needed to hear, words uttered with the compelling force of what can be uttered in the light of the day, with the liberty of one who is completely absorbed by what he has to say, and with the practicality of one who is hitting the nail right on the head. His word is drawn from the holy scripture and inspired by it alone. It is equal to the overwhelming task demanded by the scriptures of translating them into the language of his own age in accordance with the principle that he himself laid down for the interpretation and exegesis of the scripture: 'You must ask the mother at home, the children in the street and the common man in the market-place, and see on their own lips how they speak, and translate accordingly, so that they understand it and realize that you are speaking German to them.'[39] The holy scriptures and the present day intersect as it were at a single point, in the conscience that hears the word. It was Luther's concern that the word of God should be heard in this way.

CHAPTER 4

LUTHER'S ACTIONS

In a letter of congratulation to a newly-created cardinal we read: '. . . All that troubles me is that you have been appointed at the very time when it seems that the Apostolic See will be overthrown . . . He (the Pope) seems to despise and to impoverish our nation . . . Church offices are no longer given to those who deserve them, but to those who offer most for them. In order to raise the money, new indulgences are granted every day. . . A thousand ways are thought out by which the Roman See presses the gold out of us with cunning devices, as though we were barbarians . . . But now the best amongst us, as though startled out of their sleep, have begun to consider by what means they can deal with this injustice. They are determined to shake off the yoke and to recover their former freedom. The Roman Curia will suffer no mean damage, if the princes carry out what they have in mind . . .'[1] This letter does not come from the early days of the Reformation, but was written sixty years previously, in 1457, from an official of the Archbishop and Elector of Mainz to Enea Silvio Piccolomini, later Pope Pius II. This brief document tells us as much as a long description would about the situation before Luther came on the scene. The complaint of scandalous abuses in the Church goes back a long way. Throughout the fifteenth century, councils and publicists concerned themselves with the *causa reformationis*. At imperial diets the gravamina of the

59

German nation were a constant theme. There was a universal longing for a 'reformation of the head and of the members'. Numerous proposals were made as to what should be done and who should do it. But as the never-ending discussion shows, virtually nothing was achieved, and nothing at least which could silence the call for a reformation. Words were never followed by action.

This cannot be said of the movement instigated by Luther. It was this event, and no other, which came to be known as the 'Reformation', so that the word became the proper name of a single historical event. It was certainly followed on the Catholic side, albeit very late and as a reaction against the Reformation, by considerable measures to remove abuses and to renew the Roman Church within and without. This process is known as the Counter-Reformation. It is possible that this purely antithetical title does not do it justice, and that it would be better known as the Catholic Reform. But to speak of a 'Catholic Reformation' would be to force the term. For the great upheaval in Church history, which for good reasons was given the name 'Reformation' once for all, brought associations which made the term difficult to apply elsewhere. And even though it is regarded as a principle of the Reformation that the Reformation should not come to an end—*ecclesia semper reformanda*—we ought still, unless we are sectarians, to respect what took place in the sixteenth century as *the* Reformation, which imposed upon the Church the obligation and gave it the ability to regard itself as *semper reformanda*.

How did it come about that the Reformation did not become a matter of words, but went on to action? The answer is a radical one, which sounds paradoxical and goes far beyond all partial and superficial responses to this question. The Reformation did not remain a matter of words, but went on to action, because the necessity of the whole Reformation and what really happened in it was so profoundly understood that it became clear that the Reformation could only be comprehended not as a matter of specific actions, but wholly as a matter of the word and of the word alone. Towards the end of the 'Explanations of the Ninety-five Theses on Indulgences', the first great theological work published by Luther, in 1518, we read: 'The Church needs reformation. But this is not the concern of an individual man, of the Pope, nor of many cardinals—both these points are obvious from the last council—but the concern of the whole world; no, of God alone. But the time of this reformation is known only to him who created the ages.'[2] Ought one to object that Luther at this time had simply not yet noticed that the Reformation had begun six months earlier, on a day which by common consent at the present time can be exactly dated, and that it was the act of an individual person—not the Pope indeed, but the Augustinian friar and professor of theology Martin Luther? To do so would be to miss completely the truth contained in Luther's statement, the point of which is that it regards the Reformation not as lying in an uncertain future, but as assured in the will and power of God, so that it is essentially the act of God, and not of man. This, of course, is not an explicit statement of our assertion in the paradoxical answer given above, that for this very reason the Reformation is a matter of the word alone. But this is the point on which Luther was to lay great emphasis, as soon as he became conscious of what was taking place in the Reformation. His real *action* in the Reformation, to return to our paradox, was to adhere strictly to this understanding throughout the changing situation.

In his 'Address to the Christian Nobility of the German Nation of 1520, in which Luther took up with great determination the themes and plans of earlier efforts on behalf of the *causa reformationis*, but understood them in a completely new spirit, transformed them and made them far more profound, he did not arrogate to himself the action that had to be taken in the name of the Reformation—how could he have done so? He was conscious of his ministry of the word. The first sentence of the dedication, 'The time for silence is over, and the time for speech has come',[3] rings out like a bell. Yet in this work, he did something which he was never to do again. He appealed directly to others to act on behalf of the Reformation, in the hope 'that God will grant help to His Church through the laity'.[4] Surely it was not merely a piece of pious rhetorical modesty which warned everyone: 'The first and most urgent thing just now is that we should each prepare our own selves in all seriousness. We must not begin by assuming we possess much strength or wisdom, even if we had all the authority in the world. For God cannot and will not suffer a goodly enterprise to be begun if we trust in our own strength and wisdom'.[5]

Here Luther is touching directly on the root of all action, which decides whether an action is good or bad. This depends on whether one relies more on one's own power or on God. This is why faith alone is the source of good works.[6] This is the very essence of the Reformation, and is the basic theme of Luther's 'Treatise on Good Works' of the same year, 1520. But it is difficult to realize that it is a clear, acute, concrete and extremely 'practical' truth, overlaid as it is with the veneer of purely edifying language, which results from its false application, or of a failure to apply it. This warning against trusting in one's own power, placed in the introduction to the 'Address to the Christian Nobility', is not so much the routine repetition of a general religious idea, but the specific application of it to the problem of reformation action, which means not particular reforming measures, but a reformation of the Church itself. Before discussing what must be done, one must be clear whether and to what extent action is appropriate at all in the question of the reformation of the Church, and thus how far action is capable of dealing with the problems that threaten the Church and make reformation necessary, and whether what makes the Church into the Church, and what has constantly to take place in its reformation, is something which can be carried out by measures and acts, and by authority and force. Luther believes that 'we must be clear that we are not dealing permanently with men in this matter, but with the princes of hell who would fill the world with war and bloodshed, and yet avoid letting themselves be caught by the flood. We must go to work now, not depending on physical power, but in humble trust in God, seeking help from Him in earnest prayer ... Otherwise our efforts may well begin with good prospects, but, when we get deeply involved, the evil spirit will cause such confusion as to make the whole world swim in blood, and then nothing will be accomplished. Therefore, in this matter let us act wisely, and as those who fear God. The greater the power we employ, the greater the disaster we suffer, unless we act humbly and in the fear of God.'[7]

At this point it becomes evident that the form of opposition which the Reformation faced made external authority and force a wholly inappropriate instrument, because such means achieved the reverse of what was intended, and only played into the hands of the enemy. The realization that the Reformation was an encounter with the power of Antichrist is one with the recognition which he expressed more and more clearly as time went on, that this force could only be met with what is apparently the weakest instrument of all, the word alone. When, two years later, the appeal to the secular arm had turned out to be fruitless, and the situation appeared confused, Luther wrote in his 'Sincere Admonition to all Christians to Guard against Insurrection and Rebellion': 'If you say, "What shall we do then, if the authorities will not make any move? Shall we go on tolerating it, and strengthen its courage [i.e. of the papacy]?" I answer, No, you should do nothing of the sort. You should do three things. You should recognize your sin, which God's stern righteousness has punished with such a rule of Antichrist ... Secondly, you should humbly pray against the papal rule ... Thirdly, you should let your mouth be the mouth of the Spirit of Christ, of which St. Paul ... says: "The Lord Jesus will slay him with the mouth of his Spirit" [2 Thess. 2: 8; R.S.V., "with the breath of his mouth"]. If we do this, we shall be strengthened to continue what has already been begun, and display the villainy and trickery of the Pope and the papists to the people with the spoken and written word, until he is stripped naked, seen for what he is, and put to shame throughout the world. For he must first be killed with words; the mouth of Christ must do it, so that he is torn out of men's hearts, and his lies recognized and despised. But once he is removed from their hearts, so that his claims are no longer accepted, then he is already destroyed. He can be better dealt with in this way than by a hundred revolts. We shall do him no damage by violence, but only strengthen him, as has happened in many cases previously. But with the light of the truth, when he is measured against Christ, and his doctrine against the gospel, then and there he will fall and be brought to ruin without any exertion or trouble. Look at what I have done. Have I not done more damage to the Pope, the bishops, the priests and the monks with my words alone, without a single blow with the sword, than all the emperors and kings have done previously with all the force they used? Why is this? Because Daniel 8 says, "By no human hand this king shall be broken", and St. Paul says, "He shall be destroyed by the mouth of Christ." Now let me and everyone who speaks the word of Christ freely boast that our mouths are the mouths of Christ. I am certain indeed that my word is not mine, but the word of Christ. So must my mouth also be the mouth of him whose word it utters.'[8]

In the same year Luther put into practice the realization that reformation action would take place through the word alone in a way which was decisive for the further course of the Reformation. In 1521, the papal excommunication was followed in Worms by the sentence of outlawry within the Empire. Luther was removed from the public eye by a cleverly concealed move on the part of the Elector. No one knew where he was staying, nor even at first whether he was still alive. In Wittenberg, the progress of the Reformation declined into chaos under the influence of radical tendencies. Thereupon Luther decided, against the express warning of the Elector, to return from the Wartburg to Wittenberg. In what concerned the gospel, the outward authority of the secular arm was not only incapable of bringing about anything positive, but was not even able to afford any protection. Here Luther had completely abandoned the usual opinion, as he explained to the Elector in the memorable letter in which he announced his decision and the fact that he had already set out. He spoke in the language of faith, which is the language of liberty: 'This I have written to Your Grace with the intention that Your Grace should know that I am coming to Wittenberg under the protection of one much higher than the Elector. Nor have I any thought of seeking protection from Your Grace. In fact I consider I could better protect Your Grace than you can protect me. Moreover, if I knew that Your Grace could and would protect me, I would not come. This is a matter in which the sword cannot give counsel or help; God must act alone in it, without any human striving or intervention. Consequently, whoever believes most, is best able to afford protection. Because I now sense that Your Grace is still very weak in faith, I shall no longer regard Your Grace as someone who can protect or save me. Since Your Grace desires to know what you should do in this matter—especially as you are of the opinion that you have done far too little—I humbly reply that Your Grace has already done far too much, and should do nothing at all. For God will not and can not tolerate the striving and activity of Your Grace or of myself. That it be left to him, this and nothing else is what he wants. Let Your Grace judge by this. If Your Grace believes this, you will be assured and have peace; if you do not believe, I do, and must let Your Grace's unbelief be tormented in its striving, as it behoves all unbelievers to suffer.'[9]

But in Wittenberg, Luther preached every day for a whole week, and by means of the word placed the Reformation on the right course, making clear that the content of the gospel must also be the decisive factor in carrying out the Reformation in practice, that is, that everything had to be regulated according to the word and to faith: 'For the word created heaven and earth and all things; this the word must do, and not we who are sinners. This is the *Summa Summarum*; this I will preach, this I will speak, this I will write. But I will force no one, nor constrain them with violence. For faith seeks to be accepted willingly, without constraint. Follow my example: I opposed indulgences and all papists, but without force. All I have done is to put forth, preach and write the word of God, and apart from this I have done nothing. While I have been sleeping, or drinking Wittenberg beer with my friend Philip and with Amsdorf, it is the word that has done great things, so that the papacy has become so weak that neither prince nor emperor has ever done it so much damage. I have done nothing; the word has done and achieved everything. If I had wanted to proceed with violence, I would have brought about a great shedding of blood in Germany, and I would have caused such sport at Worms that the Emperor would not have been safe. But what would it have been? It would have been a game for fools. I have done nothing, I have let the word act ... it is all powerful, it takes hearts prisoner, and when they are taken prisoner, the work that is done comes from the word itself.'[10]

Little value is usually placed upon the word, on the grounds that it needs to be fulfilled by human action. Words are empty and cheap; the only thing that is real and has value is action. Goethe gave classic expression to this, when he made Faust say of the translation of John 1: 1: 'I cannot place so high a value on the word. I must translate it another way, if the Spirit guides me aright. . . . The Spirit helps me, all at once I see a way, and write with assurance: "In the beginning was the act!" '[11] This outbidding of the word by action, and of doctrine by life, is clearly something right and proper, especially in so far as it applies to the word that calls for action and works, that is, the word which demands without giving anything itself, which Luther called 'the word of the law'. What he has to say concerning the superiority of the word and of doctrine is not true of any and every word, or of every doctrine, but only of the word which creates what it says, because it is the word of promise and brings what it promises, the word of faith, which is the word of God, and reveals the true nature and purpose of the word. All that matters in the Church is the gospel, and the reformation of the Church can only consist of giving full value to the gospel. Consequently, the utmost care and consideration must be given to true doctrine, contrary to what conventional opinion holds. For doctrine belongs to God, and life to us—a distinction Luther makes in the longer series of lectures on Galatians in 1531. If doctrine is corrupt, everything becomes corrupt. If it is sound, everything is in order.[12]

But it follows that everyone must be fully prepared for the Devil to be hard at work wherever the pure gospel is proclaimed. Luther knew of the grievous temptations which arose from the consequences of the Reformation. They were such that people could ask, seeing all the tumult and strife that arose, whether the gospel was worth all this. Here the certainty of faith is at stake. Luther could say that if no more than a single person was comforted by the preaching of the gospel, he would consider it worth the shaking of the whole world. It is better that everything that belongs to this life should be destroyed, than that a single soul should be lost.[13] Consequently, where the word of God is at issue, one should not humbly give way, but should even be prepared to draw on oneself the suspicion of pride. 'In this matter I am prepared to be stubborn, blinkered and obstinate, and am glad to be called such, for here the thing is never to yield.'[14] The distinction between word and act, and between doctrine and life consequently corresponds to that between faith and love: 'In matters of love one must give way, because it bears all; but in matters of faith this is not the case ... faith must suffer nothing, and not yield. It must be stubborn and stiff-necked to the utmost degree. On the other hand, where love is concerned, man's duty is different. But through faith, man is as it were God, who cannot suffer anything. God is unchangeable, and so too is faith.'[15]

In following the indications that for Luther reformation

action was wholly concentrated upon the word, we have not lost sight of our starting-point. We set out to ask why in this case, unlike every reformation discussed previously, this Reformation did not remain a matter of words, but actually took place. The paradoxical answer we gave is now perhaps somewhat clearer. We said that the Reformation did not remain a matter of mere words, but was actually carried out, precisely because the Reformation was not regarded as a matter of action, but purely as a matter of the word. The apparent contradiction is resolved when it is realized that the question of the power of the Reformation goes back to that of the authority of the Reformation word. Consequently, the question of the events of the Reformation, of that in it which possessed the nature of action, can be answered by going back to the question of the gospel itself, as it was proclaimed in the Reformation. To understand the distinctive nature of the events of the Reformation, we need first to understand the essence of Reformation preaching. Reformation action is not the putting into practice of the Reformation word, but is the very reality of the Reformation word, and is therefore subordinate to the logic of the content of the Reformation, or, if one may so phrase it, to the logic of the gospel. The kind of action of which the Reformation consists, the conditions under which such action can take place, and therefore, the form taken by the *modus procedendi* of the Reformation, is not a formal or a tactical question, for however superficial these aspects may still be it is ultimately identical with the question of the substance of the Reformation gospel. But this means that the course taken by the events of the Reformation forms a singularly illuminating commentary on Reformation doctrine, that is, a testimony to the word, which does not have to be expressed in action, but is itself active work. We can make this clear by considering certain characteristic phrases of the events of the Reformation.

1. *Natura verbi est audiri*.[16] Luther's statement, that the nature of the word is to be heard—or, as it may also be translated, the birth of the word, the life of the word, the history of the word, the arrival of the word consists in its being heard—forms a kind of leitmotiv in what can be called his pre-Reformation phase. We are not dealing with an outward-looking person, who analyses and diagnoses what is taking place in the Church and in politics, and draws up a programme of reform. The compulsion to diagnose the ills of his time was the unintended fruit of his attentive listening, with the utmost devotion, concentration and self-criticism, to the word of the scripture, which he was passionately concerned to understand, not from philosophical or historical curiosity, but because he was personally and intimately affected by its message. His starting point was not anger at abuses within the Church, but his utter preoccupation with his own disorder and failure. His purpose was not to appear as a reformer and an improver of the world. He longed earnestly for only one thing: the redeeming and justifying word, and to receive for himself and experience in himself what it was his profession to teach.

In the course of this persevering study of the scripture, of which we are given a striking picture in his early lectures, he came increasingly to be scandalized by what he was taught about the Church and theology. But subsidiary causes of offence, of which full details are nowadays given even in Catholic accounts of the end of the Middle Ages, played no fundamental role in his search for the word of salvation. What was of vital importance was his bewilderment at what the Church's teaching and scholastic theology in general asserted as self-evident, that is, that the grace infused in the first place in baptism, and renewed after each mortal sin in the sacrament of penance, inhered in the person who received it as a new supernatural faculty enabling him to live a saintly life, even though still imperfectly. Thus grace ultimately cast man back upon himself, towards his own striving for sanctification, and consequently also into uncertainty regarding himself. It was on this issue, the scholastic interpretation of which raises numerous subtle problems, that there took place, so far as we can see at all into the mystery of the genesis of Luther's theology, what we might call the hidden atomic fission which set up a chain reaction leading to the events of the Reformation. The grace of the Holy Spirit never becomes our own *virtus* but is always effective as the *virtus* of God.[17] This was the change of outlook, as great as that brought about by the Copernican view of the universe, which led to a certainty based upon the relationship between the word and faith. Thus one cannot say simply that the Reformation began on the 31st October 1517. This was not the beginning of the Reformation in the strict sense—for those who were taking part in it, still more or less unconsciously, it had already begun long ago in the monastery, the lecture-room and the pulpit. What began on that day was rather the consequences of a reformation, the scope of which was still unrecognized, and which was still moving hesitantly out of its concealment into the public eye.

2. We cannot describe here the dramatic events of the years 1517 to 1521; we shall only point to a number of distinctive features which illustrate what we have already said concerning the relationship between word and action. The real drama of these years consisted only in a secondary sense of impressive, tense and critical scenes such as the hearing before Cardinal

Cajetan in Augsburg in 1518, the disputation in Leipzig with Johannes Eck in 1519, the burning of the bull of excommunication in 1520 or the appearance before the Emperor and the Imperial Diet in Worms in 1521. This course of events was not one which, once set in motion, continued automatically. Each further step depended to an astonishing degree upon the word of a single person, who had unintentionally presented a challenge to the contemporary world. If he had recanted at Augsburg, if he had been more cautious in Leipzig, if he had not rejected the judgement of the Pope, and if he had followed the advice of numerous well-intentioned friends and had been prepared to compromise, and if in some way he had come to an arrangement with the Imperial Diet, the course of the Reformation would have been different. Many would consider that it would have taken place in a better way, without a schism in the Church. Luther, however, was quite clear that he would have abandoned more than the Reformation if he had denied the word which it was his duty to vindicate as a professor of holy scripture. During these years, Luther's responsibility for the word of God resolved itself simply into clinging firmly to this word—something that was simple and straightforward in essence, but which represented for Luther, who stood alone and whose endurance was being tested, an ordeal by fire with a thousand trials and temptations, in a constantly changing situation.

From the extensive evidence for this, we give a number of passages from letters written in 1520: 'What honour do I seek, wretch that I am, for I have no other desire than to live in peace and concealment away from public affairs? Anyone who wants can have my offices; anyone who wants may burn my books. I ask you, what more can I do? But at the same time, I declare this: If I am not set free *from* my teaching office and the duty

I owe to the word, I will at least be free *in* carrying out this office. I am already sufficiently burdened with sins; I will not draw upon myself this further mortal sin of neglecting the post in which I have been placed, so that I am found guilty of a criminal silence, and the neglect of the truth and of so many thousand souls.'[18] 'It is hard to stand opposed to all the bishops and princes. But there is no other way to escape hell and the anger of God. So take note whether those who are scandalized by my stubbornness are not such as to despise the affairs of the word and replace it by I know not what human considerations. If someone judges [the gospel] by the standards of his earthly rank, it is no wonder that he should cry out and that it should rend him.'[19] 'For myself, once I receive the summons, as far as it depends on me I will have myself taken there sick, if I cannot come in good health. For there can be no doubt that I am called by God, when the Emperor calls ... we have no right here to be concerned about the dangers or about a fortunate outcome. On the contrary, what we have to do is to take care that we do not abandon the gospel with which we have come forward to the mockery of the godless, and do not give our opponents any opportunity to triumph over us, as though we did not dare stand up for what we have taught, and were afraid to shed our blood for the gospel. May Christ in his mercy protect us from cowardice on our own part and such boasting on their part.'[20]

3. In the dramatic events of the years 1517 to 1521 the word is manifested as a confession of faith. But these events seem to me to present another aspect which is necessary for a full understanding of the interrelationship between word and action. In 1517 Luther did not present a programme of reform. Because of his pastoral responsibility he was obliged by the central

message of his theology to take a stand with regard to a contemporary question of Church practice, but his primary purpose was not to attack its more evident abuses, as had already been done by numerous earlier critics of the system of indulgences, but to tear up the whole institution of indulgences by the roots, on the basis of a true understanding of repentance and of what it means in general to be a Christian.

Looking back upon the subsequent course of events, one can see how each theme developed step by step from the first: the question of doctrinal authority, the doctrine of the sacraments, and the understanding of the Church. It is easy to say that all that was necessary was for the consequences to be drawn from the first basic principle. But it is immensely instructive to see how Luther did this during these four years. We can see how on the one hand he hesitated, and allowed himself to be driven, even against his will, to new insights, and was forced to accept the consequences. Then, however, he would suddenly reject traditional ideas, without being expressly challenged to do so by his opponents, in a process of intellectual liberation, the suddenness of which can only be realized from a distance. The most remarkable step in this whole process was his attack on the Roman sacramental doctrine in the work *De captivitate babylonica ecclesiae praeludium* of 1520,[21] which from the point of view of the teaching of the Roman Church about its own nature, attacked its very foundations, and was completely heretical.

To all appearances, this course of events was heading directly for a revolution. It is odd that in Luther's case it was never in any danger of developing into a revolution, and that Luther in fact stoutly resisted the assaults of every kind of sectarian enthusiasm. The hold which the gospel had upon him, and which gave him the freedom to make criticisms and revise judgements even on primitive Christianity, also enabled him clearly to maintain what was of decisive importance, and to adopt a cautious and conservative attitude to the carrying out of his reforms of worship, of Church order, and of public and cultural life, which had been stirred to the very depths. All this, however, was strictly orientated to the requirements of the gospel, which were that the Reformation should not be brought about by the setting up of a new law, but by the liberation of the conscience, which brings certainty and assurance.

We do not propose to follow these individual stages in the development and the fortunes of the Reformation. Our studies of the person, the word and the action of Luther have provided an outline, and we shall now try to penetrate more closely into his way of thought. We shall begin with Luther's view of the relationship between philosophy and theology.

CHAPTER 5

PHILOSOPHY AND THEOLOGY

In one of Luther's earliest extant letters there is a statement concerning his attitude to philosophy and theology which gives an entirely personal view reflecting the circumstances of his work at that period. But this personal note unconsciously expresses a principle of fundamental significance for the entirety of his subsequent career, not merely for the future course of his approach to a simple intellectual problem, but for the basic orientation of his thinking as a whole. The letter was written in the spring of 1509, that is, during his study of theology, and was actually sent from Wittenberg, where he had been temporarily moved from Erfurt by his order six months previously, in order to teach as a Master of Arts in the faculty of arts at the same time as he carried out his own studies in the theological faculty. This was in accordance with the academic custom of the time. The foundation of the university required the Augustinian Hermits of Wittenberg to fill two chairs, that of biblical studies, which Luther took over in 1512 from Staupitz on his second and final stay in Wittenberg, and that of moral philosophy. In the latter post the twenty-five-year-old theology student had to comment on the *Nicomachean Ethics* of Aristotle. At that time, he had also received the degree of *baccalaureus biblicus*, which meant that he had also to expound books of the Bible as part of the course. He describes the situation by saying that through God's grace things were going well with him; but that the study was hard, especially that of philosophy, which from the first (he is referring to his period at Wittenberg) he would rather have exchanged for theology, and notably for a theology which explored the kernel of the nut and the germ of the wheat and the marrow of the bones.[1]

We see Luther making a decisive choice here, in favour of theology and against philosophy, not in the sense of a choice of study—for this had already been decided for him by the instruction given him by his order to study theology—but in the sense of a decision about the way of practising theology. For although the primary point is that of a change from one task, one intellectual discipline, to another, it is no accident that his statement goes on to define in critical terms what Luther certainly did not expect from philosophy, but looked for only from theology. Nevertheless, he did not expect to find it automatically in theology, but only in a true theology conducted in a way appropriate to its matter, a theology not superficial or satisfied with mere outward appearance, but penetrating to what is really decisive, and touching the heart of the individual through a real understanding of the central point at issue. We can already see the passionate determination which was no longer satisfied with conventional scholastic theology, but, with great claims on the subject and on itself, strove for a truly theological theology. The demand Luther expresses here was certainly not satisfied by a theology in which philosophy still represented the dominant element, a theology overgrown with philosophy, such as was to be found in systematic scholastic theology at least, and in some respects in its most extreme form in late scholastic theology.

This statement already sounds the basic note that can be heard throughout Luther's subsequent work, and which he formulated a few years later in a lecture on the Epistle to the Romans: 'I certainly believe that I owe it as a matter of obedience to the Lord to bark against philosophy and speak words of encouragement to the holy scripture. For if perhaps another were to do this, who was not acquainted with philosophy from his own observation, he would not have the courage to do so, or would not have commanded belief. But I have worn myself out for years at this, and can see quite clearly from my experience and from conversations with others that it is a vain and ruinous study. Therefore I admonish you all, so far as I am able, to be done with this form of study quickly, and to make it your sole business not to allow these matters to carry any weight nor defend them, but rather to do as we do when we learn evil skills in order to render them harmless, and obtain knowledge of errors in order to overcome them. Let us do the same with philosophy, in order to reject it, or at least to make ourselves familiar with the mode of speech of those with whom we have to deal. For it is time for us to devote ourselves to other studies, and to learn Jesus Christ, and him crucified.'[2]

Of course we should learn little of Luther's meaning, and should certainly misunderstand him, if we looked no further than this general affirmation of an antithesis between theology and philosophy. Luther considered himself entitled to adopt such an attitude because he had made a thorough study of philosophy. We in our turn ought not to suppose that we can understand his statements on the subject without knowing their historical background. Far less have we any right to adopt his polemic as our own without further thought, without a similar intensive personal experience in the practice of philosophy, and without considering how much our situation is different from that of Luther. Of course we must be equally careful not to dismiss these utterances as showing a frivolous contempt for philosophy, without having gone deeply into what Luther understood by philosophy. For he was an acute and thorough thinker. In all his judgements he was motivated not by a flight away from thought, but by the discipline of the kind of thought that was appropriate to theology. Consequently, the question which concerns him here is not that of an antithesis between philosophy and theology in general, but that of an antithesis between good and bad theology, between true theology and pseudo-theology; and it is the significance for this purpose of the distinction between theology and philosophy that interests him.

In fact theology and philosophy represent two traditions fundamentally different in their origin and nature: on the one hand the Christian faith, the historical origin of which is in the world of Judaism, dominated by the Old Testament; and on the other hand Greek thought, in which the freedom of the human mind to inquire rationally into the basis of being was first manifested in a unique way. The drawing together of these two traditions was the source of a very powerful and complex historical relationship, but could never hide the tension that resulted from this duality. Yet it is a foolish illusion to suppose that it was ever possible or right for this connection to be dissolved, in view of the actual course of history—as though events could be reversed, and as though it were possible to escape the historical pressure of the link between Christian faith and Greek thought. Such a view also overlooks the fact that by its origin the situation is not one that can be reduced to the simple formula of combination of two contradictory traditions, which as far as possible ought to be kept separate. However deeply the Christian faith is rooted in the Old Testament, it never purported to be understood as a form of

Israelite or Jewish religion. By accepting its mission to the world, and by realizing that the Gentiles were called to the Christian faith, without having to become Jews, primitive Christianity achieved in its very earliest stages a clear and decisive understanding of the essence of the Christian faith.

Thus Paul does not regard himself as forced to adopt a ready-made attitude as the propagator of a teaching hostile to Greek thought. He takes up an intermediate position, in which he has an obligation both to the Jews and to the Greeks, and speaks to both with the same sincerity, the same commitment, but also with the same willingness to oppose them, in the certainty that in the Christian faith the division between Jew and non-Jew, or between Greek and barbarian, has been abolished. For as he says in I Cor. 1: 22 ff., in a context which is of fundamental importance for Luther's attitude to the question of theology and philosophy, 'Jews demand signs and Greeks seek wisdom, but we preach Christ crucified, a stumbling block to Jews and folly to Gentiles, but to those who are called, both Jews and Greeks, Christ the power of God and the wisdom of God.' Thus the entry of the Christian message into the Greek and Hellenistic world was not a fortuitous event and a great threat to the purity of the Christian faith, but a necessary consequence of the real substance of the Christian faith, and therefore also essential for the purity of the Christian faith. It is profoundly significant that the New Testament was not written like the Old in Hebrew, but in Greek. But if it was in the nature of the Christian faith that the missionary encounter with the Greek world should be exercised with such speed and power, it was equally proper that it should also be prepared to encounter the most powerful element in the Greek world, philosophy.

The encounter between Christian faith and Greek philosophy

was first systematically carried out by the early Christian apologists, and was intensified and extended by the Alexandrine theologians, Clement and Origen, in a way that was decisive in determining the subsequent course of theological history. In considering how this was done, it is tempting to make the judgement that an extraordinarily dangerous course was followed, and that essential elements of the Christian faith were, if not abandoned, at least obscured, weakened and diminished. However much justification there may be for such a critical judgement (and of course it requires much modification in detail), one cannot overlook the fact that this ready acceptance of an encounter with philosophy is an expression of the understanding that Christian faith is not a flight into the ghetto, but a mission to the world, and that if it is to be maintained in its purity, it must expose itself to the critical process called for by this encounter.

Thus the rise of Christian theology is inseparable from the readiness to give a responsible account of its faith, which Christianity, by contrast with all other religions, made possible to an astonishingly radical degree. The word 'theology' is in fact drawn from Greek, but originally meant that aspect of language about the divine which was *not* capable of an encounter with philosophy: mythological and cultic language. The word 'theology', in the sense with which we are familiar, the intellectual responsibility of faith itself, is not Greek in origin, but was first made viable by Christian faith, and even then was not entirely respectable in its associations. Consequently, since the time of the early Church Christian theology has in fact always found itself in dialogue with philosophy to a greater or lesser degree. And it is noteworthy that the resolute acceptance of this situation has always been the mark of orthodox theology.

Nevertheless, the basic consciousness of an irreducible difference was always present. While conversion to Christianity naturally meant the abandonment and abolition of pagan religion, in principle at least, if not always entirely in practice, it by no means entailed the abolition of philosophy as well. Similarly, the victory of Christianity was not followed by the disappearance of the distinction between Church and State; instead, it was only then that the profundity of this problem was consciously realized and exercised any influence. In the same way, when Christianity had achieved general public recognition, and had brought to an end not only the remnants of pagan religion but also the existence of independent non-Christian philosophical thought, it certainly could not desire the cessation of philosophy as such, or its complete fusion with the statements of Christian faith, in such a way as to reduce theology merely to a Christian form of philosophy. Rather, it was in the interests of Christian faith and Christian theology that the legacy of the philosophical tradition should be pursued separately, and should be clearly distinguished from theology. This is what happened throughout the whole of the Middle Ages, where although in practice philosophy and theology were conducted by the same persons, they were not regarded as identical tasks. The problem of the right relationship and distinction between philosophy and theology is an essential one for Christianity; it is the inevitable tension which must be maintained between knowledge and faith, reason and revelation, which the Christian cannot lightly reject, and which is an obligation upon him.

It has been necessary to give this brief sketch of the wider background of our present subject, in order to make clear the dimensions of the problem. The main emphasis has perhaps been placed in a way which seems to run contrary to Luther's intention, but this is as it were a preventative measure, to make sure that in considering the direct confrontation, which provided the context and the explanation of Luther's statements, we do not lose sight of the basic substance of the problem. However, we must now give a brief account of the situation which was the background to Luther's dispute.

A basic feature of scholasticism was its distinctive theory about academic disciplines, which was valid on principle for all branches of scholarship in the same way, whether for mathematics or for medicine. It was based upon two principles, that of authority and that of reason. 'Authority' was not meant only in the sense of biblical and Church tradition; even branches of secular learning drew their inspiration from the extant works of the ancient world, the knowledge attained by which was considered to be of decisive authority. Thus, for example, even in the natural sciences, the method employed was that of the interpretation of authoritative texts, not that of independent empirical investigation. This emphasis on traditional authorities, of course, derives from the whole attitude of the medieval mind, in which the authority of the learning of the ancient world and the authority of the tradition of revelation were so involved with each other that where a conflict arose a decision could be made on the basis of the authority of revelation. Thus scholastic learning as a whole, and not merely theology, was ecclesiastical learning, and the places in which it was taught, including the universities which arose during the middle centuries of the medieval period, were Church institutions, or at least had ecclesiastical privileges. In this form of scholarship, based upon authority, the task of reason was to reconcile contradictions, refute objections and develop consequences by the use of the syllogistic method, that is, by means of dialectic. Strict limits were imposed by authority on these activities, but within these limits there was ample room for an intellectual activity which, perhaps as an actual consequence of the numerous hindrances placed upon free and untrammelled inquiry, led to extraordinarily high achievements in the form of comprehensive systems of thought which possessed great acuteness and power.

In the early Middle Ages, the philosophical armoury available as a legacy from the ancient world had shrunk to the point of disappearance, but at the beginning of the classical medieval period the publication of the complete works of Aristotle formed an important turning-point in intellectual history; and it was no accident that this coincided with the crowning achievement of the papacy in extending its influence over secular rulers, and with the remarkable drive of the mendicant orders towards a world mission. At first, the use and acceptance of Aristotle met with powerful resistance, even from the official ecclesiastical side. But this caution was overcome with the realization of the great possibilities which this philosophy made available to theology itself, of bringing faith and reason into a harmonious relationship, and of constructing a comprehensive and systematic intellectual unity embracing both natural and supernatural. The great achievement of Thomas Aquinas was to work out this comprehensive vision down to the finest details, in accordance with the principle that 'since grace does not destroy nature, but perfects it, the natural reason must serve faith, in the same way as the natural inclination of the will follows love'.[3] Thus *a priori* there can be no contradiction between theology and philosophy. Revelation is beyond reason, but not contrary to reason. It is true that a compelling proof of the truths of faith is not possible, but neither is a refutation of them, while at the same time they can be demonstrated to be without inner contradictions, and to be related by analogy to natural reality.

In this way, far greater scope was given to reason. In one direction it was limited, but in the other it was inspired to produce a triumphant achievement, and set upon a course in which it became conscious of its hitherto dormant possibilities and inevitably came to appear more independent and autonomous, and more inaccessible to attempts to bring it into harmonious relationship with the truth of revelation. It was the legacy of Augustine, still a powerful force amongst the Franciscans, which cast doubts upon the idea of a smooth harmonization between a rational understanding of the world and the Church's doctrine. The Aristotelian concept of knowledge was firmly maintained and even elaborated in detail, but theology could then be called a form of rational knowledge only in a limited or an altered sense. In late medieval nominalism, introduced by William of Ockham, the arguments were concentrated, by contrast with those of Aquinas, on demonstrating the point at which reason and faith parted company. This view was supported by a similar distinction in regard to God, who according to his *potentia absoluta* could quite well have ordained everything in a totally different way, so that his acts were not subject to higher standards and necessities beyond himself, although in accordance with his *potentia ordinata* he had bound himself to the actual conditions of reality set up by himself once and for all. Here an acute tension was set up between philosophy and theology, but in a unique and ambiguous sense. On the one hand it revealed the influence of a genuine religious feeling, emphasizing the completely different nature of the subject of theology, the antithesis between theology and reason, and the basis of theology in faith and in the authority of revelation. On the other hand, this tension was obtained by an intensified and formalist use of reason which delighted in demonstrating that Church doctrine was beyond truth and demonstration, and that its authority was of value only as a positive source of an otherwise unknowable fact. It was never clear whether it was faith or reason which was most exalted by this division.

Luther was trained in the Ockhamist way of thought in Erfurt. The tendency to see a degree of tension between philosophy and theology, and even to submit Aristotle to criticism, was therefore entirely natural to him. We find characteristic traces of this in his earlier marginal notes. Outbursts against the 'putrid philosophers',[4] the *'fabulator* Aristotle',[5] and against the 'shameless nonsense that Aristotle does not disagree with the Catholic truth'[6] can hardly be regarded as the earliest evidence of his Reformation teaching. Nevertheless, however cautiously all the signs may be interpreted, they cannot be ignored as merely the jargon of the Erfurt school of nominalism. There is unquestionably a distinctive personal note present, which is similar to that in the letter quoted above, at least in the strength and direction of its emphasis. We can see how careful we must be not to dismiss everything as being a result of Erfurt nominalism, when we turn to the letters which record his dispute in 1518 with his former teacher in Erfurt, Jodokus Trutfetter. Although Luther testifies to his highly respected teacher that it was from him that he first learned that one should accord faith to the canonical scriptures alone, and test and pass judgement on everything else,[7] at the same time he considers himself poles apart from Trutfetter, the *princeps dialectorum*. To him Luther seemed to be no kind of logician—Luther adds, 'perhaps I am not'.[8] He himself was accounted by Luther as one of those who had fallen victim to Aristotle and was consequently incapable of understanding the meaning of a single chapter of the Bible.[9] The revelance to exegesis of his anti-philosophical attitude, which is evident in the early marginal notes, was something which Luther certainly did not learn from Trutfetter.

Thus Luther's real concern in his dispute with the dominant philosophy of his time is that a genuine understanding of holy scripture should be made accessible to theology, from which it was concealed by the terminology and method of inquiry of Aristotelian thought. Consequently, from the very first the main principle of his exegetical work was to understand the distinctive nature of biblical modes of speech and thought, by contrast to the traditional philosophical language of scholastic theology. Thus, for example, he asserts that *intellectus*, instead of being understood as in philosophy as a human faculty, is used in the Bible in a sense which is defined by its object, so that the formal concept is replaced by a concern for the particular thing towards which the mind is orientated. Accordingly, true *intellectus* is not the knowledge of an arbitrary object, but something specifically biblical, namely the wisdom of the cross of Christ, that is, faith. By contrast, the so-called human intellect is mere *sensualitas*, and this includes the human *ratio*, since it is likewise incapable of understanding spiritual things (*spiritualia*).[10]

Again, in philosophy *substantia* signifies the inner nature of a thing, while in the Bible it is used in the opposite sense of something external, which gives a thing duration, and provides permanence, something on which one can rely, as in the sense of the means of life from which someone derives his existential being; the rich man from his riches, the healthy person from his health. However, it has this in common with the philosophical concept of substance, that it is concerned with the question of what makes a thing what it is. But while philosophy proceeds logically from the phenomenon to the timeless inner nature, the *quidditates rerum*, in the sense that it is evident that the nature of richness lies in riches, so that riches form the logical *essentia* in the concept of richness, the scripture, as Luther confirms, is not concerned with the *quidditates*, but merely with the *qualitates*, that is, with the external element, the external relationship of a thing, its links with other things, and therefore also with what impinges on it from outside. This concept is concerned not with the *essentia*, but with the *existentia*, not with the logical and metaphysical aspect, but with the historical. In this mode of thought, the fact that it is riches which make a rich man rich sees his riches from the point of view of time and of events; he is rich only as long as he keeps his riches. At the same time, the relevance of one's attitude is introduced: a rich man is rich only in so far as he understands himself on the basis of his riches, lets them be his substance, and places his trust in them, so that it depends upon the person himself what he makes his substance. One's substance corresponds to the way one exists and the attitude one adopts.[11]

Here is a third characteristic example, slightly different in its implications. In Romans 8: 19 Paul speaks of the *expectation of the creation*. Luther considers that the way the apostle philosophizes about things is quite different from that of the metaphysicians. They look only at what is present here and now, and contemplate the essence and the attributes of things. The apostle, on the other hand, enables us to turn our eyes away from contemplation of the present, and therefore away from a concern with *essentia* and accidents. He enables us instead to consider things with regard to their future being. This is a quite different idea, in which existent being is contemplated not simply as timelessly present, but is seen as the apostle sees it, as a creation full of expectation, sighing and pregnant with the future, taken up itself into the process of despising what now is, and reaching out with longing towards what does not yet exist. It is only with regard to their existence in time that creatures can be regarded as creatures.[12]

The rigour of Luther's opposition to Aristotelianism was revealed to the academic world by the *Disputatio contra scholasticam theologiam* of September 1517. Here he uttered an unsparing condemnation, in elegantly formulated terms: 'It is an error to say that without Aristotle no one becomes a theologian. On the contrary, one only becomes a theologian when one does so without Aristotle. The assertion that a theologian who is not a logician is an abominable heretic, is itself abominable and heretical ... in short, the whole of Aristotle is related to theology as darkness is to light.' But it is worth noting the observation which follows this, that it is exceedingly doubtful whether Western theologians have rightly understood Aristotle at all.[13] This doubt, which Luther expresses elsewhere, as to whether the Aristotle of scholasticism was the true Aristotle, is a significant indication not only of the necessity of a critical investigation of the scholastic understanding of Aristotle, but above all of the real purpose behind Luther's criticism of Aristotle. He was quite aware that he was not concerned with Aristotle as such, but with the use that had been made of Aristotle in theology. It may be asked whether this usage may have harmed not only theology, but also Aristotle himself. In this sense, Luther's criticism of Aristotle may imply a defence of Aristotle. But Luther was not interested in this aspect of the matter. His attack on Aristotle was a struggle for true theological thought. A proper understanding of his outlook is consequently to be obtained not from his general invective against Aristotle, but only by a study of the concrete theological context in which the use of Aristotelian thought forms was in fact harmful.

A decisive issue for Luther was the use of Aristotelian

psychology at the heart of scholastic theology, in the doctrine of grace, where it served as an instrument for the interpretation of what takes place in grace. Grace was understood in a way analogous to the intellectual and moral virtues, as a *habitus* perfecting man in the faculties of his soul, and as the essence of the theological virtues of faith, love and hope. He refers on one occasion to an example used by the Aristotelian scholastics to explain a *habitus*: one becomes a harper by playing the harp, that is, one develops this faculty by practice in repeated acts. Here he points out that: 'We do not become righteous by doing what is righteous, but being made righteous we carry out righteous acts.'[14] It is not Aristotle that he is really attacking. For Luther intends neither to dispute the Aristotelian description of the acquirements of technical skills, nor their application to the moral sphere, so long as the distinction between the latter and the proper concern of theology is understood. Why should anyone dispute that a particular virtue can be achieved, even in the moral sphere, by practice? The danger in Aristotelian ethics is not this view itself, but its introduction into the doctrine of grace. Of course it is questionable how far the ethical approach of Aristotle is fundamentally opposed to the subject matter of theology. It is true that the scholastic doctrine of grace was only vulnerable to Luther's polemic against the Aristotelian description of the coming into being of a *habitus* by repeated acts, in its extreme nominalist perversions, and not in its true form. Scholasticism distinguishes quite clearly between a *habitius acquisitus*, a *habitus* acquired by oneself, such as only exists in the sphere of the natural virtues, and a *habitus infusus*, an infused *habitus* bestowed as a gift, which is only possible through the process of grace. Nevertheless, the interpretation of what takes place in grace by means of the categories of the Aristotelian concept of virtue leads to the introduction of the concept of merit, and to an inability to make a clear distinction between the moral and the theological aspect. Luther saw this quite clearly.

Luther's attack on the scholastic conception of the relationship between theology and philosophy, both in its Thomist and in its Ockhamist forms, brought with it tasks which for obvious reasons Luther himself made little attempt to carry out. This does not mean that they may be overlooked, but rather that they should be regarded as having been left to posterity. Luther himself did a considerable amount of preliminary work, but his achievements are no more than the first steps, which need to be followed up.

In the first place, Luther's criticism of scholastic thought forms faces us with problems in which the task of theology comes into contact with that of philosophy. These are the problems involved in working out appropriate and adequate concepts and methods of inquiry for describing the historical being of man. This does not mean that theology must simply submit itself to the discipline of another philosophy, different from Aristotelianism. Theology is responsible for its own language. But its dialogue with philosophy is part of its responsibility. Theology would not be responsible theology, if it restricted its responsibility for language itself. It also shares a responsibility for the language of philosophy. Moreover, in many respects more attention has been paid by philosophy than by theology to what Luther has taught us about the appropriate way of describing man in his historical being.

Secondly, the most striking example of the fact that Luther does not simply play off theology against philosophy, but regards their relationship as one which makes a proper distinction between them and accords its own sphere to each, is the

'Disputation concerning Man' of 1536.[15] Rightly understood, the reason of man is actually something divine.[16] If it kept within its limits, and concentrated on what concerned it, it would be truly reasonable, and could not be too highly praised. The reverse is true of reason when it tyrannizes the conscience and puts itself in the place of God; in this case, it is the duty of faith to slay it.[17] The task posed by Luther's theology is that of giving a fuller exposition of the relationship between theology and philosophy in the light of his extremely contradictory assertions concerning reason.

There is a third associated task. The study of Luther's understanding of theology must be extended to cover the theological epistemology which is implied in it, and therefore to the hermeneutic principles which follow from it. The purpose of the chapters that follow is simply to illuminate from different points of view the basic problems of his thought, which have been mentioned in this chapter.

CHAPTER 6

THE LETTER AND THE SPIRIT

FOR Luther, theology was two things at once. It was his calling, his trade, a subject of which he had a thorough understanding, and which it was his duty to understand thoroughly. It was also the essence of what is decisive in human existence, the truth that brought assurance, certainty, salvation and life. Thus, on the one hand it was the object of cognition, of a human faculty, of the activity of knowledge; on the other hand, it was a matter of faith, of grace and of the act of God. From the first point of view it was concerned with the holy scriptures, with the task of interpreting them, and with the exposition of doctrine in accordance with them; in the second respect it was concerned with man's own existence, his own personal experience, and with the Holy Spirit. Thus on the one hand it was concerned with the ability to understand and utter something, and on the other with the understanding of oneself on the basis of what is uttered.

As modern men we have a tendency to emphasize vigorously the distinction between these two aspects. The leading spirit of the theology of the Enlightenment, Johann Salomo Semler, did much to establish this view: according to him, a distinction must be made between theology and religion. The former is a matter of the understanding, a specific intellectual skill, a method to be learned; the other is a matter of the heart, of experience and emotions. One need not be a theologian in order to be a Christian. Nor does a theological training make one a Christian. Theology is knowledge about religion, whereas religion is life itself directly experienced. Of course there are certain links between the two. Because religion, that is, religion as the Church, is concerned with public life and the community, it needs theology. Furthermore, it is obvious that it is also of value to theology that the theologian himself should have a living relationship to his subject; above all he ought to take what he teaches seriously with regard to himself and be personally involved. Nevertheless, the dominant theme is the distinction between the approach of knowledge and that of faith, the objective presentation and exposition of the material (the *explicatio*) and one's own subjective involvement, one's own personal response or the appeal and challenge to make such a response (the *applicatio*). Although it is not denied that these two aspects are related at every point, a sharp distinction is still made between, on the one hand, what can be objectively verified, methodically demonstrated, and can stand up to a scientific inquiry, and, on the other hand, subjective convictions, the obligation of conscience, and personal involvement—or in other words, between historical truth and existential truth. It has consequently been supposed that the exposition of traditional texts, and therefore their interpretation, as a matter of understanding, is only concerned with historical truth, and is therefore subject to methodical and historical considerations; while their application to the present and their personal acceptance can be left to chance or to personal inclination, being no more susceptible to discussion than matters of taste.

Theology is concerned on the one hand with texts handed down by tradition, that is with historical data, and on the other hand with the word and with faith; in it the written text and the spoken proclamation, history and faith, are intimately interwoven. As a result, in theology, hermeneutics, the problem of interpretation, is of fundamental importance. This is generally agreed. What can be disputed is the way in which the problem of interpretation is tackled in theology, and whether the approach is sufficiently radical. Theology is bound to fall into decay if we separate what it claims to unite: the understanding of the biblical tradition, and the faith implied by this understanding. If theology is not to be defeated by the problem of interpretation, it cannot be reduced to mere historical understanding, but must maintain the association between the different aspects of understanding within the existential situation in which understanding takes place, so that an existential response becomes possible. The special concern of theology with the particular problem of interpretation ought not, of course, to be taken to imply that it is in any sense an exclusive concern of theology. Theology is only a particularly acute manifestation of something which is true of any responsible treatment of traditional material and texts which are relevant to a contemporary situation, whether in philosophy, law, classics, philology or anything else. Hermeneutics is the carrying out of a process of understanding which would be inadequate, one might say crippled, if it did not lead on to the present situation.

This recent change in the understanding of the problem of interpretation is to be found not merely in theology, but throughout the intellectual activity of the present day. It leads us back to the problem as we find it in Luther, and indeed it is affected, sometimes directly and sometimes indirectly, by influences which go back to his hermeneutic principles. For Luther, theology as the object of intellectual inquiry and theology as the sphere of a personal encounter, formed an indivisible unity. Let me quote again a passage from a letter to which I have already referred.[1] Luther was looking for a theology which would explore the kernel of the nut, the germ of the wheat and the marrow of the bones. It was with this desire that he studied holy scripture. Although, looking back, he later expressed the view that during the rule of the papacy and of scholasticism, the scripture had been 'pushed under the seat',[2] he was referring more to the practical influence of the Bible than to its theoretical evaluation. For in theory, of course, its unique authority was always fully affirmed. The question of the relationship between scripture and tradition was barely discussed in the prevailing theology of the time. It was the Reformation which first subjected the problem to a closer examination. Appealing as it did to the scripture alone, it was able to adopt a position which was still possible in the dogmatic theology of the time, and even to some extent to follow tendencies which seemed to point explicitly in the direction of what later came to be known as the scriptural principle of the Reformation. In this respect, Luther gratefully acknowledged his obligation to his former teacher at Erfurt, Trutfetter.[3] We can see in the very earliest extant records of his theological thought, long before the scriptural principle of the Reformation was formulated in theoretical terms, that Luther concerned himself for practical purposes with the scripture alone. For him, theology consisted of the interpretation of the holy scripture. This task was completely identified in his mind with the question which constantly pursued him of his standing in the sight of God. For he never doubted that the will of God was revealed and comprehensible to men solely through the holy scripture.

This did not yet mean that he was certain *how* this was so. There are many difficulties in a formal scriptural principle.

Such a principle can turn the scripture into an oppressive law. Obviously, if the scripture alone is valid, everything depends upon how this validity is understood, and how the scripture is interpreted. A proverbial saying with which Luther was acquainted sums up these hermeneutic difficulties: 'The scripture has a wax nose':[4] that is, its countenance can be changed and distorted in many ways by an arbitrary interpretation. An extraordinary degree of devotion to the scripture is necessary, in order not to do it violence by approaching it from individual and isolated points of view, but trying instead to understand the fundamental message. The less one approaches the scripture from a previously established position, looking for specific answers to specific questions, or in order merely to enrich one's knowledge, and the more radically one accepts the challenge to one's own existential life of an encounter with the scripture, concentrating upon a single fundamental question aimed at human existence itself and touching one's very conscience, the more one looks ultimately for only one thing in the scripture, the word which brings certainty in life and in death, the better will be one's prospects of a real understanding and adequate interpretation of the scripture. For its fundamental theme is clearly the unique and ultimately valid word, which is called the word of God because it is a decisive utterance about our existence as human beings.

Luther's later account of how the basic insight of the Reformation came to him[5] is an impressive testimony to his struggle to understand the scripture, and to find an answer to the question of what brings certainty and assurance to the conscience. It would, however, be an error to suppose from this passage that Luther was only concerned here with the right understanding of a single biblical passage. It is true that Luther himself emphasizes that once he had attained a right understanding of Romans 1: 17 the whole Bible took on a new appearance for him, and that this one verse gave him an understanding which was of immense hermeneutic importance. But there is a danger here of seeing what took place in Luther's intercourse with the scripture from too narrow a point of view. His preparatory work for his first commentary on the Psalms is a unique testimony to the way he strove to understand the scripture in such a way that it did not remain merely the letter, that is, something alien, remote and external, but became the Spirit, that is, something alive in the heart, which takes possession of man. For the question of the true spiritual understanding of the holy scriptures, that is, an understanding through which the Spirit itself can take hold of man, is identical with the question which tormented Luther, that of the reality of grace and the certainty which brings assurance to the mind and the conscience. For what is grace, except the presence of the Holy Spirit?

Consequently, Luther formulated the principle of interpretation for his first exegetical lectures as follows: 'In the holy scriptures it is best to distinguish between the Spirit and the letter; for it is this that makes a true theologian. And the Church has the power to do this from the Holy Spirit alone and not from the human mind.'[6] And in his commentary on Psalm 45 he says of the way in which we should hear and read the word of God, that it is not something we should attempt to do through our own powers, nor should we be content with the letter and with the mere outward hearing of the word, but should make it our concern to listen to the Spirit itself. It is not by the word as it is uttered outwardly that we are really taught inwardly, for it is merely the tool and instrument of him who writes living words in the heart. What is uttered *vocaliter* by the voice, must be understood *vitaliter* in the heart through the Holy Spirit. Thus the Spirit must be drawn out from the letter. The Spirit is concealed in the letter. But this must be understood in a profound and theologically very significant sense. The letter is not a good word, for it is the law of the wrath of God. But the Spirit is a good word, good news, the gospel, because it is the word of grace.[7] Or, to phrase it differently again: what the law says, and the events it recounts, are mere words and signs. But the words and events of the gospel are reality, the very substance of what they describe.[8]

This striving for a true understanding of the scripture, with its concern for the Spirit, is of necessity concerned with the present existential situation. For the Holy Spirit is a present and life-giving Spirit, by contrast to the letter, which owes everything to the past and consequently speaks of the past. Thus, in this early lecture, does Luther not merely sharply criticize the historical understanding of the Psalms as practised, for example, by Nicholas of Lyra in the fourteenth century, following rabbinic exegetes. The hermeneutic principle from which Luther starts, with its antithesis between the letter and the Spirit, also leads him to the realization that the understanding of the scripture is not something that can be preserved and passed on. As existential life continues, so the understanding of the scripture is a continuous task which can never be brought to a conclusion. For there is a constant threat that an understanding once achieved will cease to be the Spirit, and return to being the mere letter, unless it is constantly attained anew and made one's own. Thus unceasing progress is necessary in understanding the scripture. The Spirit turns into the letter; but the letter must in its turn constantly become the Spirit once again. One stage of understanding is always the letter from which the Spirit comes in the next stage. This reveals an astonishing insight into the historical limitations of our understanding. When the Psalmist prays: 'I am thy servant give me understanding, that I may know thy testimonies!',[9] Luther's interpretation is as follows: 'The Psalmist prays for an understanding against the mere letter, for the Spirit is understanding. For as the years have passed, so has the relationship grown closer between the letter and the Spirit. For what was a sufficient understanding in times past, has now become the letter to us. Thus at the present time, as we have said, the letter itself is more subtle in nature than before. And this is because of the progress of time. For everyone who travels, what he has left behind and forgotten is the letter, and what he is reaching forward to is the Spirit. For what one already possesses is always the letter, by comparison with what has to be achieved . . .' And Luther is sufficiently bold to draw an example of this from traditional dogma: 'Thus the doctrine of the Trinity, when it was explicitly formulated at the time of Arius, was the Spirit, and only understood by a few; but today it is the letter, because it is something publicly known —unless we add something to it, that is, a living faith in it. Consequently we must always pray for understanding, in order not to be frozen by the letter that kills.'[10]

In using the antithesis 'the letter and the Spirit', Luther was following a far-reaching tradition. The antithesis was first formulated by Paul, and its influence in the history of thought is mainly due to 2 Cor. 3: 6: 'The letter kills, but the Spirit gives life.' (R.S.V.: 'the written code'). This distinction between an understanding based purely on the outward meaning of a text, and an understanding based on its inner significance, between remaining satisfied with the lifeless letter and going on to penetrate the living Spirit of a text, has become a general hermeneutic principle. This goes far beyond what Paul had in mind in this antithesis. He was not thinking of a basic principle for understanding written texts in general, but of the distinction between the law of the old covenant and the Spirit, as the determinative element in the life of the new covenant. Nevertheless, the essential character of the former was that of a 'written code' handed down by tradition, to which is opposed the event of the imparting of the Spirit through the proclamation of faith. Thus for Paul, the distinction between the letter and the Spirit, in the sense of the law and the gospel, is associated with the question of understanding and interpretation in a very profound sense.

However, in the course of theological development, this relationship was soon distorted. Origen interpreted Paul's antithesis in a Platonizing sense, taking it to mean that one should pass beyond the sphere of what is perceptible to the senses to that which is intelligible to the mind. It thus became a justification for allegorical exegesis, which went beyond the literal meaning to the spiritual and figurative sense. This interpretation of 2 Cor. 3: 6 by Origen had a decisive effect on the history of exegesis, since it seemed to draw a legitimization of allegory from the very heart of Pauline theology. In the course of his dispute with the Pelagians about the true understanding of Paul, Augustine succeeded in recognizing that in 2 Cor. 3: 6 *littera* and *spiritus* were not general exegetical terms but were used to refer to the distinction between the law and grace. However, he too used the terms elsewhere in the sense given them by Origen, although he weakened the distinction by according to the letter a necessary function as a sign. Thus in medieval exegesis, which was based upon Augustine, the literal sense of the scriptures continued to be regarded as the true and valid meaning, the only one on which a proof could be based in matters of theological dispute. But it was still regarded as right and proper, in passages in which the literal

meaning was obscure or offensive, or not immediately edifying,
or where it could be made more edifying by revealing deeper
mysteries in it, to supplement and go beyond it, giving it a
spiritual and allegorical sense. This extra meaning had always
to be one that could be demonstrated from the literal meaning
of other passages in the Bible.

Thus an attempt was made to limit the dangers of allegorical
interpretation. Its scope was firmly restricted by the biblical
texts as a whole, and above all by Church doctrine. Furthermore, the possibilities of allegorical interpretation were given
systematic dogmatic form in the idea of the fourfold sense of
scripture. In addition to the literal meaning, three methods of
spiritual interpretation are possible, although they are not
applicable to all texts. The terminology is somewhat arbitrary.
They are the allegorical application to the Church and to
dogma, the tropological or moral interpretation, applying to
individual persons, and the anagogical interpretation, applying
the text to metaphysical and eschatological mysteries. It was
admittedly possible by these methods to make a fruitful use
of the biblical text without risk to Church dogma. This,
however, concealed the dangers inherent in this procedure.
There was no longer any serious respect for the biblical text
itself. It was always possible to avoid strict attention to the
actual text. And wherever there was any risk of conflict with
prevailing Church teaching, the art of interpretation had to be
used in such a way that it became in fact the art of concealed
reinterpretation.

Surprisingly, when Luther began to study the holy scriptures, he expressly affirmed this traditional fourfold meaning of
scripture. To a certain extent, it was actually of value to him as
he progressed towards the Reformation understanding of the
scripture. Of course from the very first Luther avoided the

frivolous approach to the text to which this method led, because for him the interpretation of scripture was an utterly serious personal necessity. Consequently, his use of the fourfold sense of scripture was due not to a delight in playing with the numerous meanings of the text, but to a determined inquiry into its unique meaning. By comparison with the scriptural exegesis of the late Middle Ages, which on the whole was dry and sterile, Luther's pre-Reformation exegesis, carried out at a time when he must still be regarded as a late scholastic theologian, presents a very unusual phenomenon. There is a change of atmosphere which is due not only to his existential emphasis, but also to the fact that Luther does not make use of the distinction between the letter and the Spirit merely in the conventional sense in which it was understood in the hermeneutic theory of scholasticism. On the one hand he tended to see it basically as an antithesis. This is an ontological view which provided the background to the thought of Origen, and similarly also to that of Neoplatonism. The distinction between the letter and the Spirit is rooted in numerous antithesis similar in their implications: between the carnal and spiritual, visible and invisible, sensible and intelligible, manifest and concealed, inward and outward, lower and higher, human and divine, earthly and heavenly, temporal and eternal, present and future, untruth and truth. Of course, in spite of certain relationships and similarities, one cannot talk of Neoplatonism in Luther's case. This can be seen from the fact that his understanding of the letter and the Spirit, apparently Neoplatonic in its overtones, was so closely related to the content of the Bible that it took on the original Pauline sense of the law and grace, and so led him to strive for a spiritual understanding which could no longer be confused with the conventional allegorical interpretation.

The way in which Luther makes use of the idea of the four-fold meaning of scripture in obtaining a true understanding of the scripture is very instructive. He did not regard the literal meaning as such as the 'letter that kills', and the allegorical, tropological and anagogical interpretations imposed upon it as the 'life-giving Spirit'. Instead, he based the fundamental distinction between the letter that kills and the life-giving Spirit on the substance of what was expressed in the whole fourfold meaning of the scripture. The whole can be the letter that kills, or the whole can be the life-giving Spirit, depending upon whether the understanding is orientated towards Moses or towards Christ. As a result, the traditional schematization fell apart. The allegorical sense, and also the anagogical, ceased on the whole to be of interest. His whole attention was concentrated instead on the relationship between the literal and the tropological sense. He understood the literal sense not, however, as the historical meaning, but as the Christological meaning of the text. That is, the basic meaning with which the study of the text of the Psalter is concerned is Christ himself. The prayers of the Psalter are to be regarded as uttered by him; that is, if they are to be understood at all, they must be understood as if the person speaking in the Psalms, the 'I' who prays in them, is not some arbitrary person, but Jesus Christ himself. To begin with Jesus Christ as the fundamental meaning and utterance of the holy scripture became Luther's basic hermeneutic principle. He says: 'Others may follow more devious routes, and as though they were wilfully fleeing from Christ, neglect this way of coming to him through the text. But whenever I have a text which is a nut whose shell is too hard to crack, I throw it at once against the rock [Christ], and find the sweetest kernel.'[11]

But if Christ speaks through the Psalter then it follows that in this understanding of Christ the details of his Passion, of his bearing the sin of the world, and even of his abandonment by God are portrayed in all their severity. In this respect Luther's Christological interpretation of the Psalms goes infinitely further than the tradition, and so prepared the way for his theology of the cross. But if Christ is the fundamental meaning, so that in him all words form a single word,[12] then their application to the individual (the tropological sense of the scripture) must consist not of disconnected useful moral applications, or of a demand for similar works on the part of man, but must be aimed solely at the faith which apprehends Christ. This is the ground on which the earliest form of Luther's doctrine of justification sprang up. We may also say that we find here an understanding of the Holy Spirit strictly orientated towards the crucified Christ, and consequently, therefore, towards the relationship between the word and faith. The concealment of God on the cross is paralleled by the structure of faith, which consists of concealment beneath a contrary. 'For who would realize that one who is visibly humbled, tempted, rejected and slain, is at the same time and to the utmost degree inwardly exalted, consoled, accepted and brought to life, unless this were taught by the Spirit through faith? And who would suppose that one who is visibly exalted, honoured, strengthened, and brought to life, is inwardly so pitifully rejected, despised, weakened and slain, unless this were taught by the wisdom of the Spirit?'[13]

It now becomes clear what 'spiritual' means here. It means everything, in so far as it is understood 'in the sight of God'; that is, in the sign of the cross of Christ, and therefore in the sense of the concealment of God beneath the contrary. Salvation is spiritual, in so far as it is not understood as the affirmation of worldly existence or as the bestowal of temporal goods, but as being crucified with Christ, and so possessing life in death. The believer is spiritual, in so far as he understands that he is hidden in God, and so affirms his concealment in the sight of the world, in order to be safe in this concealment beneath the contrary. The Church is spiritual, as long as it regards itself as hidden in this life, and does not place its trust in earthly instruments of power, but realizes that it must be persecuted, and that the most dangerous temptation is the temptation not to be persecuted and to live in safety. Even sin is spiritual, in so far as it is recognized in the sight of God as self-righteousness, as pious self-assertion against God, and as a flight from proclaiming the righteousness of God into self-justification. 'The spiritual' is not a specific area of existence, the realm of pure spirituality, of inwardness and of the invisible. To understand the concealment of the spiritual in that sense is to understand it not as spiritual, but in a carnal way. 'The spiritual' is the category of true understanding. Someone whose existential being is spiritual exists of course in the visible world, but his real existential being is not manifest. What can be seen exists, but it is the contrary, and not the spiritual life as such. Consequently, to live in the Spirit means to live in faith. The Spirit and faith are the same.[14]

It is this Christologically orientated understanding of the Spirit which gives rise to the concentration on the relationship between the word and faith which is fundamental to Luther's theological thinking: 'The glory and power of the kingdom of Christ is so hidden that it cannot be recognized, if it is not revealed to the hearer through the word of preaching; for what the eye can see is its extreme opposite, shame, weakness, loneliness, and utter contemptibleness in every believer.'[15] 'For faith is the reason why we can show what good things we have through the word alone. For faith is concerned with what is not visible, with what can be taught, shown and inspired through the word alone.'[16] In his comment on Psalm 119: 148 Luther expresses his wonderment at the constantly repeated petition for the word of God: 'This is a strange prayer, which begs God for mere words, not for things, but for their sign. Whoever cried out so fearfully for words?' But his answer is: 'But because invisible things are concealed in words through faith, he who possesses the words possesses everything through faith, although in hidden form.'[17]

This early form of Luther's theology raises many questions. For Luther himself it was a transitional stage, but at the same time a preliminary step in which, in spite of all that required correction, what was to come could already be seen. We shall now go on to describe two later corrections to the theme of the 'letter and the Spirit', which do not really represent a contradiction of his earlier position, but rather developed its consequences, and made them more precise.

The first concerns Luther's hermeneutic method. The hermeneutic principle which he laid down in his early period implicitly and inevitably implied the abandonment of the fourfold meaning of scripture. Once its meaning was reduced to the relationship between Christ, the word and faith, the whole mighty hermeneutic system became meaningless, and was quite clearly replaced by a concern for the fundamental theme of the scripture in its literal sense. Thus at the beginning of the *Operationes in Psalmos* of 1519, Luther explains: 'Our first concern will be for the grammatical meaning, for this is the truly theological meaning.'[18] It is now clear that he considers that there is only one genuine meaning of scripture, and that is the literal sense, which as such is spiritual because of the content of the scripture. The justification of allegory on the basis of 2 Corinthians 3: 6 is now sharply rejected. Admittedly, it was still possible for Luther to use allegory as a homiletic device to obtain a more striking application of the text, particularly in his sermons, though he did this with decreasing frequency. But allegory was no longer regarded as a valid hermeneutic principle. This was the beginning of a process which eventually made it impossible to avoid the problems of historical and critical exegesis—although the historical and critical method is not itself adequate to provide a hermeneutic answer to the problems it raises.

The second point in which Luther's earlier discussion of the letter and the Spirit was corrected in the subsequent period concerns the understanding of the word as it was worked out in conflict with a sectarian enthusiasm which presented an extreme radical version of the Reformation. The inner word was opposed to the external word, which strictly speaking was a return to what was in fact a distortion of Augustine. In the teaching of Karlstadt and others, Luther saw himself faced with an understanding of the Spirit which was simply worked out in an ontological sense as the antithesis of corporeality, and which consequently, in spite of superficial similarities, cannot in any sense be derived from the works of Luther's early period. At first sight, the position of the enthusiast was completely opposed to that of the Roman Church. 'His [i.e. the Pope's] spirit did more to make the spiritual bodily, for he made spiritual Christianity into a bodily and external Church. But the main effect of this sectarian spirit is to make spiritual what God made corporeal and external. That is why we steer between the two and make nothing either spiritual or corporeal, but keep as spiritual what God made spiritual, and keep as corporeal what he made corporeal.'[19] Nevertheless, both extreme views are fundamentally identical in an enthusiastic understanding of the Spirit, against which Luther had only to define more closely the understanding of the Spirit which he had already begun to work out on his own account in his first lectures on the Psalms. 'In these passages, which concern the spoken and external word, it must be firmly maintained that God gives no one his Spirit or his grace except through or with the outward word which precedes it, and this is our defence against the enthusiasts, that is, the spirits which boast that they have the Spirit without and before the word, and judge, interpret and expound thereby the scripture and the spoken word as it pleases them, as Müntzer did, and many still do at the present time, claiming to be able to distinguish accurately between the Spirit and the letter, without knowing what they say or assert. For the papacy is also a vain enthusiasm, since the Pope boasts that all that is right is locked within his heart, and that what he decides and enjoins upon his Church is to be regarded as the Spirit and as right, even when it both goes beyond the scripture and the spoken word and is contrary to them . . . Thus, to sum up, enthusiasm lurks in Adam and his children from the beginning up to the end of the world, as a poison placed in them by the ancient serpent, and it is the source, power and might of all heresy, including that of the papacy and of Mahomet. Thus we must firmly maintain that God desires to do nothing with us men except through his outward word and sacrament. But everything which boasts that it is of the Spirit, without the word and the sacrament, is the Devil.'[20]

CHAPTER 7

THE LAW AND THE GOSPEL

THE form taken by Luther's early theology, as we see it in the first lectures on the Psalms, was dominated by the antithesis between the letter and the Spirit. This distinction, subject as it was to ambiguity as the result of a long and varied conceptual history, enabled Luther to treat as one two apparently separate questions which concerned him. Firstly, how should the biblical word be interpreted so that it speaks directly to the reader, affects him and comes to life in his heart? Secondly, what is the message of the holy scripture concerning its real subjects, Christ, faith and the Holy Spirit. The twin concepts, the letter and the Spirit, were handled by Luther like a plough, with which he broke through the hard surface of the scripture and made deep furrows in it. Admittedly, he did not continue to use this conceptual approach, which reflected his early thought. It was replaced by the distinction which it already implied between the law (the demand) and the gospel (the promise and the gift). In the interests of theological clarity, he expressly made this distinction between the law and the gospel his standard terminology. This linguistic change, which came about as a result of a gradual transition, does not signify a change in the substance of his teaching, but merely the maturity and confirmation of what had already been prepared for in his early period.

The continuity can be clearly seen from the fact that both

forms of expression have the same purpose: to define the true essence of theological thought, the fundamental message of the holy scripture. It is dedication to this purpose that makes a man a theologian. 'In the holy scripture it is best to distinguish the Spirit from the letter; because this is what makes one a true theologian'—so he says in the first lectures on the Psalms.[1] Luther repeatedly clarified this point in similar terms later on: 'Virtually the whole of the scriptures and the understanding of the whole of theology depends upon the true understanding of the law and the gospel.'[2] 'Anyone who can properly distinguish the gospel from the law may thank God and know that he is a theologian.'[3] Again, he says in a sermon: 'Both depend on this distinction. Thus Paul desires that in Christianity both of these, the law and the gospel, should be clearly distinguished . . . don't confuse them! When that happens, you lose one of the two, or even both; just as under the papacy no one knew what was the gospel as opposed to the law, or what was the law as opposed to the gospel; for they had a faith which was only in the law . . .'[4] Or again, in his introductory speech to the first disputation with the antinomians, that is, on an academic occasion which was of particular value for the clarification of the pure doctrine of the gospel: 'I have often heard before that there is no better way to hand down and to maintain true doctrine than by following this method, that is, of dividing Christian doctrine into two parts, the law and the gospel.'[5]

The first thing we notice about this distinction, which tends to sound like a cut and dried formula, is the remarkable fact that the touchstone of theology, the point which decides whether one has really grasped its true substance, is presented as a *distinction*. Thus Luther does not specify a particular idea, making it the centre of his thought and subordinating everything else to it. This might have been possible, for example, with repentance, the forgiveness of sins, love, the kingdom of God, or something similar—that is, a dominant religious idea which could have been placed at the head of a scale of values and turned into the principle by which a whole system was ordered. A superficial judgement would be that Luther himself gave pride of place and a forced and one-sided emphasis to one favourite theme, that of justification by faith. As far as the scriptures are concerned only a very limited amount of text is devoted to this doctrine; the idea only occurs in one section of the Pauline epistles, where it is called for by a specific dispute. For this reason, Luther has been accused of offending against the scriptural principle which he himself proclaimed. It is suggested that the scripture is much richer than Luther implied by his arbitrary insistence on one specific idea, and by his Paulinism, which it is suggested represents a very narrow version of Paul's real thinking. He has been reproached for not paying attention to the whole message of the scripture, and for reducing everything to a single point with a reckless subjectivism. It is argued that the fundamental scriptural principle of the Reformation, the 'scripture alone', *sola scriptura*, must be accompanied, by contrast with the use Luther made of it, by the further basic principle of exegesis, that of *tota scriptura*, 'the whole scripture'.

But the issue is not adequately treated if the discussion is abandoned at this level. Of course this line of argument needs several important clarifications. It is certainly dangerous to lay absolute importance on something which is only a partial aspect of a much greater whole, and obstinately to pursue a single and limited purpose. This is the basic intellectual approach of the sectarian, who is obsessed by a partial truth, proclaims it blindly without any sense of legitimate countervailing truths and distinctions, and thereby turns it into falsehood. On the other hand, it would imply a fundamentally false attitude to holy scripture to suppose that everything in it should be regarded as of equal importance. This, of course, is not possible and whenever this principle has been advanced, its sole effect in practice has been to deprive uncomfortable biblical insights of their force, or even to legitimize a one-sided emphasis on certain aspects. Nor does Christian faith of its nature require one to orientate oneself towards a particular idea, or even towards a profusion of specific ideas. Luther does in fact lay great weight upon the doctrine of justification, but his purpose is not to give preference to one Christian doctrine amongst many others, but to make possible a thorough approach to all Christian doctrines, or, to use more radical language, to make possible a proper treatment of all conceivable doctrine. The proper function of the doctrine of justification is that of giving a true significance to all other doctrines. But it can only be understood as Luther saw it if it is identical with what is implied by the distinction between the law and the gospel as the basic guiding principle of theological thought, and therefore as the decisive standard of theological judgement.

Although this distinction between the law and the gospel seems at first sight to be narrow and doctrinaire, we must be prepared to be drawn by it into a realm of thought of immense scope, and yet unusually close to reality. Of course we must also be prepared to accept and tolerate unusual ideas, which require the utmost concentration for their understanding. There is no reason to regard this suggestion of intellectual exertion as an evident symptom of deficiency. It is characteristic of our technical age to accept the utmost intellectual complexity as something natural and proper, and yet very marvellous, in fields where the appropriate methods are calculation and mechanical manipulation. On the other hand in the case of the intellect, that is where the task of giving a comprehensive account of reality is concerned, and also where the intellectual exposition of faith is called for, a primitive mode of expression, concepts which make no demand on the intellect, and unthinking repetitions are taken for granted, and even regarded as adequate for such matters.

Thus when Luther presents the decisive issue in the form of a distinction this does not of course mean that he is really proposing to replace a single idea with a twofold idea as the standard of judgement, as though the pattern of his thought were not that of a circle about a single point, but that of an ellipse about two *foci*. Nor is the recognition of this sufficient in itself to counteract the misunderstanding that he was concerned merely with the proper hierarchy of individual doctrines, and not with an attempt to find the specific process of thought and method of judgement which is appropriate to the inner structure and content of all Christian doctrine. But if we attempt to define the role of the distinction between the law and the gospel by saying that it is concerned with the structure of doctrine, and is limited to Christian doctrine, we must go on to test this approach, and see if it is adequate and appropriate.

What does 'distinction' really mean here? Obviously it does not mean a division, a separation. There is not merely an alternative: either the law or the gospel. It is not as though one can be replaced by the other. In a series of passionate conflicts, Luther attacked the antinomian misunderstanding which alleged that because Christian preaching was the gospel, it had nothing to do with the law. Moreover, he regarded it as obviously necessary, for the sake of the purity of the gospel, to defend the law. If the gospel were meant simply to compete with and replace the law, it would itself be no more than a form of law. But whereas the relationship is not such that within it one simply excludes the other, like light and darkness or good and evil, neither is it accurate to consider both as complementary, as though the law were not sufficient, and the gospel had to be added to it, or as though the gospel alone were not sufficient, and the law was required as well. The need for a proper distinction seems to face us with a task which is more difficult than that of mere separation or mere association. This task is to maintain an opposition between the two which is of the nature of a mortal enmity—so that the law slays the gospel, and the gospel the law—but also, *at one and the same time*, to reduce this enmity to order, by bringing both into a proper relationship, in which each remains in its own place and within its own limits: the law does not claim to be the gospel, and the gospel does not attempt to take over the role of the law.

This reflection on the distinction between the law and the gospel impels us to define the distinction more closely and in more concrete terms. For we must not appear to be content with an abstract game with purely formal relationships, but must recognize the real and serious problems with which Luther was concerned. For the moment, however, let us ignore this demand. A further observation on the nature of this distinction will make the need for such a concrete explanation even more urgent, but this is necessary if our painful advance is to make any progress. The distinction between law and the gospel would be a simple one if it were concerned with a theoretical understanding, which, once it had been grasped, could be applied like any other piece of knowledge. Of course something of the sort is also involved. But this is not the real issue. A distinction here does not mean a difference which simply exists, and has only to be established, understood and recognized. The issue is a serious one for the very reason that the difference does not exist in practice, but is rather experienced only in a mixed and confused form, and that even where it is clearly recognized, it must be repeatedly clarified, and can only be maintained against a constant and pressing threat of confusion. Thus 'distinction' here is in the strictest sense a *nomen actionis*, and does not mean—except in the deepest sense of the term—the mere affirmation of a difference which already exists, but refers to the actual carrying out of the distinction, which demands total involvement and sustained commitment. The distinction between the law and the gospel is not modelled on the harmless and peaceable business of a logical operation, a process of definition by which one tries to draw a line between two entities or two sets of ideas, as one does in establishing the difference between the short story and the novel, or between murder and manslaughter. The appropriate model here is that of the process of a legal dispute, in which a distinction has to be made in concrete terms between two different legal claims relating to an extremely complicated situation. Perhaps an even more appropriate example is the course of a battle, which seems all the more embittered and hopeless because the two opposing fronts are completely locked together.

Thus the distinction between the law and the gospel cannot be carried out by means of a theological definition, which at best can only maintain the process in being. For theology as a whole is not an occupation whose aims are fulfilled in itself. Theology—in the specific sense of Christian theology—is only meaningful at all for the purpose of preaching. 'Preaching' here must be taken in a very broad sense, or more accurately, in the very exact, real and consequently very comprehensive sense of the word which is spoken and must be spoken, in concrete circumstances, for Jesus Christ's sake. Only when we have something to say for Jesus Christ's sake, appealing to him and speaking in his name, which means speaking with an authority received from him, is there any point in theology. And the distinction between the law and the gospel is only the central issue of theology because it is concerned with what is the true word of Christian preaching.

Christian preaching *is* the process in which the distinction between the law and the gospel takes place. This must not be misunderstood. The purpose of Christian preaching is not primarily that of instruction concerning the distinction between the law and the gospel—though it is so in a secondary sense. Rather, the concern of Christian preaching is to put into practice the distinction between the law and the gospel, that is, to carry on the progress of a battle, in which time and again the distinction between the law and the gospel is newly at issue and is made in practice. This means that making the distinction in practice between the law and the gospel is not fortuitous and incidental to the process of preaching, but is what is really meant to take place within it. But if the process of preaching is what it claims to be, that is, the process of salvation, then as the distinction is made between the law and the gospel, so the event of salvation takes place. And a confusion of the two is not a misfortune of little significance, a regrettable weakness, but is evil in the strict sense, the total opposite of salvation.

In order to express these strange sounding propositions in all their rigour, let us add that to fail to make this decision, to confuse the law and the gospel, is the normal occurrence, the state of affairs which exists everywhere. This is the situation with which Christian preaching is always faced and which is the only cause of its taking place, but Christian preaching is also constantly being drawn into it and is in continual danger of being submerged in it through mistaking its task. For the confusion becomes wholly evil when the very preaching which ought to distinguish between the law and the gospel confuses them. The failure to distinguish the law and the gospel always means the abandonment of gospel, leaving only the law. Yet when the law is not distinguished from the gospel, but is itself presented as the gospel, it is no longer properly recognized as the law. The final outcome is that the law itself is lost, because the law is all that remains. On the other hand, the gospel is of its very nature a distinction between the law and the gospel. Thus the gospel is not present in a pure and undefiled form when it stands on its own, untroubled and undisturbed, with its relation to the law never considered. In such isolation, the gospel could not be the gospel. For the gospel only comes into action when it does so in distinction from and in opposition to the law—and when as a result the law is really the law.

But to what in fact do these two terms, the law and the gospel, which become more enigmatic the more we use them, actually refer? They certainly refer to something which is brought forth by the word and is effective through the word. If the central issue of theology is the distinction between the law and the gospel, then the decisive task of theology is to learn to make this distinction with respect to the word. It is concerned to acquire the knowledge, and above all the ability to make right use of the knowledge, that anyone who deals with the word is ultimately concerned with a *twofold* word, and that if the word is to be handled aright, it is necessary to penetrate into this inner conflict within the word and to take part in it oneself.

The distinction with respect to the word which we are now approaching reveals certain fundamental insights. It would be wholly inadequate to consider the word merely in abstract terms, with regard to the different ideas it contains. The word is only apprehended as such in concrete terms when the relationship is understood between what it *says* and what it *effects*, that is, when it is understood as an active and effective word and so is not separated from the situation in which it is uttered and which is changed by the word, but is regarded as one with it. This is the only way in which it can be meaningful to speak of a distinction with regard to the word which does not point to a number of arbitrary ambiguities, but touches on an ultimate duality. And this is the only way in which it is possible to understand, as Christian preaching asserts, that salvation depends upon the word: for evil also becomes powerful through the word, and therefore the proper use of the word requires the knowledge that one is accountable for what leads to death and to life.

Luther could describe the duality of the word as that between the word of God and the word of man: 'As often as God's word is preached, it creates a joyful, open and assured conscience before God; for it is the word of grace, and forgiveness, a good and beneficent word. But as often as man's word is preached, it creates a troubled, cramped and fearful conscience within man, for it is the word of the law, of anger and of sin, and shows what we have failed to do and how much we have to do.'[6] In the first place, this reveals very closely the extent to which the word possesses the character of an event with power to bring about an ultimate decision. It has the power in so far as it touches and strikes man at his most sensitive point, the very heart of his being, where the decision is made as to what his position should be ultimately—that is, in the sight of God. Luther calls this point the 'conscience'; but he is not following the idealist interpretation of the conscience as an independent voice within man's own heart which gives him independence, and is thus the basis for man's autonomy. What he means is that man is ultimately a hearer, someone who is seized, claimed, and subject to judgement, and that for this reason his existential being depends upon which word reaches and touches his inmost being. This may be a word that imposes a burden on him which he has to carry himself, throws him back upon himself, makes an unlimited claim upon him as one who acts and who acts, therefore, on his own behalf, and then presents him with the account of everything he has not done, everything in which he has failed and everything he still owes. Or it may be the word which sets him free from this imprisonment within himself, this abandonment to his own resources, and reveals to him a hope which is not founded upon himself, and promises him a courage which is not derived from himself. Such a word lays claim to him not as an active agent who has to justify himself by his works, but as one who owes nothing to himself, who has become a gift to himself, and who, moreover, is able to understand himself as one who loves through a gift, through grace, and through forgiveness.

The first kind of word, which places upon man a burden to be borne by himself and his own abilities, and lays claim to him in respect of his activity and his powers, but ultimately leaves him on his own, is in one sense, a qualified sense, 'the word of man'. For it is a word which results in nothing *more* than what a man can do of his own power to another, as one who is imprisoned within himself. How could such a word of man, though outwardly it may be a mighty word, be other than powerless to set the conscience free? If the word of man is considered with regard to what ultimately takes place through it, it is clear that it is a word in which the only effective powers are those by which man is held captive. Thus ultimately it is not the word of man, but—in so far as the power which holds man imprisoned is ultimately the power of God, the law which accuses him the law of God, and the anger which terrifies him the anger of God—it is in fact the word of God; but it is the word of law, the word of anger, a word in which God remains absent and concealed—that is, in which he is present as one who is absent and concealed. On the other hand, the word in which God comes as one who is present and revealed is the word of God in a different and special sense. That is, it is the word through which he creates and brings about my acceptance of him as God, my honouring of him as God, my faith in him, my readiness to receive him, my trust in him and my self-abandonment to him, so that I am set free from myself and from all the powers to which I sold myself. God's word in this strict sense can only be the word of faith, that is, the word which makes a total demand upon man that he should receive what is given him and accept the gift of grace. For in the sight of God, man is not one who acts, for he can become righteous in his sight through faith alone.

Thus the distinction between the law and the gospel reveals what is distinctive in Christian preaching. It would be quite wrong to base this claim to validity on a formal claim to be a revelation, such as all religions make in one form or another, and which means nothing in itself. The substance of the Christian faith is not a new or even a better and more perfect law, nor is it even a law which is purged of all ceremonial laws and concerned with pure morality but which is ultimately no more than a word of the same nature and the same structure as in all religions, a doctrine consisting of human words. It is a word of radically different nature, the word of faith. This is because its sole concern is to evoke faith, and because it is nothing other than the pure word of God, bringing a promise, giving a gift full of grace, and omnipotent. Thus the understanding of the gospel as justification through the word alone, through faith alone, is identical with the distinction between the law and the gospel, and to lose sight of the distinction between the law and the gospel is to lose sight of the pure gospel.

For the distinction between the law and the gospel is identical with the distinction that must be made with regard to what makes man truly righteous, and truly saved. Of course there is such a thing as a righteousness brought about by man himself through his works. But this is not the righteousness which can bring peace to the conscience and give it assurance. Christian righteousness is the very opposite: not the righteousness of works, but the righteousness of faith; not active righteousness, but passive righteousness, given as a gift; not our own righteousness, but a righteousness from outside ourselves, imputed to us and because of this never becoming our own possession, even when it is given to us. It is in the strictest sense righteousness accepted by faith. Thus the Christian is in himself and on the basis of his own powers a sinner; but at the same time, outside himself, on the basis of what God does, and in the sight of God in Christ, he is one who is righteous.

'The righteousness which derives from us is not Christian righteousness, and we are not justified by it. Christian righteousness is the direct opposite, the passive righteousness which we merely receive, in which we effect nothing, but through which we allow someone else to work within us, that is, God. This is not understood by the world ... even Christians only understand it with difficulty ... This distinction must be carefully considered. I am not yet master of it. Anyone who does not apprehend passive righteousness in danger and in temptation will not endure ... The whole world thinks that this is an easy thing; but it is not, for it lies beyond the law, beyond our powers and even beyond the law of God, which goes far beyond Christian righteousness. The evil that seizes hold of us in temptation is that we have no prospect except to cry, "Ah, if only I were devout!" This attitude has become our normal one: "Ah, how I have spent my time, how wickedly I have lived!" Human nature cannot escape this contemplation of its own righteousness and raise itself up to contemplate Christian righteousness . . . And yet there is no other means of salvation. Either we are faced with eternal death, or we take hold of passive righteousness. We should say, I do not strive for active righteousness. I may very well have it, and can point to the case in which I have acted accordingly. But that does not mean that one ought to rely upon it. It will not endure. I must remove the law from my sight and act as one who receives; I will acknowledge that I am justified, and desire to receive the righteousness of grace, of the forgiveness of sins, of mercy, of the Holy Spirit and of Christ, which he [God] gives, while we receive it and let it happen to us. The earth receives the rain in this way. It does not create it through any work, and cannot obtain water through any work of its own, but it receives the rain. As much as the rain is the earth's own, Christian righteousness is our "own". This is easy for us to hear and understand. But when it comes to the point, we do not understand this distinction aright. God grant that we may appreciate this distinction at least a little. The greatest art of Christians is to be ignorant of the whole of active righteousness and of the law; whereas outside the people of God, the greatest wisdom is to know and to contemplate the law. Would it not be strange if I should learn, and teach men, not to pay attention to the law and to act as though there were no law, and in contradiction to this to insist on the law in the world and to act as if there were no grace? For if I do not remove the law from my sight and turn my thoughts to grace, as though there were no law and only pure grace, I cannot be blessed.'[7]

So far we have only made a first tentative step towards the distinction between the law and the gospel. But at this point we find ourselves at the very heart of Luther's theological thought, and have reached the basic theme which we shall now develop further.

CHAPTER 8

THE TWOFOLD USE OF THE LAW

THE distinction between the law and the gospel results in a distinction with regard to the law itself. We turn to this, not in order to obscure the questions which still remain unelucidated from the previous lecture by introducing new problems, but in order to return to the real meaning of the distinction between the law and the gospel, and inquire into it more deeply. It is often only possible to understand a matter from its consequences, because it is in these consequences that its nature is expressed.

If the distinction between the law and the gospel results in a further distinction with regard to the law, but not with regard to the gospel, this clearly means that the gospel has only a single significance, whereas the law has a double significance. It may be somewhat premature to formulate the matter in these terms, and we may be required to correct them later. But they are clearly correct in one respect: it is because of the gospel that the law appears in a different light than hitherto. This relationship is not reversible; the understanding of the gospel is not altered in the light of the law. For the law is not added to the gospel, but the gospel is added to the law.

Some of these statements may be somewhat lacking in caution and in need of qualification. But if the distinction between the law and the gospel is valid at all, there is no doubt that the gospel would not be the gospel if it were not the final and ultimate word. For if 'good news', that is, preaching which brings joy and liberty, which increases courage, reveals hope and creates faith, is not to be a mere interlude which provides a passing relief, a diversion, a slight illusion, a momentary forgetfulness, and a kind of opium, but instead is to dominate the future, be adequate to all temptations, resolve all confusion and shine brighter than all darkness, then it must be a word which is unequivocally clear, true and certain and cannot be shaken or explained away. It must be a word which is true unconditionally and without qualification, which is reliable and therefore evokes trust, and which illuminates the man who permits it to be spoken to him, liberates him from the curse of the lie and brings him the truth, sets him free from doubt and gives him certainty, saves him from death and hell, and gives him life and blessedness. Thus, in this sense, if the gospel is to be taken at its word, and if it is to carry out what is promised, it must be not merely *something* unequivocal; it must be the unique and unequivocal word, which makes everything else unequivocal.

By contrast, it seems right to us to describe the law as something with a double significance. Nevertheless, this statement must be made with caution; if only to avoid the use of the term 'with a double significance' in a trivial sense. The law is clearly anything but trivial, equivocal, and frivolous. With good reason we associate with 'the law' the concept of something stern, binding, and unyielding, which in one way or another always prevails. One cannot joke with the law. Moreover, this is true in both of the fundamentally different spheres in which we customarily use the concept of law: both in nature, and in the intellectual and moral life of man. Of course in these two cases the rigour of the law is quite different in form. The law of nature, a basic category of modern science, which has not been shown to be invalid in spite of the notorious crisis concerning the basic principles of modern science, but has merely been reinterpreted and made more precise, is concerned with what takes place as a matter of fact, necessarily and without exception. On the other hand, the law which refers in one way or another to man with his freedom of choice is concerned with what *ought* to take place, and what in fact very often does not take place. It is valid only as a demand, a stipulation, an ideal or something similar. At first sight the difference seems to be so great that one might suppose that the two have nothing in common except their name. When we speak of the law in our present context, we naturally do not mean the so-called law of nature, which is carried out automatically within nature, without requiring any command or prohibition to be uttered. Our subject is what is called the moral law, which appeals to the human will and which is carried out or not, fulfilled or not, depending upon human action. From this point of view the content of the two forms of law is completely opposed.

The law of nature seems to be the very essence of what we can count upon without question, of what we can rely upon. Technology is a unique example of this. The source of failure is always man. He is the unreliable element, and consequently it is man whom it is the purpose of an increasingly technological society to make more and more reliable. For the law in the sense of the law of nature is at the same time the essence of irresistible power and controlling force. The law which is valid for the universe is the key to universal power. It is no accident that the law of nature has arrogated to itself the traditional divine attributes of immutability, reliability, and omnipotence, and has thereby taken the place of God.

By contrast, the law of obligation, which assumes man's

freedom of choice, seems to be the essence of unreliability and impotence. This law is constantly changed, transgressed and broken. It has many loopholes, through which one can slip past it. It seems to be defenceless and abandoned to contempt. Nor is this all. It changes with time and with men. Man makes and chooses his own laws, even if he then presents them as God's law. And since what man says about God is usually associated with this kind of law, God himself is drawn into the doubtfulness and impotence of the law, of which modern man in particular is becoming increasingly aware, and which consists of the disappearance of absolute obligations, the growth of intellectual disorientation, the relativization of all standards, the confusion of higher and lower values of good and evil, the loss of privacy, and the decline into the unknown, into emptiness and into nothingness.

Of course these two contrary spheres which we associate with the word law, as the law of nature on the one hand and as the moral law (in the widest sense) on the other, can be shown to be more closely related than appears at first sight. From the point of view of their power, it is true that the law of nature is exercised with infallible and irresistible power. But if we take men into consideration here—and it is an artificial abstraction which cannot be maintained in reality to ignore man's part in science and technology—two things can be seen. Firstly, the law of nature is the very way in which nature is put at man's disposal and subjected to him; that is, it is the way in which the power of nature is not withheld from man, but is handed over to him, is placed under his control, and becomes the instrument of his power. The power of the law of nature is transformed into the power of man. There is no need to illustrate the problems that arise from this. For the second point is that the law of nature is powerless against this power of man. What

man in his freedom can do with the powers of nature, by
making use of their laws, is not controlled by the law of
nature, and cries out for another law of a different kind and
different in its power, a law which has power over human
freedom, and which restrains man and keeps him within
bounds. It may well seem that the law of obligation is weak or
impotent, because it does not take place automatically through
the working of natural forces, but has as its sole instrument the
mere word, and consequently relies upon the will of man and
breaks down when he is unwilling. But this is evidence of its
peculiar power, and of the fact that it never leaves man in
peace, but is always present, if only as an irritant. Even when
this law is transgressed, it is by no means overcome, but takes
its revenge in the consequences which result from disregarding
it. This revenge does not take place, of course, in any automatic
or calculable fashion. But the law is a force that constantly
pursues man, as can be seen both from his urge to carry out
achievements on a titanic scale, and also from his outbursts of
dismal despair.

With regard, however, to the double meaning of the law,
which is the contrary concept to that of the one meaning of the
gospel, and which provided us with our starting-point, let us
reflect first of all, in isolation from Luther's ideas, on the
phenomenon of the law in general. From this point of view,
we see that there is a characteristic relation between the two
kinds of law, even though modern man regards them as
parallel and apparently unconnected entities. Of course by
definition the law of nature is in the strictest sense unambiguous,
clear and capable of mathematical analysis. Its motto is that
the account can always be balanced, that there is no trickery,
and that there is nothing in any way uncanny about it. But the
result of this kind of unambiguity is that man himself is not

unambiguous. The question of his real obligation—which includes another, that of his real identity—is one of terrifying complexity and ambiguity. One might say on the one hand that the law of obligation is equally unambiguous, in so far as it undoubtedly concerns man and makes a demand upon him. But there are evidently many contradictory views of what this means, how it is to be interpreted and how expressed, and so one can say at once that the law to which man is subject is a complex and ambiguous law. This complexity may be regarded as its richness, or as the curse of an unending task imposed upon man. Man does not know what is his ultimate concern. He must choose and decide. But how can he decide when everything is ambiguous? How can he be certain of his choice, if the choice is of his own free will?

If the ambiguity of the law is properly seen as the co-existence of different elements of a double meaning, we have not in fact touched, in what we have said so far, on any aspect of the double significance of the law which Luther understood as a consequence of the distinction between the law and the gospel. For of course he was not thinking of the double meaning which we derived from the modern use of the concept of law. And if he was not thinking simply of the contrary of the single significance of the gospel, but of the consequences of that single meaning, then there is no question of a vague and uncertain double meaning. Rather, he must be referring to something which brings clarity into the complex ambiguity of the law, but which, since he is concerned with the law and not with the gospel itself, is a clarity and unambiguity which consists in applying to the law a distinction with regard to the proper way of dealing with the law, and the right attitude to it. His clear intention is to assert that the proper attitude to the law can clearly be seen in the light of the gospel only when one has learned to distinguish between two aspects of the law, a double use of it, a *duplex usus legis*, as Luther puts it.

The situation with respect to the gospel is quite different from that concerning the law, since essentially there can only be a single use of the gospel, while there must be a double use of the law. This is due to a difference between the two, which is evident from a quite superficial observation. The law is clearly a much more difficult and problematical concept. When one speaks of the gospel, there cannot really be any doubt about what is meant. Naturally, it does not refer to one of the four New Testament gospels. This new literary category which came into being with primitive Christianity is merely a secondary phenomenon. For there is only one gospel, which is the message of Christ. 'Those who proclaim at the greatest length and in the loftiest terms how only faith in Christ makes us righteous are the best evangelists. Consequently, the Epistles of St. Paul are more of a gospel than Matthew, Mark and Luke. For the latter do not describe much more than the history of the works and miracles of Christ. But no one gives a finer account of the grace which we have through Christ than St. Paul, especially in the Epistle to the Romans. Now because much more depends upon the word than upon the works and deeds of Christ, and because if we had to do without one or the other, it would be better to lack the works and the history than the word and the doctrine, it is fair to give the highest praise to those books which deal more with the doctrine and the words of the Lord Christ. For even if the miracles of Christ did not exist and we knew nothing of them, we would nevertheless have enough with the word, without which we could not have life.'[1]

This concentration on the true substance of the gospel is

directly related to a concentration upon oral preaching. For 'the gospel ought not really to be written, but should be a spoken word ... That is why Christ himself wrote nothing, but only spoke, and why his teaching is not called scripture, but the gospel, that is, the good news or preaching, which ought not to be proclaimed with the pen, but with the spoken word.'[2] That the gospel should be given a fixed written form is basically inappropriate, and is at best the result of necessity. 'That it was necessary to write books is in itself a great breach and decline from the Spirit; it was caused by necessity and is not the proper nature of the New Testament.'[3] Thus when Luther speaks of the gospel, he is referring strictly and exclusively to the Christian proclamation, which, although it depends upon the biblical text for the testimony which provides its norm, is enabled to testify on this basis at the present day; and without this the gospel would not be put into effect as such.

This unambiguous definition of what is meant by the gospel of course does not exclude the possibility and inevitability of disputes concerning the true understanding of the gospel, nor the possibility of doubt about the extent to which the extant tradition concerning Christ is truly the gospel at all, that is, whether it can still be understood at the present day as the gospel. But anyone who acknowledges the preaching of Christ as the gospel can only do so by acknowledging that he owes this certainty to the gospel itself. For the gospel is made the gospel by the fact that it is manifested to those who believe as the 'spiritual light which is much brighter than the sun'.[4] Thus the kind of word appropriate to faith is that of the confession of faith, the utterance of a rock-like certainty. For 'the Holy Spirit is not a sceptic, and has not written doubtful matters and mere opinions in our hearts, but assertions which are more certain and sure than life itself and all experience.'[5] Consequently, faith is the only appropriate *usus evangelii*.

On the other hand, when we come to speak of the law, we are faced with something quite different in content. Of course Luther's use of the word 'law' is derived from biblical usage, and Pauline usage in particular, and is consequently connected with the special status which the Mosaic law, the Torah, has in the Old Testament. But this linguistic connection raises difficult problems, since for historical and practical reasons the Pauline concept of the law is not simply identical with that of the Old Testament; and in its turn, Luther's concept of the law is not simply identical with that of St. Paul. Nor must one try to define the law in biblicist terms, such as by identifying the Old Testament with the law and the New Testament with the gospel, for in fact the New Testament also contains law in a certain sense, and the Old Testament already contains the gospel. Nor again can what is meant by law be defined according to a stylistic standard, by labelling all biblical sayings which contain demands as law, and all assurances, promises, consolations, etc., as the gospel. It is clearly not a matter of linguistic form, nor of allocating individual sayings by definition to the law or to the gospel, for one and the same saying can have the effect of the law, or can be taken as the gospel. It is possible to let the coming of Jesus and even the cross have such an effect on oneself that it is treated as a statement of the utmost severity of the law. Or else, for example, one can understand the first commandment in such a sense that the voice of the gospel is heard in it. If what we have said is true, that the only true use of the gospel is faith, then we may be so bold as to state the reverse, so long as it is properly understood: every word to which I listen in true faith, and in accord with Jesus, that is, every word which is the word of God for me, in that it becomes for me the word of faith, becomes for me a testimony of the gospel—even if it is the birds of the air and the lilies of the field. On the other hand, everything to which I do not listen in faith is the word of the law.

This formulation, however, seems to be so broad that the ground seems to be slipping from under our feet in our search for an understanding of the law. But an infinite horizon opens up before us when we speak in theological terms of the law. This is so, of course, for the sake of the gospel. For in theology everything must be done for the sake of the gospel, because this is true of preaching. The idea of the distinction between the law and the gospel would be completely misunderstood if the two were simply parallel to each other. It is unquestionably right to say that preaching and theology are concerned with the gospel alone, and not with the law as well, outside the gospel and in isolation from it. But it must be carefully noted that because our sole concern is with the gospel, then the law ought properly to be included as well. For the gospel is the fulfilment of the law. If the law is not there, crying out for fulfilment, the gospel becomes meaningless, because it is no longer necessary. Where there is no sin, it is not possible to preach the forgiveness of sins. Where death has no power, the message of the resurrection cannot be proclaimed. Where there is unbelief at work, the word of faith cannot be uttered. Only when it is spoken to the godless does the word of God have somewhere for its power to be revealed. For, as Luther says, 'It is the nature of God that he makes something out of nothing. Consequently, if someone is not nothing, God can make nothing out of him. Men make something into something else. But this is a vain and useless work. Thus God accepts no one except the abandoned, makes no one healthy except the sick, gives no one sight except the blind, brings no one to life except the dead, makes no one pious except sinners, makes no one wise except the foolish, and, in short, has mercy upon no one except the wretched, and gives no one grace except those who have not grace. Consequently, no proud person can become holy, wise or righteous, become the material with which God works, or have God's works in him, but he remains in his own works and makes a fabricated, false and simulated saint out of himself, that is a hypocrite.'[6]

Thus the reason why our account of the law has to be so astonishingly wide in its scope is because the universality and reality of the gospel is at stake. But if we follow this indication, we must readjust, in more than one respect, our ideas about the understanding of the law and the use of this term. Anyone who seeks to comprehend the reality of the law need look no further than the Ten Commandments. It would be difficult to find elsewhere so elementary, so striking and so concrete a formulation of the absolute demand made upon him in the sight of God, as a human being in relation to his fellow-men. But we must take care not to fall into the foolish assumption that the law is a doctrine which first came to man as something preached to him, that is, that the law is something which had to be added to man, and that man was not, by the very fact of his being human, affected by the reality of the law. The preaching of the law only reveals 'what already exists in human nature'.[7] 'For the law is already there in fact.'[8] 'For the law is there in fact, without our being necessary to it, and even against our will, before justification, at the beginning of it, during it, at the end of it, and after it.'[9]

Not that the exposition of the law, the setting-out in concrete terms of what is demanded of man, can be carried out without explicit teaching. Similarly, it is essential that man, who so easily makes his love loveless, and his reason unreasonable and blind, should repeatedly be told what is good and evil. This, indeed, is one indispensable function of Christian preaching. But that is not its true task, and it is not Christian preaching alone which teaches the law. The teaching of the law takes place in various and innumerable forms of jurisdiction and education, instruction and upbringing, learning and civilization, philosophy and religion. And it would be doctrinaire and totally unchristian to assert that nothing true, good and right was recognized anywhere except in the Bible, or that nothing true, or right, ever took place outside Christianity (not to speak of the scandalous things that have taken place within Christianity!).

The attempt has been made to interpret the idea that the law is always present to man on the basis of the biblical expression concerning 'the law written in the heart', and from Stoic doctrines of natural law, as though every man knew the content of the law through innate ideas. This view, which was sometimes naïvely accepted even in Reformation theology, has been rightly criticized. The law which always makes this demand upon man is not a compilation of timeless ideas, but is something which is effective in an historical form, and is the very essence of the linguistic innovation. Nor is it effective in man only in the form of theoretical instruction, but it is effective also as a force in the very reality of his life, making demands on him, challenging him, urging him on and carrying him with it. In every reality he encounters, he encounters the law. It is present to him not merely in the form of thoughts and ideas. We are only dealing with the reality of the law, what one might call its living historical presence, when we bear in mind not only what the law says, but also what it brings about, what it is capable of.

According to the conventional view, the law teaches, urges

to do good, is beneficial to life and makes righteousness possible. This is actually true, and takes place in practice, in so far as the demand of the law can be limited to partial aspects. But it is totally false if one considers how radical a demand is made upon man, and if one bears in mind the judgement which will ultimately be made upon him. If man is not divided into thousands of partial functions and tasks, but considered in himself as a person, and if attention is paid to more than merely the fragmentary objectivizations of man in the deeds and acts which he initiates, the inevitable conclusion is that the law teaches less about what we should do than about what we have not done in practice, less about the good we should achieve than about the evil we have already committed, and less about the possibilities of man than about what it is no longer possible for him to alter.

From this ultimate and radical point of view it is an illusion to suppose that the law sets man free. Rather, it burdens man and imprisons him in what he is already irrevocably committed to. Consequently, it is also an illusion to suppose that the law in this radical and ultimate sense can serve to justify. Rather, it accuses, and man encounters it as a judge or an executioner. Instead of giving life, it kills. This is clearly only manifest when it drives man to despair. But despair is merely the reverse aspect of blinded pride. And one is just as fatal to man as the other. The mad attempt to cope alone with oneself and the world, with one's failure and with death, and with the law in the whole violence of the force by which it calls into question man's whole being—that is, the attempt to justify oneself— invariably means, either in the form of an explicit atheist conflict with God, or in the religious disguise of a pious attempt to justify oneself, a refusal to be made dependent upon God.

True godlessness is not the abstract denial of the existence of God, but the denial of one's own dependence upon God, that is, the denial of one's own existential being as God's creature. Thus unbelief is man's fundamental sin. And unbelief means to persevere in the principle of self-justification. Consequently, existence outside faith, whatever variations there may be in the form it takes, is existence under the law in the sense that it is existence which has fallen so helplessly prey to the law, that it is no longer possible to realize what the true function of the law is. Faith in the law, which is the very opposite of faith in the true sense, that of the gospel, is the common element underlying every kind of unbelief, and especially religious unbelief. 'Religion that can be comprehended by reason is false religion . . . In this respect there is no distinction between the Jews, the papists, and the Turks. Their rites are different, but their hearts and thoughts are the same . . . That is, they say, "If I have acted in such and such a way, God will be well disposed towards me." The same feeling is found in the hearts of all men.'[10]

Thus if the law is used in the sense of the gospel—and to do this is the task of the Holy Spirit—then what the law effects in practice, but which remains unknown and uncomprehended, is now revealed. We see that it cannot assist in our justification, while at the same time its accusations and the death it brings are now manifest. But because this takes place in the context of the preaching of the gospel, the accusation brings about a saving renunciation of self-justification, and the death it brings becomes the first step towards life. Luther says that to understand, teach and carry out the law in this way is the true, 'theological' use of the law, for it furthers the aim of God's action towards man. It serves the true work of God by carrying out his 'strange works'. For God kills in order to bring to life.

But it would be complete confusion to suppose that the gospel played the role of a new law, ordering life in the world. In the world, the law is still necessary and still has its place, and remains distinct from the gospel. What matters is to recognize the necessity and the proper place of the law in the world, and to distinguish them clearly from the gospel. There is a positive necessity for the law, in forming, ordering and maintaining life, making righteousness possible. This is the 'civil use of the law', the *usus civilis* or *politicus*, as Luther described it. If the law is limited and restricted in this way and regarded soberly and without illusions, its valuable earthly function becomes clear. The law provides in the world as it now is, a sinful world, an irreplaceable and necessary service, so long as it is not misused to provide justification in the sight of God, but is intended to lead no further than to worldly, secular righteousness, by limiting the consequences of sin and subduing man.

This distinction between the double use of the law, the *usus civilis* and the *usus theologicus*[11] is not a theory developed in isolation, but is intimately connected with the true understanding of the gospel. At a first superficial encounter with this doctrine, it is difficult to perceive its profound basis and its immense consequences. We shall go into it more thoroughly in the lectures that follow, and shall conclude our preliminary observations by briefly rejecting three misunderstandings.

It is a misunderstanding to divide the two ways of using the law between different groups of persons, although numerous utterances might be taken to imply the need for this—as though the first, civil use of the law was only for uncultured people who have to be coerced into maintaining outwardly good order, while the second, spiritual use of the law was as it were for a higher and more sensitive group of persons. Since a Christian is both a sinner and righteous at the same time, as a sinner he lives under both uses of the law at the same time.

Again, it is a misunderstanding to suppose that the law itself is twofold, consisting of a profane law, and a religious law which goes beyond this. In fact it is one and the same law, through which God deals with man in two ways.

Finally, it is a misunderstanding to suppose that the two uses of the law are parallel to one another, but unconnected. Of course the civil use of the law is not put into force through sermons, and exists in fact in a fundamental independence from Christian preaching. Nevertheless, a true understanding of the civil use of the law can only be obtained from the gospel. For only faith can liberate secular righteousness from the foolish attempt at self-justification in the sight of God. Thus the value of faith for man's life in society extends to such concrete purposes as that of setting him free for sober and reasonable political understanding and political action.

CHAPTER 9

PERSON AND WORK

T HE pairs of contrary concepts which have guided us so far
in our attempt to penetrate more deeply into Luther's thought,
have in common the fact that each one of them represents an
antithesis in a double sense. However sharp the antithesis may
be there can be no doubt that the affirmation of one side does
not simply mean the denial of the other, and vice versa. There
is no question of a purely exclusive opposition, such that one
side or the other must be chosen, as is the case with good and
evil, or life and death. However critical of philosophy Luther
may be in his understanding of theology, he nevertheless does
not go so far as merely to deny and reject philosophy. Nor
does the Spirit do away with the letter, or the gospel with the
law. Finally, we saw how this conjunction of two aspects
which are not mutually exclusive, but which must be sharply
distinguished, dominated in particular the theme of the twofold
use of the law.

In formulating this relationship of mutual tension, we have
used in each case the word 'and'; it is meant not merely to
separate the contraries we have been discussing, but also to link
them together. It is meant to emphasize that each in its turn
has its own proper function, in its own place and within its
own limits. In fact one might be even more precise and say that
one is not merely inevitably tolerated in conjunction with the
other, but rather is accorded its own proper function as a result

of this conjunction and distinction. According to Luther, however, this influence is only exercised in one direction. The civil use of the law can only be understood in the strict sense on the basis of the theological use of the law. The law can be properly interpreted, that is, understood as the law, only on the basis of the gospel. Only the Spirit makes it genuinely possible to take the letter seriously. In the same way, the proper approach to philosophy is revealed only by the content of theology. Every one of these statements is attested many times in Luther's works, even the latter, which appears the most surprising. Thus, for example, in Luther's theses for the disputation at Heidelberg, we read: 'Just as it is only a married man who makes a proper use of the evil of concupiscence, so no one philosophizes aright except the fool, that is, the Christian.'[1]

Of course such an interpretation gives rise at once to serious doubts. Surely it is obvious that we are misrepresenting Luther's mode of thought if we regard its main concern as that of harmonization, of striving to reconcile contraries and strike an acceptable balance between them, as polarities of thought, each dependent upon the other. Surely we are not dealing with a compiler of systems who restores all conflicting matters to order by means of careful distinctions, and regards his task as complete when everything is put in its place. Surely the basic structure of Luther's thought is not that of Catholicism. For the description of Luther's intention which is suggested by this interpretation of the word 'and' is disconcertingly reminiscent of the way in which nature and grace are brought into a harmonious relationship, the one carefully related and subordinated to the other, in Catholic thought. There the purpose is to bring into an appropriate harmony all relationships in which a similar tension is present, such as that between theology

and philosophy, the Church and the State, or even the tension
in the Church itself between the imparting of grace and judicial
severity, and between the divine work of grace and human
merit. According to Thomas Aquinas, grace does not do away
with nature, but perfects it. Consequently, grace assumes
natural knowledge, and natural reason serves faith.[2]

It is obvious that Luther's thought is not based upon this
fundamental continuity between nature and grace. On the
other hand his mode of thought must not be so sharply contrasted with Catholic thought that the surprising links with the
hierarchical thought of Thomism which we have uncovered
are overlooked or ignored. The marked difference which we
can perceive in comparing Luther and Aquinas, and which,
over and above the personal characteristics of these thinkers,
is relevant to the denominational differences between Protestantism and Catholicism, cannot easily be reduced to a formula.
Certainly, Luther's view is not adequately represented by the
mere negation of the hierarchical Thomist relationship between nature and grace. The difference which is unquestionably present clearly does not lie only in a different definition
of the relationship between nature and grace, for it cannot be
understood within the same conceptual scheme. The difficulty
lies in the fact that the difference goes very much deeper than
this. It is the basic concepts, or more precisely the fundamental
questions they pose, which are different.

The distinctive characteristic of the way in which Luther
handles these antitheses only becomes clear when, in spite of
the conjunction between the two aspects which prevents them
from being mutually exclusive, one also becomes aware of an
extremely bitter and hostile conflict between the two. How
these two apparently opposed points of view can be reconciled
is the heart of the problem with which Luther's thought con-

fronts us. The situation is at first sight confused, but there is no doubt, especially in comparison with the tradition of scholasticism and Catholicism, that the dominant point of view in Luther is that of the conflict, which he makes as acute as possible, treating it, as one might almost think, with a delight in paradox. Although on the one hand he can praise reason as the highest thing in this life, and even as something divine,[3] we must contrast this with the hard saying, 'that reason is the Devil's whore, and can do nothing but shame and disgrace everything which God says and does'.[4] Thus there is a mortal enmity between faith and reason. 'Faith strikes dead this reason, and kills this beast, which heaven and earth and all creatures cannot destroy.'[5] And likewise, in a way even more offensive to pious ears, the law and Christ, and the law and faith, each fall into a contradictory antithesis.[6] 'The law is the negation of Christ.'[7] 'If one has to give up one or the other, Christ or the law, the law must be given up, not Christ.'[8] What takes place in faith can consequently be expressed in the following dramatic terms: 'When sin and the law come into the conscience, both should be turfed out: I know nothing of the law and sin', but only of Christ.[9]

The impression that Luther's main concern was to drive a wedge between irreconcilable opposites has led in the conventional picture of Luther either to the suppression of the other aspect, that of their conjunction, so difficult to reconcile with that of their separation, or else to Luther's being regarded as a confused thinker who said one thing one day and another the day after, and who is not to be taken seriously either in his exaggerations of the antithesis nor, apparently, in his rare attempts to compromise, to bridge the gap and to reconcile the differences. But it is all too easy to talk like this, and abandon the task of understanding Luther. Our task is precisely to understand the inner connection between Luther's utterances, which at first sight are so contradictory. Only when we have understood the contradictory assertions which form the antithesis can we come to understand the other non-contradictory and related assertions, to understand, moreover, something which is profoundly different from the Catholic doctrine of nature and grace, in spite of a confusing impression of similarity. In order to do this, however, it is necessary to define more precisely the context in which Luther's thought is conducted, which is also the one within which we shall attempt to understand his utterances.

Now the antitheses in Luther's thought which we have mentioned so far have, of course, much in common apart from the mere fact of the recurrent similarity in their formal structure which we have already outlined. An inner relationship can be detected which leads to the conclusion that the recurrent structural similarity has the same origin in each case, and is an expression of the fundamental conception which determines Luther's thought. Of course one must not jump to the conclusion that all the antithetical pairs of concepts we have discussed, together with those that follow, can be regarded as equivalent. The distinction between the law and the gospel, which we found to be fundamental, cannot simply be equated with that between philosophy and theology. Similarly, the twofold use of the law—as we see from the way it is formulated —cannot be identified with the distinction between the law and the gospel. Again, the two pairs of concepts which are closest to each other, the letter and the Spirit, and the law and the gospel, represent different aspects of the matter. Thus although the task of interpreting and establishing the connections between the individual antitheses must be carried out with great caution, we cannot fail to observe that ultimately each one is concerned with the same thing. That is, proceeding from the distinction between the law and the gospel, it is possible to obtain in similar ways both a specific understanding of the relationship between theology and philosophy, and an insight into the distinction between the civil and theological uses of the law, which is fundamental to the understanding of the law. Associated with these are further important offshoots of this basic antithesis, which we shall discuss later.

This undoubtedly difficult problem is present in the most widely separate areas of Luther's thought, and is the aspect of his thought which is most worthy of consideration. How can a fundamental antithesis, which has both a contradictory and also a non-contradictory sense, be validly developed and extended throughout numerous different forms? To find a proper answer to this question we have to identify a level of experience where what is difficult for reflective thought to understand is encountered as elementary reality, and in which the immediate suspicion that we are faced with exaggerated and artificial contradictions gives way to the impression that we are dealing simply with the conscientious consideration and vindication of the *sole* necessary principle. As we set out to identify this level of experience, we shall follow two important indications which arise from previous discussion of the subject.

The first indication is that the characteristic dual and antithetical structure which we met cannot be reduced to an abstract system; that is, it cannot be considered without taking time into account. These antitheses cannot be resolved by a kind of mathematical exercise. Luther is not expressing an individual taste or a mere witty conceit, but an insight into the very heart of the matter at issue when he says: 'Mathematics is more inimical to theology than anything else. There is no part of philosophy [that is, learning in general] which conflicts so much with theology.'[10] Although this observation in its direct context, a disputation concerning the doctrine of the Trinity, is not without its difficulties, it is rooted in a much wider context, and this leads to the realization that theology is not concerned with a state of affairs which is timeless, but with an event which concerns time so radically that it does not merely bring into being a time of crisis, but does something even more profound, and brings about a crisis in time. Luther can characterize the distinction between the law and the gospel as one between different times. He does not mean a conflict between two consecutive historical periods of time, but a conflict about what time really implies. 'Consequently, the Christian is divided between two times: in so far as he is flesh, he is under the law; in so far as he is spirit, he is under the gospel . . . The time of the law does not endure. "Christ is the end of the law." [Rom. 10: 4] The time of grace will be external.'[11] This difference between times is experienced by the conscience, and existence in the time of the law taking the form of fear, and existence in the time of grace taking the form of faith. 'These times are sharply distinguished; and yet they remain very close to one another, that is, sin and grace, the law and the gospel.'[12]

In order to work out the dual antithetical structure which we have observed, we must concern ourselves with the event which is the subject-matter of theology and must be understood simultaneously as the process of the history of revelation, as the event of preaching, and as an event which takes place in the human conscience. Only when the antitheses which provide the tension within Luther's thought are not balanced one against the other in the context of a formal and neutral understanding of the time, like pieces on a chess board, but are related to historical time, which is ultimately the real field of dispute, so that these antitheses are considered as themselves historical, do they lose their appearance of confused contradiction.

This leads us to the other indication. If the theological structure on which Luther's thought is built up (and to call it a 'structure' does not really accord with its close relationship to 'events', to history in the broadest and most concrete sense) is not to come under suspicion of being mere speculation, but is to be understood as corresponding to historical reality and doing it justice, then it must have some kind of foothold in human existence. There is no need at this point to raise the premature objection that this would evidently reduce the content of theology to an anthropological account of human potentialities; this objection is improper, whether the intention is to protect Luther against such a misinterpretation, or even to accuse him of slipping into the error of turning theology into an anthropology. There can be no question of our trying to break away from the concrete historical basis which is the only way to make a serious distinction in theological terms between the law and the gospel, that is, the appeal to the holy scripture, which in its turn means the appeal to Jesus Christ. Nor can there be any question of our ignoring the word, the event in which Christian preaching is carried out, the gospel is proclaimed, and the distinction between the law and the gospel is put into practice. But if this process is not to be regarded merely as an optional addition to human existence, or as a superstructure built upon it by religious fantasy, it must be made clear that the distinction between the law and the gospel, together with all the other distinctions associated with it in Luther's theology, is directly related to a contradictory situation brought about by the very fact of human existence, inseparable from it, and introducing profound difficulties into it. And it is this original distinction between the law and the gospel which brings the situation from obscurity and confusion into the light of day.

Luther discusses the situation in terms of the distinction between person and work. Our modern idea of the meaning of the dual concept 'person and work' is unconsciously formed by the romantic doctrine of artistic apprehension. A work— by which is meant in the proper sense a work of art—is the expression of the creative personality of the artist, which is what is really worthy of consideration. Consequently, reproduction becomes the ideal of interpretation, that is, the re-experiencing and re-living of the original productive experience to which the work owes its origin. Thus the work is an expression of the person, and mediates a return to the person, for the person is the decisive element in the whole process. But the nature of this cult of personality is such that the person is regarded as fulfilling itself in works which are a representation of it. In fact one could even say that the person itself forms the ideal work. The true aim of all works is the self-realization of the person.

Luther came from and lived in a tradition to which this romantic understanding of a work as a work of art, and of the person as the artist, and thus as itself the true work of art, was utterly foreign. Anyone who spoke of a 'work' at that time was automatically referring to a good work. Admittedly, there is, in spite of the distance between the two, something in common between what we may somewhat tentatively term the conventional medieval understanding of a work as a good work, and the romantic understanding of a work as a work of art. This connection lies in the fact that in both cases the person is expressed in the work, and so fashions itself, though of course in the medieval sense this idea was in no way aesthetic in meaning, but meant that man should fulfil his calling and endure in the last judgement. In contrast, however, to the popular understanding of man's justification, and the role played in it by works, scholastic theology in fact introduced into this concept important qualifications, limitations, distinctions and objections. Nevertheless, the basic view which was maintained by the Church and put forward in theology, and which also underlay popular ideas, was that however the relationship between the grace of God and human works might be precisely defined, the aim was the perfection of the person, which gave men the ability to perform meritorious works.

In clear contrast to this background of ideas, which we have only been able to describe in a rough and inadequate way, Luther developed extraordinarily early an understanding of justification in which the question of justification is concentrated strictly upon the person, and completely disregards works as in any sense the cause of justification, however important they may be as its consequence—when of course they would no longer be concerned with the question of justification. He presents this view by laying great emphasis on the irreversible movement from the person to works, in a stereotyped polemic against Aristotle. Thus for example in the first lectures on the Psalms he says, '. . . his [the righteous man's] righteousness does not spring from works, but his works from righteousness . . . This is contrary to Aristotle, who says, "by doing right one becomes righteous." Rather, by being righteous, one does right.'[13] Or in the lectures on Romans he says, 'The situation in the sight of God is not that someone becomes righteous by doing right . . . but that the righteous man, by being so, does right . . .'[14] 'For God does not accept the person on account of his works, but the works on account of his person, that is the person before the works, as it is written: "The Lord had regard for Abel (first) and (afterwards) his offering [Gen. 4: 4]." '[15] Or in a letter of 1516: 'For we do not become righteous, as Aristotle holds, by doing right—albeit in a hypocritical way—but, if I may so express it, by becoming and being righteous, we do right. The person must be changed first, and then the works are also changed. Abel was pleasing to God before his sacrifice.'[16]

The starting-point of the polemical attitude he adopted towards Aristotle is the latter's doctrine of the *habitus*. This concept came to be of great importance because with regard to the life of the soul, the characteristic phenomenon which it emphasized was that of taking on what is described as a second nature (through habit or practice). That is, it taught that abilities could be attained, to which, admittedly, there must have been some tendency already naturally present, but which were not in themselves present by nature; yet which, once they were obtained, represented a natural condition from which equivalent acts proceeded as though automatically. In the moral sphere, this theory accords a central position to the concept of virtue, in which a number of important aspects are combined. The first is that of the continuity and reliability of the subject of moral action. Individual acts are not isolated from one another, as though they were strokes of good fortune, but arise from a condition, a moral property, which can normally be relied upon. The second aspect is that of ease and facility. Just as an acquired mastery of a musical instrument, for example, makes it very easy to play, and thereby makes the enjoyment of the musician's art perfect since there is no longer any trace of exertion, the ideal of virtue is similarly that it should be practically automatic, unconfined, natural in the highest sense, voluntary and completely at one's disposal. Finally, the principal ethical aim implied by the concept of virtue is that of perfection. Just as the virtues themselves are the perfections of particular faculties in a particular respect, so man as a whole is perfected according to the degree of his moral excellence.

If Luther had been merely concerned with the argument that action proceeds from being, there would have been no real cause for any polemic against Aristotle. For it is precisely with this that Aristotle himself is concerned; not merely in the general sense in which it is obvious that human nature underlies human actions, but also in the special sense that if individual acts are to be virtuous and right, they presuppose an appropriate state, a particular attribute on the part of man—that is, something in the nature of his being. One cannot judge that someone is righteous in the ethical sense simply because on one occasion he may have acted righteously, but only when one can be sure, as a result of the attribute of righteousness he possesses, that he will always act righteously.

Thus Luther's criticism of Aristotle is in no sense directed against the precedence of a state of being over an individual act, but against the Aristotelian conception of the way such an attribute comes into being. For according to Aristotle a *habitus*, whether it is a technical or an intellectual skill, or even a moral virtue, comes into being through practice and habit, that is through repeated acts. However much the *habitus* may in the final analysis have precedence over the *actus* in attaining this goal the reverse is true, that is, the *actus* has precedence over the *habitus*. And whatever one may say, there can be no objection to this, at least as far as technical and intellectual skills are concerned. Some people learn them more easily than others. But without practice no one becomes perfect. In the moral sphere too, the disciplinary function of practice, habit and experience is indisputable. If one's utterances are limited to this sphere—which is the case with Aristotle—there can scarcely be any objection. Only when we ask whether someone who is righteous in the moral sense should really be regarded as righteous in a radical sense, and when we ask whether in this latter respect it is meaningful to say that by acting righteously, that is, through repeated righteous acts, one can acquire the attribute of righteousness, can there be any objection.

This is the starting-point of Luther's criticism of Aristotle. Otherwise, it would not have been meaningful, for he certainly does not intend to argue that the Aristotelian doctrine of the *habitus* is not justified in its proper application. But he is in total accord with the whole of Christian theology, which, whatever the degree of respect in which it holds the ethics of Aristotle, must naturally deny that by acquiring virtues in the Aristotelian sense man can be ultimately righteous—that is, in the sight of God. Thus we must go on to ask how far Luther was right to criticize the scholastic doctrine of justification. Ignoring the fact that the nominalist tradition which formed Luther's intellectual background in fact displayed weaknesses in this respect which did not exist in Thomism, it is nevertheless possible, taking into account the main features of the doctrine of justification common to the whole of scholasticism, to assert quite firmly that there was no question of any one scholastic theologian advancing the opinion that man became righteous in the sight of God through his righteous works. It was always beyond question that man could not become righteous in the sight of God without grace, but only did so through grace, and the only possible variation was in the degree in which this decisive role of grace was reflected in the approach of different theologians.

Nevertheless, in general, scholastic theology made use of Aristotelian psychology, including the concept of the *habitus*, in order to interpret the doctrine of grace. Thus Luther's criticism of Aristotle in this respect is strictly speaking a criticism of scholastic Aristotelianism. What was the effect of the application of the concept of the *habitus* to the interpretation of the doctrine of grace? Limiting ourselves here to its more elementary features, we are bound to say that in its doctrine of grace scholasticism used the concept of the *habitus* in a way completely contrary to that of Aristotle. For the doctrine of grace is not concerned with self-acquired skills and virtues in the natural sphere, that is, in respect of those things of which man is capable by his own powers and potentialities, but with a supernatural *habitus*. There are two elements in this emphasis on the supernatural character of the *habitus*. The first is that a faculty is added to man which endows him with potentialities which perfect his nature beyond its natural level and towards the supernatural, that is, towards his eternal goal, God. Secondly—this is already implied—this faculty is not acquired by man in a natural way and by his own powers, but is always given to him as a gift, in a supernatural manner. Man receives it through grace alone. Consequently, when the concept of the *habitus* is used in the doctrine of grace, it refers to a supernatural *habitus*, which is therefore in no sense self-acquired, but is infused. The term is an allusion to Romans 5: 5 ('God's love has been poured into our hearts through the Holy Spirit which has been given to us'; Vulgate: *diffusa est*).

Why could Luther not be satisfied with this? That an 'infused *habitus*' is meaningless in Aristotelian thought as such need not have troubled him. Rather, he would have been bound to see in this a decisive guarantee of the precedence of the person over works. The *habitus* of grace cannot be acquired by any human work. Only when man is equipped with this *habitus* as by a gift, as takes place in the sacramental action, is he capable of doing works in accordance with it, and these alone are truly good works, pleasing to God. And according to scholasticism, the idea of merit can only have any place in the doctrine of grace because the meritorious works of man are nothing more than the consequences of grace, and therefore do not in any sense limit the idea of *sola gratia*, but only interpret it. In this sense, the basic principle put forward by Luther seems in fact to be preserved in the scholastic doctrine of grace by the use of the concept of the *habitus*, for it implies that a person must first be righteous in order to do right. Or, as Luther taught time and again, the tree makes the fruit and not the fruit the tree.

If, in spite of this, Luther's criticism of the scholastic doctrine of grace is not to be dismissed as unfounded, or explained away as provoked by a deficient nominalist form of the doctrine of grace, and if it is not possible adequately to interpret his criticism of the concept of *habitus* simply as a further and positive development of ideas inspired by nominalism, it must be discussed at a more profound level. Why did scholasticism lay such emphasis on the concept that grace was imparted to man in the form of an inner quality, as the endowment of a *habitus*? One can certainly say, following Luther's observations on the precedence of the person over works, and of being over action, that the primary reason was to give proper weight to the element of grace, without which no truly good work can be done. Anyone who is not righteous in the sight of God through the reception of sacramental grace cannot carry out works which are righteous in the sight of God. Nevertheless, however much the intention may have been to give absolute precedence to grace, another aspect must be emphasized in explaining the particular function performed here by the Aristotelian doctrine of the *habitus*. This will enable us to understand why Luther disagreed with the scholastic doctrine of grace.

The use of the idea of the endowment of grace in the form of a *habitus* to express the precedence of grace over human works led at once to the problem, resulting from a psychological interpretation of the event of grace, of the location of the *habitus* of grace in the human soul. Was it situated in the potentialities of the soul which gave the power to know and to strive, and which were now endowed with the so-called theological virtues of faith, love and hope? Or was it, as Thomas Aquinas taught, in the essence of the soul, the *essentia animae*, which underlay the potentialities of the soul and was to be distinguished from them? This problem is only worth mentioning here, because it was no accident that something within man was defined as the point at which the transformation takes place. Luther, by contrast, made use of the concept of the person, rarely used in the doctrine of grace before him, and never emphasized; and the reason why he did so is that grace does not alter something within man, but alters his situation, and so alters man himself in respect of his standing in the sight of God, the way he is regarded from God's point of view. Whereas the concept of grace as a *habitus* directs attention within man, Luther, from the point of view of the concept of the person, considered grace only and wholly as an event which affects man in his being with regard to something outside him, his being in the sight of God.

But this difference is merely an indication of the principal point at issue. According to the scholastic theory, the value of the concept of the *habitus* is that it interprets grace as a new and supernatural faculty, as a supernatural virtue. A righteous person is one who is endowed with the power to carry out righteous acts. Although this *habitus* is not self-acquired, but is infused through grace, nevertheless the way in which the acts of a justified person proceed from this *habitus* is conceived entirely in moral terms. That is, the life of the righteous person is located within himself as a new, albeit supernatural quality, but one which is as it were his nature, in so far as the new life of the righteous person must be realized on the basis of this endowment. The basic tendency must now be directed towards its realization. Habitual grace must now be actualized. Thus a person is only truly justified to the extent to which grace is realized in works. For within the limits of an understanding of man which is conceived of in terms analogous to those of morality, everything depends upon man's actions, upon his freedom, and upon his self-realization in the course of attaining perfection. For grace does not do away with nature, but perfects it.

Luther, however, understands the person not on the basis of its potentialities and its activities, that is, not within the categories of morality, but regards it, in sharp contrast to the active behaviour of man towards the world, as the passivity which constitutes man's being, as his existence as a creature, as his relationship to God and his standing in the sight of God. This leads us to a fundamentally different understanding of the distinction between person and work. In this distinction, of course, the one does not exclude the other, but it requires that in a given case each must be regarded strictly in isolation from the other, in order that the distinctiveness and purity of both may be maintained. For it is clear that for Luther it is the distinction between the relationship of man to God and his relationship to the world which is at stake in the distinction between person and work. Now we begin to see why we have had to consider the distinction between person and work, in seeking to identify the level of experience on which Luther's thought is conducted. This will become even clearer when we go more deeply into the distinction between person and work, taking as our guide the distinction between faith and love.

CHAPTER 10

FAITH AND LOVE

To the distinction between person and work there corresponds that between faith and love. 'How often have we said that faith and love must be distinguished in such a way that faith is referred to the person and love to works. Faith destroys sin and makes the person pleasing and righteous. But when the person has become pleasing and righteous, the Holy Ghost and love are given to it, so that it takes pleasure in doing good.'[1] There is an even more brief and precise formulation of this idea: 'Thus faith remains the doer, and love remains the deed.'[2]

This takes us to the very heart of what it means to be a Christian, and also to an understanding of the fundamentally simple but at the same time all-inclusive content of Christian preaching: 'All Christian doctrine, works and life can be summed up briefly, clearly and more than fully in the two terms faith and love, whereby man is placed midway between God and his neighbour, receiving from above and giving out below, and becoming as it were a vessel or a tube through which the stream of divine goodness flows unceasingly into others. See how closely those are conformed to God who receive from God everything he has to give, in Christ, and in their turn, as though they were Gods [Luther uses an irregular plural, implying something different from the ordinary form, which would mean 'gods'] to others, tender them benefits. The words of Psalm 82:6 are true of them: "You are gods, sons of the Most High, all of you." We are children of God through faith, which makes us heirs to all the divine goodness. But we are Gods through love, which makes us do good to our neighbour; for the divine nature is nothing other than pure goodness ... and friendliness and kindness, pouring out its good things every day in profusion upon every creature, as we can see.'[3]

Our progress through the great antitheses in Luther's thought has led us to the distinction between person and work, and the further distinction, which makes it clear, between faith and love. Here we come to the fundamental essence of Christian doctrine. This confirms our supposition that we have now reached the level of experience on which all the numerous antitheses can be understood as springing from a single root, and therefore as ultimately aiming at one and the same goal.

Yet does this not bring us in fact to the point where all the contraries seem to be reconciled and resolved in one single and indivisible unity? Just as the person and works, the doer and the deed, cannot be separated, neither can faith and love. They form a single event, a single living reality. 'For just as faith brings you blessedness and eternal life, so it also brings with it good works and is irresistible. For just as a living person cannot restrain himself, but must move, eat, drink and have something to do—and it is not possible for such works to go by default, because he is alive; and no one needs to call and urge him to do such works, for as long as he is alive he does them—so, similarly, no one need do anything else to get someone to do good works than to say, "Only believe, and you will be able to do everything yourself." Consequently, you do not have to demand good works at length from someone who has once believed. For faith teaches him everything, and everything that he does is well done, and all his works are good and precious, however slight they may be; for faith is so noble that it makes everything good in a man.'⁴ Just as the unity of person and work is nothing less than the living man himself, so it is clear faith and love have their unity in the fact that they sum up the true life of saved man, who has attained to a unity with himself.

It may seem that in faith and love we are dealing with a whole and unbroken unity, such that we could hardly hope to find there the key to the understanding of the antithetical theme which in so many respects dominates the whole thought of Luther. This impression is not maintained on closer examination. The very fact that this unity is expressed through the *duality* of faith and love, and that the inseparable link between them must be expressed in the form of a *distinction*, points to a tension even in this, the profoundest and innermost heart of the matter.

Ought we to be surprised at this? If we are dealing here not with a static situation or ideal, but with the life itself, that is, with events, then there must be tension, process and distinction, and everything, in fact, which is brought about by movement from place to place, or even from one time to another. Because man exists as such only in this movement, he can only be defined in terms of this form of transitional existence. Luther's apprehension of this existence in constant movement, of the temporal nature of man's being, formed a determining factor in his theological thought from the very first. There is impressive evidence of this as early as the first lectures on the Psalms: 'For it is not sufficient to have done something, and now to rest, but, as philosophy tells us, movement is an uncompleted act, always partly comprehended, and partly still to be comprehended, always lying midway between two contraries, and belonging at the same time both to the starting-point and to the goal. If we existed in one only, there would not be any movement. But this present life is a kind of movement and passage, or transition . . . a pilgrimage from this world into the world to come, which is eternal rest.'[5] The active life (*vita activa*) 'is constantly a progress from act to act, from potentiality to potentiality, or as that passage describes it [Luther is referring to 2 Corinthians 3: 18, where the true *vita contemplativa* is referred to], from understanding to understanding, from faith to faith, from glory to glory, from knowledge to knowledge'.[6] For 'progress is nothing other than constantly beginning. And to begin without progress is extinction. This is clearly the case with every movement and every act of every creature.'[7] Thus one must 'constantly progress, and anyone who supposes he has already apprehended does not realize that he is only beginning. For we are always travelling, and must leave behind us what we know and possess, and seek for that which we do not yet know and possess.'[8]

Thus what is true of every human life, and indeed can be perceived in every creature, is also and especially true of Christians. In the lectures on Romans, he says: 'Your life does not consist in rest, but in moving from the good to the better, as the sick man moves from sickness to health.'[9] Luther goes on to expound this in ontological terms, non-being, becoming, being, activity and suffering: 'Man is constantly in non-being, in becoming, in being, in deficiency, in potentiality, in reality'—and he interprets Christian existence accordingly —'always in sin, in justification, in righteousness, that is, always a sinner, always repentant, always righteous. For repentance is the movement from what is not righteous to what is righteous. Thus repentance is midway between un-righteousness and righteousness. And thus its being is in sin as its *terminus a quo* and in righteousness as its *terminus ad quem*.

Thus if we are constantly repentant, we are always sinners, and nevertheless, in fact consequently, always righteous and in the process of being justified ...'[10] 'Consequently the whole life of the new people, the people of believers, the spiritual people, consists only of longing, seeking and praying with the sighing of the heart, with the spoken voice and with the work of the body, to be justified, right up to the moment of death; it consists of never standing still, never having apprehended, never setting oneself any works as the goal of righteousness to be attained, but constantly looking forward to righteousness as though it were always to be found outside oneself, while one lives and exists oneself always in sin.'[11]

Luther spoke in this way not only in his early years, but also in the later disputations on the nature of a Christian: 'That man is justified we understand in the sense that man is not yet righteous, but is constantly in movement, in progress towards righteousness.'[12] 'Thus our righteousness is not yet completed. It is still being carried out [by God, that is as the *opus Dei*] and is still taking place. The work of building is still going on. But it will finally be completed in the resurrection of the dead.'[13] Again, as he observes with marvellous perception: 'The person who believes in Christ is righteous and holy through divine imputation. He already sees himself, and is, in heaven, being surrounded by the heaven of mercy. But while we are lifted up into the bosom of the Father, and are clad with the finest raiment, our feet reach out below the garment, and Satan bites them whenever he can. Then the child struggles and cries out, and realizes that he is still flesh and blood, and that the Devil is still there, and plagues him constantly, until the whole man grows holy and is lifted up out of this wicked and evil world. Thus we are saints and children [of God], but in the spirit, not in the flesh, and we dwell under the shadow of the wings of our mother hen, in the bosom of grace. But our feet must still be washed, and because they are unclean must go on being bitten and tortured by Satan, until they are clean. For you must draw your tiny feet with you under the garment, otherwise you will have no peace.'[14]

This theme seems to have led us completely astray. We were trying to understand the duality of faith and love as the expression of a fundamental tension, from which all the antitheses of Luther's thought could be derived, and to which they were all linked, and which would make clear that they all referred to a single fundamental situation. Since faith and love, corresponding to 'person' and 'works' refer to human existence as such, that is, to the movement it possesses as a temporal, historical and existential form of existence, we were led on towards the tension which constitutes the very nature of this movement, the fact of being midway between a *terminus a quo* and a *terminus ad quem*. Then, following Luther's exposition of this fundamental condition of human existence, we found ourselves in the midst of his utterances concerning justification. But this clearly means that we have ended up with a duality, and in fact with the most extreme and contradictory duality of sin and righteousness, and not with what seemed to be the harmonious duality of faith and love. And yet it is clear that both are concerned with the same situation, because those passages which speak of justification refer, no less than those which speak of faith, to human existence as such, that is, in its historical nature. Thus Luther can claim that theology defines man far more accurately than the traditional definition of a man as *animal rationale*, when it defines him with regard to the fact that human existence is a continuous event, and that this event, seen from its furthest *terminus a quo* and its ultimate *terminus ad quem*, is justification.[15]

This change of theme, whereby the subject of justification

intrudes into our discussion of the duality of faith and love,
is no accident, and really means that our theme has been made
more precise. For we can only understand the necessity of this
duality between faith and love, not to speak of the astonishing
fact that a high degree of tension is possible between faith and
love, on the basis of the doctrine of justification. The different
ways in which human existence can be characterized as a
transitional state, between birth and death, between creation
and resurrection, between sin and righteousness, between God
and our neighbour, and therefore also between God and the
world, may not of course be equated. But they must be considered together if man's existence in a transitional state is to be
properly understood as the fundamental tension to which all
the antitheses in Luther's thought are related.

For it is by no means obvious and undisputed that human
existence can be interpreted by means of the duality of faith
and love. Perhaps it may be generally agreed, whatever qualifications are made, that human existence can be interpreted as
love, including all perverted and deficient forms of love,
because it is existence in motion, historical existence. But why
is it also necessary to bring in the idea of faith? If we follow
Luther, we find that he decisively excludes the interpretation
which speaks of two realms unrelated to each other, on the
one hand the earthly and moral life of man's relationship with
his fellow-men, and on the other the religious relationship with
God, reduced to the inner life, and concerned only with the
salvation of the individual soul. One cannot emphasize more
strongly the inseparable connection between man's relationship
to God and his relationship to his fellow-men, that is, the connection between faith and love, than by saying that man, in
his position between God and his neighbour, is as it were the
passage through which the encounter between God and the

world takes place.[16] But how can we conceive the necessity of this connection? For it must be made clear that faith is necessary for love, and love for faith, and it must be made clear why this is so. But how is this connection to be understood? One alternative is impossible for Luther from the very first, and in any case is manifestly a quite inadequate interpretation. That is the suggestion that faith is no more than the religious basis on which the obligatory nature of the commandment of love is founded. It is true that faith is not without its consequences for our apprehension of the commandment of love, and for a true understanding of it. But the real nature of faith cannot be regarded as that of faith in the law.

Luther's view seems to be accurately represented by the statement that faith gives the power to love. Numerous utterances by Luther seem to be in accord with this interpretation of faith as the 'moral driving force'. One has only to think of the image of the tree and its fruits which he uses so often, and which portrays the precedence of the person over works. Or again, there are numerous statements concerning the effectiveness of faith, which is not a quality lying idle in the soul, but an active force effective outside man: 'Oh, faith is something living, busy, active and powerful, and it is impossible that it should not unceasingly bring about good. Nor does it ask whether there are good works to be done; before one can ask, it has done them, and is always doing them. But someone who does not do such works is a faithless person, groping and looking around himself for faith and good works, and knowing neither what faith is nor what good works are, and yet chattering and babbling many words concerning faith and good works.'[17]

A question arises at once, however, from this interpretation of faith as the power to love. What is the necessity for bringing faith in at this point? Would it not be simpler to say that love itself is the power to do works of love? Is not Luther strangely misrepresenting the situation by placing love entirely on the side of works, understanding it as a work, and then, instead of allowing love to be regarded as the effective force in itself, introducing faith as the active agent of love? In fact, as long as one thinks in the categories of power and effect, of potentiality and act, it is meaningless to describe anything other than love itself as the power to do works of love. Of course poverty of love, the inability to exercise true love, and powerlessness to fulfil the commandment of love in a radical way, are part of human experience. We have always to face the question of the liberation of love, and of the courage to love. But this question lies in a different realm, and cannot properly be understood in the context of human powers. Immediately following the passage quoted above, we read: 'Faith is a work of God within us, which transforms us and makes us born again from God ... and slays the old Adam, makes us completely new persons in heart, courage, mind, and all our powers, and brings the Holy Spirit with it.'[18] Of course the conventional understanding of faith and the Holy Spirit is that additional powers are imparted to man, of which it can be affirmed that they do not derive from man himself, but from God. But what does this really mean? Does it mean any more than an emphasis on what is miraculous, given as a gift, and not at man's own disposal? Such an experience could by no means be restricted to what Luther means by 'faith', if indeed such an experience is connected at all with faith in this sense. Is not man's endowment with additional powers from God to be found in experiences such as inspiration, illumination, ecstasy, in the experience of being filled with the power of love, rather than in the concealment and obscurity of faith?

Luther means something quite different when he speaks of
faith. His real and primary concern is not with the imparting of
additional powers to human existence, but with man's becoming something radically new, with a rebirth that includes
the end of the old man, and with a change in regard to man's
very existence as a person. But this cannot mean a change *to*
the person, for this will be no more than the alteration of certain
attributes and abilities—but an actual change of man's person
itself. Expounding Gal. 2:20 ('It is no longer I who live, but
Christ who lives in me'), Luther says: 'These are the words of
Christian righteousness. If I wish to dispute concerning Christian righteousness, I must throw away [my own] person ... All
I must have in mind is Christ, crucified and resurrected.'[19]
'Faith makes of you and of Christ as it were one person, so
that you cannot be divided from Christ, but cling to him, as
though you were called Christ, while he says: I am that sinner,
because he clings to me ...'[20]

How is this to be understood? And how near does it bring
us to an adequate understanding of how and why faith takes
precedence over love? In his sermon 'On Good Works' Luther
laid great emphasis on faith as the sole fulfilment of the first
commandment, and consequently on the precedence of faith
over all good works, and in fact on faith as the essence of all
good works. But it is notable that what he really stresses is not
the power which it provides to do good works—though this is
present as a secondary element—but a much more radical
aspect: what it really is which makes good works good. Luther
says: 'The first, highest and most sublime good work is faith
in Christ [his actual words are *in Christum*] ... for all works are
summed up in this work, and receive from it the influence of
their goodness as it were in fief.'[21] Thus, to sum up, faith is not

the power to act which makes good works, but is the power of the good which makes works good.

What am I referring to when I try to express Luther's meaning by speaking of the power of the good to make works good? Luther's answer is as follows. Faith, as the power of the good to make everything good, and therefore as the one good work, the work of God pure and simple, is certainty of conscience. For whatever the position and belief of the conscience are with regard to God, so are the works which derive from them. Where there is no faith, there is no clear conscience before God. 'This means the head is cut off the works.' Consequently, works which take place outside faith are nothing and are dead.[22] Thus one cannot create a clear conscience and the resulting certainty from works—this is not merely impossible, but actually brings all truly good works to an end; instead, the certainty must be there first. Man must know that he is ultimately—that is, in the sight of God—affirmed, accepted and loved, in order to have freedom to love, and to carry out works that are completely real and truly good. 'Thus a Christian living in this trust in God knows everything, is capable of everything, and dares to do everything which is to be done, and does everything joyfully and freely, not in order to amass merits and good works, but because it is a pleasure to him to please God in this way; and he serves God wholly gratuitously, content that it pleases God.'[23]

This faith is a good conscience. And faith which makes conscience certain—which means that it makes it good—makes works good, because in the first place it frees them from the inappropriate purpose of providing man's justification, of giving him assurance in the sight of God through works, or, one might add, of providing him with a refuge and hiding-place from God behind works. Secondly, however—and this point is closely related to the first—faith liberates works from the hierarchy of a religious scale of values, in which some works are more meritorious than others. Faith gives the freedom to do what is necessary for the sake of one's neighbour, that is, to do what is demanded by love. 'Thus here everyone can observe and feel for himself whether he is doing good or not doing good. For if his heart is assured that it is pleasing to God, the work is good, even if it is as small as picking up a blade of straw. If this assurance is absent, or if there is any doubt, the work is not good, even if all the dead were raised by it and a person gave himself for burning.'[24] 'In this faith all works become equal, and one is like another, and all distinctions between works fall away [although within the realm of works proper, distinctions do exist[25]], whether they are great or small, brief or lengthy, many or few. For works are not pleasing on their own account, but on account of faith . . .'[26]

Thus the distinction between faith and love is necessary, because each affects man, makes demands on him and calls him into question in a fundamentally different way. He is challenged by faith with regard to his very self, in so far as he has not power over himself, whereas he is challenged by works with regard to that over which he has power and which is the object of his actions. Precisely because both are so closely connected, it is dangerous for no distinction to be made between faith and love, between what is God's affair, and what is man's affair. If this distinction is not made, both conscience and works, the whole of human reality, fall into hopeless confusion. Love needs faith, because only when an ultimate certainty takes away from man his anxious care for himself can love be pure love. And faith does not need love, but brings love with it unasked through its own inner necessity. For faith, which is the life-giving work of God in man, cannot exist without human creative life proceeding from it.

Thus the distinction between faith and love guards against a confusion, fatal to human existence, about the place of human existence. Only when this distinction is made is man's existence set in its proper place. He is only truly man when he does not imagine that he is anything on his own account or that he can depend upon himself, but endures, in a transitional situation between God and his neighbour, his transitional situation between birth and death, and between sin and righteousness. But if this is so, then the inseparable conjunction of faith and love reveals an understanding of man fraught with tension, which Luther expressed at the beginning of his work on 'The Freedom of a Christian' in two propositions: 'A Christian is free and independent in every respect, a bondservant to none. A Christian is a dutiful servant in every respect, owing a duty to everyone.'[27] Faith and love mean the simultaneous conjunction of radical freedom and radical subjection to service. Although this is in no sense a meaningless paradox, but, rightly understood, a unique relationship necessarily required by the nature of the matter, it is not formulated in such a paradoxical way merely for the sake of appearance. A true association between the radical freedom of man and his radical subjection to service means that both must be preserved in their identity, something which in its turn can only take place if freedom and subjection to service co-exist and overlap. But to express this fact in a paradox points to a further fact that this association involves a struggle fraught with conflict and full of temptation, which cannot take place in theory, but only in life itself, by the maintenance of the extreme contradiction it implies.

For this reason, temptations can arise in which the different nature of faith and love is experienced in the most acute fashion.[28] To attempt to give way in matters of faith for the sake of love means to abandon the truth of the gospel and to deny God. 'If *one* friend has to be left in the lurch, then let it be the friend and fellow-man rather than God the Father: away with love, that faith may prevail.'[29] But this antithesis can only be understood when one realizes what is at stake for one's fellow-men if faith is allowed to waver. For if the true substance of faith is at issue, so is the doctrine that expresses faith. But only he who places doctrine higher than life, for the sake of life itself, has understood what is at issue in faith: 'We must distinguish between life and doctrine. Doctrine belongs to God's side, and life to our side. Doctrine does not belong to us, but life belongs to us ... With regard to doctrine I can let nothing go, but with regard to life, everything.'[30] 'Doctrine must be pure throughout. And this is utterly necessary. For it is our light, to light us to heaven ... This distinction between doctrine and life [which merely represents the distinction between faith and love in another form] is very necessary: doctrine is heaven, life is earth ... sins with regard to doctrine cannot be forgiven, for that would mean that God's word, which brings the forgiveness of sins, would be abolished.'[31] Thus by a false application of the idea of the forgiveness of sins, the source of the forgiveness of sins is itself destroyed.

Against the background of these considerations of the relationship between faith and love, the profound difference between the Reformation understanding of the gospel as justification through faith alone and the Catholic and scholastic understanding of justification through grace appropriated in the form of the *habitus*, once again becomes clear. There is no question that faith and love are equally important on both sides. For the formula 'by faith alone', although it excludes love as the basis of justification, is far from excluding love as the consequence of justification, so that in fact *sola fide* is a battle on behalf of pure love. By contrast, the Catholic and scholastic interpretation is solely concerned with faith, through its explicit emphasis that what is at issue is a true and living faith. For mere faith is dead faith, and only becomes living and true faith through the practice of love, through faith formed by love. It is faith that justifies; but—in this view—not faith alone, but *fides charitate formata*.

To formulate the opposition between the different confessions which came to a head in the Reformation by saying that what is ultimately in dispute is whether faith makes love living, or whether love makes faith living, seems difficult to grasp. These opposing positions can be elucidated from the interpretation of Gal. 5 : 6, where it is said of faith that it works through love. Luther denies that this means that faith justifies through love. What it means is that faith works through love, in the sense that love becomes the instrument of faith, and does not appear independently as the cause of works.

This extreme formulation of the opposed denominational attitudes to the relationship between faith and love can be experienced in concrete terms with regard to two points.

There is first the question, what event or process makes a person into a person? Is it man himself who is active and effective, in so far as he is considered as a person in his individual being? Is it man ultimately who acts? Or is this view merely a variation of the definition of man as *animal rationale*, which fails to express the true nature of man? But what does it mean to say that man as a person is ultimately someone whose being is passive, who receives what he is. And how does this take place? Does it not take place by his being *called* into being? Has his personal existence any other basis than in the word? Does man receive his individual existence otherwise than in hearing, than in affirming the word of affirmation spoken to him, that is, otherwise than in faith? Is it not in fact true that *fides facit personam*: faith makes the person?[32]

This leads us to a second concrete form in which our extreme expression of the relationship between faith and love becomes a matter of experience. This is the situation of temptation. What is it that ultimately makes man certain in his conscience? Is it the love which he practises himself, albeit through the grace he has received? Or is it imputed love, which in the strict sense is *extra nos*, but in such a way that it lifts *extra se* anyone who accepts this imputation in faith, and accords him certainty in this way alone, through faith alone. For man, even man who has received grace, is uncertain in himself. Certainty only exists when God is with man through the word, and therefore when man is with God through faith. 'Our theology is certain', says Luther, 'because it sets us outside ourselves.'[33]

CHAPTER II

THE KINGDOM OF CHRIST
AND THE KINGDOM OF THE WORLD

T o suspect Luther of retreating into the inner life and into a religious individualism is not merely absurd in view of the revolutionary historical consequences of his career, but is also contradicted by the responsibility which he explicitly assumes in his teaching for the most varied spheres and events of public life: the Church and secular authority, marriage and economic problems, schools and universities, the question of the Peasants' Revolt and the Turkish war, and in general for the contemporary historical situation of the world. But there is something which provokes this suspicion amongst those who understand him. He concentrates all his utterances, with an intensity rarely equalled elsewhere, upon the conscience. But this emphasis upon the conscience, properly understood, is the reason for the unparalleled range of responsibility which he assumes in his work.

In what is admittedly a different context, referring not to the historical but to the universal eschatological effect of what Christ brings about in the conscience, Luther says of the unimaginably great inheritance promised in Galatians 4: 7: '... so assuredly you are children, not slaves, and therefore without the law, and also without sin, without death; and salvation is there, and no more evil, and the state of being a son brings with it an all-embracing and eternal kingdom with all salvation, etc. No one can describe this exhaustively. I have only the centre point; as soon as we die, we shall also have seen the circumference. Yet anyone who comprehends this in faith possesses nothing but the hearing of the voice of the promise, and yet in this I have something which is greater than heaven and earth. What Christians have is just as great in itself and as unlimited as this, yet as far as we can see and feel, it is very narrowly restricted and is as it were merely the centre point. Thus someone who apprehends the fatherhood of God in his heart and through his hearing should not be judged by what the eye can see, but should be compared with the greatest circle, and that is called God, who is infinite. Thus the promise is also infinite, although it is summed up in the *verbum centrale*.'[1]

This eschatological dimension of what is promised to faith, defined as it is by the infinity of God, stands in a mutual relationship to the historical sphere of influence centred upon the conscience. To say that faith possesses a kingdom which is greater than heaven and earth, would be mere words, if it did not bring the believer into a relationship, fraught with tension, with the kingdom of the world. The eschatological hope would be mere rhetoric if it was understood in isolation from history, and not in the enduring of history. It would no longer be possible to identify the kingdom of Christ as a kingdom which is not of this world, if it were not understood, and witness were not borne to it, in this world, and if it were not in confrontation with the kingdom of the world.

Here we are leaving behind the elucidation of the relationship between person and work, and between faith and love, and discontinue our attempt to reduce our whole theme as it were to the single mathematical point of the process that takes place in the individual conscience. We turn instead to the historical sphere, to the process of world history, and to the eschatological sphere, to the process which God is carrying out in the world. Our inquiry is now into the relationship between the kingdom of Christ and the kingdom of the world. Yet in adopting these universal themes we do no more than draw two circles which, with this same point as their centre and the world and God as their respective radii, include everything that exists. But one must not allow oneself to be misled by this image into deriving from it a solution of the difficult problem of the relationship between the two kingdoms, seeing them as two spheres of reality which embrace human existence in the manner of concentric circles. The doctrine of the two kingdoms cannot be represented in a diagram. The relationship is one of movement, activity and conflict. The situation that presents itself is one in which the two kingdoms are intermingled. And the distinction between the two kingdoms cannot be put into force by an explanation made once for all, but only by incessant preaching. 'I must always drum and hammer and force and drive in this distinction between the two kingdoms, even if it is written and spoken so often that it becomes tiresome. For the Devil himself never ceases cooking and brewing up the two kingdoms together. The secular authorities always seek, in the name of the Devil, to teach and instruct Christ how he should conduct his Church and his spiritual rule. Similarly, the false priests and sectaries, not in the name of God, always seek to teach and instruct people how they should conduct secular rule. Thus the Devil is unrestrained on either side and has much to do. May God defend us from him, amen, if we are worthy of it.'[2]

The expression 'the doctrine of the two kingdoms' has become so closely linked with Luther's thought that the false impression has arisen that a doctrine of the two kingdoms as such is one peculiar to Luther. Consequently, the different associations suggested by the very term 'the doctrine of the two kingdoms' tend to be taken without further examination as opinions of Luther, mostly in the sense of an agreed and peaceable division between the two spheres. But anything like the modern separation of Church and State, which is what people usually have in mind, is a totally inadequate picture of the scope of Luther's doctrine of the two kingdoms. This is true, regardless of whether this new interpretation of the term as a separation between two distinct spheres has a religious or a secularist emphasis, or whether it is meant to legitimize, by means of a doctrine of the two kingdoms with a religious or secularist slant, either the withdrawal of the devout from the world or the retreat of secular life from God. From Luther's point of view, both variations of the doctrine of the two kingdoms, interpreted as a separation between them, fall into the same error, and in fact are merely modifications of the basic mistake of confusing the two kingdoms. For one can only be deceived into making such a separation through an inability to make a proper distinction between God and the world, and a consequent unawareness of their inseparable interrelationship.

The significant fact about Luther's much disputed, misinterpreted and misused doctrine of the two kingdoms is not the fact that he held such a doctrine, but the nature of the distinction which he makes between the two. We cast light on the problem by relating it to more remote historical phenomena, which, however, are also symptomatic of the basic problem of the radical duality which manifests itself in human existence, by pointing to the phenomenon of the tension between 'sacred' and 'profane' in the genuinely cultic sense of these terms, or to the conjunction in apocalyptic of the present aeon and the aeon to come. In a similar way, we can also point to the Augustinian conception, a direct ancestor of Luther's thought, of the two cities, the *civitas Dei* on the one hand, and the *civitas terrena*, sometimes characteristically alternating with the *civitas diaboli*. From this the medieval theory of history derived two ideas. In the first place, the whole course of history was seen as determined by the co-existence and opposition, and to some extent even by the intermingling of two peoples, going back as far as Abel and Cain. As God has a people who belong to him, so has his opponent. Just as the Church is the body of Christ, so there is a similar human and historical *corpus* belonging to Satan. Secondly, this idea of a dichotomy in history was used to explain the inner structure of the *corpus christianum*, and to describe the hierarchical order within it, the *sacerdotium* and the *regnum*, the spiritual and the secular authorities, which existed, as the two swords, or as the sun and the moon, with each other, for each other, and exercising numerous influences upon each other, but which nevertheless belonged to a definite and fixed hierarchy, just as the *regnum gratiae* was higher than the *regnum naturae*. In accordance with this theory, the world of the Middle Ages was characterized by the harmonious spiritual and secular dual structure of Christianity. However the concrete form this should take became a source of severe conflict. The Middle Ages in the West represents an attempt, which ultimately failed, to set up a world order on the basis of a doctrine of the two kingdoms projected into the kingdom of Christ itself, thereby becoming a doctrine of two rules or two authorities, but developing at the same time, from the personal point of view, into a doctrine of two classes.

However much the medieval and Catholic conception of the doctrine of the two kingdoms can be condemned from Luther's point of view for confusing the two—one has only to think of the institution of prince-bishops, of the papal states or of the claims of the papacy to universal rule—it is nevertheless far from easy to define the exact difference between this doctrine and Luther's. For in spite of all the confusion of powers which existed in practice, the theoretical distinction remained in principle undisputed in the Middle Ages. And in spite of his emphasis on the distinction, Luther had no intention of propounding a division into two separate and unrelated spheres. Nor have we reached the heart of the matter with the observation that within Christianity itself Luther rejected the division into clergy and laity. He did so on the basis of his understanding of the word and faith, and the new understanding this gave him of the sacraments. As a result he submitted the traditional sociological structure of Christianity, which was built up on this division, to a radical revision. His programme for this is set out in the address 'To the Christian Nobility of the German Nation': 'To call popes, bishops, priests, monks and nuns the religious class, but princes, lords, artisans, and farm-workers the secular class, is a specious device invented by certain time-servers; but no one ought to be frightened by it, and for good reason. For all Christians whatsoever really and truly belong to the religious class, and there is no difference among them except in so far as they do different work ... This applies to us all, because we have one baptism, one gospel, one faith, and are all equally Christian. For baptism, gospel, and faith alone make men religious, and create a Christian people ... The fact is that our baptism consecrates us all without exception, and makes us all priests. ... Those who exercise secular authority have been baptized like the rest of us, and have the same faith and the same gospel; therefore we must admit that they are priests and bishops. They discharge their office as an office of the Christian community, and for the benefit of that community.'[3] This does not mean that different functions and tasks overlap. But the distinction to be observed here is not derived from the different qualifications of the persons concerned, but from the different tasks laid upon them, yet in such a way that their personal equality is not a basis for the rule of one over the other, but of mutual service, which cannot be divided up into special privileges for each class. Just as a deposed priest becomes a peasant or a citizen like anyone else,[4] so even persons of the so-called secular class can and must in certain circumstances accept ecclesiastical tasks.

This critical stand taken up by Luther, not so much against the existing sociological order as against its basis and interpretation, necessarily resulted in a reconsideration of the nature of the ecclesiastical ministry, as well as of the function of the secular authority. But at first sight one might have the impression that all that was taking place was a degree of reform within the structure that had come down from the Middle Ages. Certainly, the idea of the two classes had disappeared, but there continued a duality of two functions and authorities within Christianity, the spiritual and the secular.

In fact, even Luther did not work out his real doctrine of the two kingdoms in direct confrontation with medieval Catholic social doctrine, but only when he was challenged by the radicalism of the enthusiastic sects. Sometimes the radicalism of these sectarians manifested itself in a pacifist form, declaring, with an appeal to the Sermon on the Mount, that to participate in the works of the secular authority was impossible, since for Christians the command not to take an oath, not to resist evil and not to kill were always absolutely valid. Sometimes it took on a militant revolutionary form, preparing the way with the sword for the kingdom of Christ and for righteousness, and attempting to set up the law of Christ by force. In both cases, the right and the necessity of secular authority were called into question. In confrontation with the

Catholic tradition it was only necessary to remove certain false interpretations of the duality within Christianity, that is, those which explained it in terms of individuals or classes of persons, in order to establish the duality, accepted by both sides, between the spiritual and the secular offices as two distinctive functions and forms of service within Christianity. But it was necessary to oppose the enthusiastic sects by a reasoned basis and justification of this fundamental duality.

Although to outward appearances Luther was allied with the existing powers against the enthusiasts, he ultimately saw a common factor in the traditional Catholic view and that of the enthusiasts. In both cases, their theological understanding of the secular world, and the necessity of being committed to it, was not properly conceived. Whereas the enthusiastic sects saw an abyss and an opposition between the spiritual and the secular, the traditional Catholic view saw them as being on different levels, both in regard to the law, as well as in regard to individual Christians: popular teaching held that the radical demands of the Sermon on the Mount were only valid as additional counsels for those who were perfect, and not as an absolute law for every Christian. In these terms, the only possible justification that could be given for secular authority was one which did not include any real moral responsibility on the part of a Christian towards the secular authority, and which, if followed to its logical consequences, meant that the enthusiasts were right. Thus for Luther to develop his doctrine of the two kingdoms in direct opposition to the enthusiasts did not mean that he was adopting a reactionary course, as has been asserted in particular with regard to his comments on the Peasants' War, but meant that his rejection of the traditional view of the spiritual and secular authorities was expressed in profounder and more mature terms.

Three symptoms reveal how deep the breach was, and how Luther tried to build on a new foundation, although in part with traditional material.

First, it is notable that two themes which had run parallel with each other in the Middle Ages, the apocalyptic vision of the two kingdoms, based on the history of salvation, and the sociological distinction between two authorities, based on the relationship between nature and grace, were not combined in a haphazard way in Luther's development of the doctrine of the true kingdom in opposition to the enthusiastic sects, but were linked in such a way that both themes underwent a reinterpretation. In his 'Address to the Christian Nobility' Luther argued entirely within the framework of the *corpus christianum*, but rejected its division into two classes of persons, as it were two peoples, priests and laity, and simply posited two different ministries within a united Christianity in which all belonged to the spiritual class. Three years later, however, in the work 'On Secular Authority, And How Far One Owes Obedience To It' he introduced a distinction in personal terms between two peoples, but in this case between Christians and non-Christians: 'Here we must divide the children of Adam and all men into two parts, the first belonging to the kingdom of God, and the second to the kingdom of the world. Those who belong to the kingdom of God are all true believers in Christ, and are subject to Christ. For Christ is the King and Lord in the kingdom of God ... The gospel should also be called a gospel of the kingdom of God, because it teaches, governs and maintains the kingdom of God.'[5] On the other hand, 'All who are not Christians belong to the kingdom of the world and are subject to the law.'[6]

The consequences of this seem to be an equivalent division of powers. Those who belong to the kingdom of Christ 'need no secular sword or law. And if everyone in the world was a true Christian, that is a true believer, there would be no need or use for prince, king, lord, sword or law. For what purpose would it serve, as long as they had the Holy Spirit in their hearts to teach them and ensure that they never did wrong, loved everyone, and gladly and joyfully suffered wrong from everyone, and even death? Where evil is always suffered and right always done, there is no need for any quarrel, strife, court, judge, punishment, law or sword. Thus it is impossible for the secular sword and law to find anything to do amongst Christians.'[7]

On the other hand, all this is necessary for the sake of non-Christians. 'But since few believe, and fewer still behave in a Christian way, not resisting evil nor doing evil themselves, God has made for them, instead of the Christian class and the kingdom of God, another form of rule, and has subjected them to the sword, so that even if they desire to do evil they cannot, and even if they do it, they may not do it without fear or with joy and success, just as a fierce wild animal is bound with chains and bonds, so that it cannot bite and tear in the way it would like; whereas a tame and submissive animal does not need this, but is harmless without chains and bonds. For if this was not done, since everyone in the world is evil and there is scarcely one true Christian in a thousand, one would devour the other, so that no one could nurture his wife and children, feed himself and serve God, and so the world would become waste. Consequently, God has set up two forms of rule, the spiritual, which makes Christians and devout people through the Holy Spirit subject to Christ, and the secular, which restrains the unchristian and wicked, so that they have to keep peace outwardly and be silent against their will.'[8]

This introduction of the doctrine of the two kingdoms into

the antithesis, eschatological in its implication, between two peoples, Christians and non-Christians, presents a sharp contrast to traditional teaching and makes quite clear the purpose served by the two forms of rule and authority. They are two different ways in which God encounters the sinful world: the first, with the gospel, which gives the Holy Spirit, and the second, with the law, which outwardly checks the consequences of sin. On the other hand, it would clearly be false to try to interpret the doctrine of the two kingdoms, set out as it is here in personal terms, in an organizational and institutional sense, as if it referred to two completely different groups of persons and spheres of life. For there has obviously to be a distinction between Christians and those who are only apparently Christian. 'For the world and the mass of people are and remain non-Christian, although they are all baptized and are called Christian. But Christians (as we say) are far from one another, so that in the world it is not possible to have a common Christian rule over the whole world, nor even over one country or the great mass of people, for there are always far more of the wicked than of the devout.'[9] But one must go beyond this, to say that it is not merely the scattered and isolated existence of Christians in the world which does not permit such a division between groups of persons. For the Christian himself, as long as he exists in this world, is both righteous and a sinner at the same time, and is therefore fundamentally in need of both forms of rule. It is true that there are considerable differences of degree in the way in which a single person can show the necessity of secular rule, not perhaps by doing wrong, but by being threatened with wrong from someone else, and even though not unwilling to suffer wrong himself, being driven by love to help his fellow-men in what is necessary for their life together.

Thus the first characteristic of Luther's new departure is that the way in which the doctrine of the two forms of rule is given theological profundity and clarity is by being related to the doctrine of the two kingdoms, with its eschatological implications. The second characteristic is equally striking in comparison with both medieval Catholic tradition, and also with the enthusiasm of the sects. Luther's doctrine of the two kingdoms assumes that the secular kingdom is on principle not meant for Christians, neither as its rulers nor as its subjects. Thus in a sermon he says: 'The world is included in these two kingdoms: the first is for despairing consciences, and the second for hard and stubborn minds. Christians are not needed for secular authority. Thus it is not necessary for the emperor to be a saint. It is not necessary for him to be a Christian to rule. It is sufficient for the emperor to possess reason.'[10] Thus secular authority is by no means to be found in Christianity alone. The intrinsic legitimacy of secular authority does not derive from the fact that those who exercise it are Christians. Consequently, Luther can actually take pagan authority as a model in order to show what the task of secular authority is. For 'God has subjected and submitted secular rule to reason, because its purpose is not to control the salvation of souls or their eternal good, but only bodily and temporal goods, which God subjects to man . . . Consequently, even in the gospel we are taught nothing of how this rule is to be exercised and carried out, but are only commanded that it should be honoured and not resisted. That is why the pagans (as they have in fact done) can speak and teach well on this subject. And to tell the truth, they are far more skilled than Christians in such matters . . . For God is a gentle and rich Lord who subjects a great deal of gold, silver, riches, dominions, and kingdoms to the godless, as though they were chaff or sand. In the same way, he also makes lofty reason, wisdom, languages and eloquence subject to them, so that his dear Christians seem to be mere children, fools and beggars by contrast with them.'[11]

While on the one hand, therefore, Luther was able to praise the Turkish state (although not without qualifications), on the other hand, even though he has been rebuked for being a servant of the princes, he submitted the so-called Christian authorities to a criticism of unparalleled frankness: '. . . from the beginning of the world a clever prince is a very rare bird, and a devout prince rarer still. They are usually the biggest fools or the wickedest fellows on earth, so that one is always well-provided with mischief from them and can expect little good of them, especially in godly matters which concern the salvation of souls. For they are God's jailers and executioners, and his divine wrath uses them to punish the wicked and to preserve external peace. Our God is a great Lord. And the reason why he also has to have such noble, high-born and rich executioners and jailers is so that they may possess in abundance riches, honour and fear from everyone. It pleases his divine will that we should call his executioners noble lords, fall at their feet, and be subject to them with all humility, as long as they do not extend their task too far and seek to become shepherds instead of executioners [i.e., to interfere in the spiritual office]. If a prince happens to be clever, devout or a Christian, this is a great miracle and a most precious sign of God's grace upon his country.'[12]

Secular authority as such, then, is independent of whether those who possess secular power are Christians or not, because in the 'first use of the law' God carries out its work even through non-Christians, sometimes better than through Christians. Yet in the end it matters very much whether those who possess secular authority are true Christians or not. And it matters not merely from their personal point of view, but also with regard to their office. For their very ability and success becomes a danger to them. 'All kings and princes, if they follow nature and the highest earthly wisdom, are bound to become God's enemies and persecute his word ...'[13] because as 'superiors' they forget that they are 'inferiors' with regard to God.[14] 'Thus whoever wishes to be a Christian prince must genuinely reject the view that he should lord it over others and act with violence. For all life is accursed and damned, lives for and desires its own good and benefit, and all works are accursed which are not carried out in love.'[15]

Thus Luther, in apparent contradiction to his usual praise even of pagan secular rule, but in fact in opposition to the contempt of the enthusiasts for secular authority, can encourage Christians to take on this task with a good conscience: 'Do not be so blasphemous as to say that a Christian may not carry out what is the work, ordinance and creation of God himself. For otherwise you should say that a Christian ought not to eat or drink or be married, for that too is also the work and ordinance of God ... and it would be quite unchristian to say that there was any form of service of God which a Christian ought not to do or may not do, for the service of God befits no one so much as Christians. And it would also be good and valuable if all princes were truly good Christians. For to wield the sword and authority as a special service of God is more fitting for Christians than for all others upon earth.'[16]

Finally, there is a third characteristic of Luther's fundamentally new approach to the doctrine of the two kingdoms. It is usual to treat it as though it were mere ethical theory, dealing with the problem of the clash between the commandments of God in their radical sense and the necessities of earthly life, a clash which apparently enforces compromises and omissions.

The prevailing discussion of the concrete forms it apparently takes tends to lead to this. It is however a misunderstanding, albeit a frequent one, to interpret the doctrine of the two kingdoms as one attempt to legitimize the inconsistency of Christian existence. Of course it depends how this is understood. A deeper truth may be implied here in some respects than is supposed by such hostile criticism. But even so, such an insight would only confirm that the doctrine of the two kingdoms reveals the basic structure of Christian preaching as a whole, in that Christian preaching does not merely oppose an ideal to earthly reality, but vindicates the reality of the word of God in the reality of the world. Consequently, the gospel is deficient, if the doctrine of the two kingdoms is deficient. And it is only from the gospel that one can judge the distinction made between the two kingdoms. If we try to express this in terms of our theological disciplines, although they are not entirely appropriate, we could say that we are dealing here not with a special problem of ethics, restricted as it were to the question of the true doctrine of the state, but with the basic problem of dogmatics itself, that is, the basic question of fundamental theology.

We are only able here to give a few fundamental pointers towards the understanding of Luther's doctrine of the two kingdoms.

First, the two kingdoms are related to one another and belong to one another, in that God is Lord in both. For 'the secular rule can also be called the kingdom of God. For he intends it to stand, and us to be obedient in it. But it is only the kingdom of his left hand. The kingdom of his right hand, which he rules himself, not placing in it father and mother, emperor and king, executioner and jailer, but dwelling in it himself, is that in which the gospel is preached to the poor.'[17] This does not prevent the kingdom of the world from still being the world, and therefore, in comparison with the kingdom of Christ, 'a poor, wretched and even a foul and stinking kingdom'.[18] 'For if heaven and earth belonged to me alone, what would I have by comparison with God? Not as much as a drop of water or a speck of dust by comparison with the whole ocean.'[19] Thus when the alternative has to be faced, there can be no question as to which has precedence: 'And shall I so shamefully reject and ignore God and his kingdom that I accept this filthy and deadly kingdom of the belly instead of the divine and everlasting kingdom that gives me eternal life, righteousness, peace, joy, and blessedness . . . ?'[20] Indeed, the kingdom of the world can even become the kingdom of Satan, if the distinction between the two kingdoms is completely confused, and God and the world are no longer distinguished. This confusion of the two kingdoms, which is a work of Satan, can in essence only take place in the kingdom of the world, though it does so in such a way that as a result even the kingdom of the world is ruined. Yet as long as life is still maintained in it, however much it may be oppressed and perverted, God nevertheless carries out his work of the law in concealment, regardless of all the destruction, and even Satan is ultimately drawn into its service.

Secondly, this means that the two kingdoms are not distinguished by possessing two separate laws, which compete with each other and contradict each other, but by being constituted by the law and the gospel respectively. If one is aware of Luther's distinction between the law and the gospel, one cannot fall into the error of thinking that the kingdom of Christ, in which the gospel rules, has nothing to do with the law, and that what is put forward as the law in the kingdom of the world is the law of God as such. Further consideration of the doctrine of the two kingdoms must consist of the concrete application in practice of the distinction between the law and the gospel.

Finally, the doctrine of the two kingdoms brings us back once again to a concentration upon the conscience, and thereby to a strange double truth. For the sake of the conscience, a distinction must be made between the two kingdoms. But again for the sake of the conscience, it is also necessary that in certain respects they should overlap or even coincide: 'For before God and in the service of his authority, everything must be the same and mingled together, whether spiritual or secular, pope or emperor, lord or servant, and there can be no distinction or respecting of persons here. One is as good as another before God. For he is the one God, Lord of all equally, of one as of another. Therefore they ought all to share the same obedience and be mingled together with each other like the pastry for a cake, and each one should help the other to be obedient. Thus in service or subjection to God there can be no rebellion either within the spiritual or the secular kingdom. For even in the world no rebellion arises from obedience or service, but from the desire to rule and dominate.'[21]

The way the two kingdoms coincide and yet remain separate within the human person will be dealt with under the theme of man as a Christian and man in the world.

CHAPTER 12

MAN AS A
CHRISTIAN AND MAN IN
THE WORLD

WE turn once again to the problem of the two kingdoms, but
here we shall concentrate upon the existence of one and the
same person in both kingdoms. If we are not to end up with a
completely schizophrenic picture, then our dominant approach
must clearly be that of the unity rather than the duality, and
our high-flown discourse must lead to generally understandable consequences for the practical circumstances of everyone's
life. There can be no doubt that it is right to look for this if
God is Lord in both kingdoms, and if faith and love are
inseparably linked as the doer and the deed.

We are coming here to the point where the theme we have
pursued so far, if it is not to be deprived of its force or even
contradicted, must be maintained to the very end, to the point
at which it has to be vindicated in the concrete circumstances of
life and death. Here too, where it might seem that the unity of
the human person could be taken for granted and would
exclude any duality, it is essential that the true unity should be
revealed. This can only be done by boldly bringing the concept
of the person within the field of tension and regarding one and
the same person both as a Christian and as one who belongs to
the world. Again, we must not reduce to mere triviality the
serious approach to doctrine which we encounter in Luther's

thought and which we have tried to achieve in pursuing his thoughts, and our attempt to speak in practical terms must not amount to a surrender or a flight from doctrine. We must therefore not be afraid, though we are on the threshold of practical ethical decisions, to elucidate and bring together a number of elements which illustrate Luther's way of thought and his understanding of reality and therefore the ontological problems to be dealt with, in order to make perfectly clear how, and in what way, doctrine is related to life.

It is not very difficult to find an expression which will characterize the very basis of Luther's mode of thought. It can be found in a preposition which might be described as the key word to Luther's understanding of being: the preposition *coram*, which can be translated into German by the word '*vor*' and into English by 'before'. To define more closely the significance of this word 'before', one might say that it is spatial and not temporal in meaning. But if this definition were taken strictly, it would be not merely inadequate but misleading. For curiously enough, it implies a determination of place which as such is a determination of time. Its precise meaning, which is also that of its etymology, is 'before the face of', 'in the sight of'. More-over, Greek and Hebrew possess equivalent expressions similar in their etymological structure. But in Hebrew, not only is the situation assumed by the expression 'to be before the face of . . .' maintained in a more living form in the consciousness of the language, but the expression concerned is also far more fre-quent than in Latin and Greek. Thus in the fundamental sig-nificance of the Latin *coram* for Luther's mode of thought, the influence of the biblical, or more precisely the Old Testament, understanding of reality is at work.

Thus what is as such a determinant of place is also a deter-minant of time. This can be seen at once from the fact that 'in the sight of' means for practical purposes 'in the presence of'. Although the situation referred to is very elementary, it is difficult to express it in abstract terms. In any case the fundamental situation is that something is defined here not in itself, but in its outward relations with something else, or more properly, in terms of the relationship of something else with it. But the relationship is not that of things which are together or adjacent in space, are a certain distance from each other, are brought into contact with one another, or affect each other physically. What is decisive in this relationship is that there is a countenance which fixes its eye upon something, looks at it, perceives it and gives existence to it as such. What is 'before' me is present to me, and exists for me. But we are concerned with more than the mere epistemological affirmation that man knows things only as they appear to him, that is, as he sees them, and does not know the thing in itself.

There is something strange about the verb 'to look'. The decisive element is not what one looks like, but how one looks. To describe what a person looks like can be done in numerous ways, by speaking of size and shape, the colour of the skin, the clothing, etc. Of course what is hardest to describe, and what is most important in what a person looks like, is his face. It is most important, because at this point a person looks literally from within himself—something appears of what exists and takes place within him. But the ultimate reason why this, the most important element in what a person looks like, is hardest to describe, is that it is really beyond the task of description. For description it is necessary to stand apart, not merely spatially but also in time, from the object. But the face of a person, at least when it is looking towards me, does not give me room or time to observe and describe it. For I experience

myself in it, as one observed, as one looked at, which results
either in my looking away or in my being completely preoccupied in holding my own against the gaze directed towards
me. My presence is determined by that of another. In the sight
of another I can certainly look away from him, but I cannot
simply disregard him. That is to say, to 'disregard' someone is
only a modification of 'being regarded' by someone. In the
presence of another I am in some way claimed by him, while
he is also claimed by me. It is true both that he is in my presence
and I am in his presence.

This means that the term 'to look' has a characteristic ambiguity. What one looks like contains in it an active element of
looking at something, but also includes the passive element of
being looked at. This is true in the strict sense of the encounter
between one person and another, face to face, but is also
applicable to the relationship to everything which is looked at
as present. This aspect of looking is also true of things when
man looks at them. Man not only looks at them, but sees
himself as looked at by them. This is so because he recognizes
that he is in a certain sense dependent upon them, though in
such a way that the way in which things look at him is inseparable from the way he looks at things. *Facies rerum est
omnia in omnibus*, says Luther: 'The way things look is everything.' And he immediately gives this a theological application:
'Just as the word of God is fearful to those who fear, a fire to
those who burn, and salve to the meek, and in general:
whatever your disposition is, so the word of God is to you.'[1]
'For whatever someone is like, God, the scripture, the creation
is like that to him.'[2] To 'look at' someone in the active sense,
that of the way a person looks at things, is transformed into
being looked at and points to the dependence of man upon how
he is looked at, on his 'looks' in the passive sense, the 'looks'

which he possesses. This expression contains in itself an element of value, more evident still in the phrase 'the regard' that one enjoys, and which is the opposite of the regard that one is refused or the contempt which one encounters. The word 'face' similarly takes on a passive significance in the expression 'to lose face'. [The German *Gesicht* means both 'vision' and 'visage, face'—Translator.]

Of course the profundity of the situation to which the *coram*-relationship leads is naturally only manifested in an encounter between one person and another. The most important element in the situation that is implied by the preposition *coram* is not the way in which someone else is present before me, in my sight, but the way that I myself am before someone else and exist in the sight of someone else, so that my existential life is affected. This can be verified from such simple and basic experiences as my dependence upon the countenance the other person presents to me, that is, whether he regards me in a friendly or hostile way, interests or bores me; whether he takes any notice of me at all or ignores me; or, to put it in slightly different terms, whether he turns his face towards me or turns away from me, and turns his back upon me. This *coram*-relationship, in which man always finds himself, is in fact the characteristic human situation, without which he would not be man at all. In it the way in which he encounters others, others encounter him, and he encounters himself are interwoven.

We are in contact here with a complex of experience and encounter about which one might be tempted to make the superficial comment that it is merely a question of man's vision, consciousness, understanding and judgement. But if we think out its more profound implications, we realize that we have been brought into contact with the situation in which a judgement is made about human existence and about reality.

In seeing and being seen, where the event which we call presence takes place, there also takes place the event in which human existence is exposed to judgement. The *coram*-relationship reveals that the fundamental situation of man is that of a person on trial. That he is subject to judgement in this way, and longs for it as much as he fears it, shows that his inner structure is that of a court of law, in the sense that the way he understands and regards himself is determined by the judgement he encounters, while what he encounters as judgement is effective because it comes to him as one who is doubtful and problematic in his own eyes. The situation with which we have come into contact cannot be described in exhaustive detail here. It must suffice to indicate two aspects of it.

It is because man exists in this *coram*-relationship that man only truly exists in being recognized. A characteristic understanding of the relevance of this situation is found in the following passage: 'So long as something is not recognized as having happened, it has not yet happened to him [man] or in him; but it takes place when it is recognized as having taken place.'[3] Again, we can point to the fact that Luther can speak of 'becoming a sinner' in a special sense, referring not merely to the falling into sin of a sinless person, but of the recognition by a sinner that he is a sinner, whereby he first becomes a sinner in the strict sense.[4] Another example of the relevance of this understanding, transforming reality as it does, can be found in the context of the doctrine of the two kingdoms itself: 'It is a completely different thing to be married and to recognize married life. Someone who is married and does not recognize married life can never live in it without disgust, pain, and sorrow . . . But those who recognize it are those who firmly believe that God himself instituted marriage, and ordained that man and woman should be joined together and beget and raise children. For they have God's word for it . . .'[5]

This brings us to the second indication. The *coram*-relationship provides the reason why reality can be spoken of; or more accurately, the *coram*-relationship involves the expression of reality in the spoken word. For Luther this has the concrete meaning that reality is only understood for what it is if the word of God, through which it has its being and which is what is truly real in it, is heard. The essence of this understanding of reality as consisting of the word can be seen in Luther's doctrine of the sacraments. Thus in the Shorter Catechism we read: 'Baptism is not only mere water, but it is water understood according to God's commandments and associated with God's word.'[6] But the same is true of all creatures: 'The whole creation is his [God's] mask.'[7] This has a twofold meaning. Firstly, the creation is only a mask, that is, it is not anything in itself or on its own account, but is only the veil which conceals the Creator, who speaks to us from it and through it. That is why the true recognition of reality requires a distinction between the creation as a mere mask and the word of God concealed in it, so that the house is not confused with the host, nor the creature with the creator, and honour and faith are accorded to God and not to the creation.[8] But this leads us to the second point. Because of the distinction between God and the creation, between the word and the mere mask, we are required to acknowledge and reverence the creation as a mask, the purpose for which it was ordained by God. 'The monarchy, the empire, secular authority, the teacher, the schoolmaster, the father, the mother, the lord, the lady, the servant, the maid, are all masks, persons whom God desires to be reverenced and honoured and acknowledged as his creation. They must exist in this life, but he does not wish divine nature to be ascribed to them.'[9]

It has already been made clear that the emphasis accorded to the *coram*-relationship in Luther's thought is not derived simply from the phenomenon of our encounter with our fellow-men, although Luther is also concerned with the encounter between one person and another when he thinks in these terms. But the essential object of Luther's thought when he considers this *coram*-relationship is presence in the strict sense, the presence which makes its object present. And the presence which makes its object present is God alone. Thus the fundamental situation of the *coram*-relationship is existence *coram Deo*, existence in the sight of God, in the presence of God, under the eyes of God, in the judgement of God, and in the word of God.

But it would be quite wrong to isolate this existence in the sight of God from the different ways in which man is involved in a *coram*-relationship. In Luther's language these other *coram*-relationships constantly recur: existence in my own sight (*coram meipso*), existence in the sight of men (*coram hominibus*), and existence in the sight of the world (*coram mundo*). The two latter forms are almost identical, though it is nevertheless worthwhile to pay attention to the difference between them. Even existence 'before myself', by contrast to existence 'before God', can in certain respects be identified with *coram*-existence in relation to men and to the world. On the other hand, existence 'before myself' is taken up into existence before God once man becomes aware that he in fact possesses this existence before God. This means, of course, that he is no longer abandoned to his own forum and judgement, but is rather translated out of himself, and thus possesses his being and existence outside himself, because he possesses it in the sight of God.

The living and overpowering force which is a constant characteristic of Luther's thought, and the concrete, immediate, relevant and compelling language he uses even in the loftiest reflections, are due to the assurance with which he moves within the framework of these *coram*-relationships. This comment would be misleading if we were to give the impression that it referred to a formal method, a subtle intellectual technique. It is easy to gain this impression, if, as we have tried to do here in outline, one analyses the structure of these *coram*-relationships as the characteristic structure of Luther's thought and language. But the impression of complication we have given is absent from the situation as it is seen by someone who is at grips with the heart of the matter, as Luther was, in a way that is remote to us. Not that the intensity with which a theologian penetrates the heart of the matter necessarily makes it easy for him to handle structures of thought with great virtuosity. But the unavoidable difficulty for anyone who engages in theology, the toil and labour that it demands, and the suffering without which no true knowledge and no authority can be acquired, are not something which can be mastered methodically by learning a technique; for it can be truly said of theology: 'One becomes a theologian through life, and even through death and through the experience of damnation, and not through understanding, reading or speculation.'[10]

With these reservations in mind let us add a few final comments on Luther's approach to the *coram*-relationship. To exist before God and to exist before the world are not two possible and mutually exclusive choices, two separate realities, but an alternate relationship which is necessarily simultaneous. Someone who possesses his existence in the sight of God does not thereby cease to exist in the sight of the world. And someone who possesses his existence in the sight of the world is not thereby deprived of his existence in the sight of God. But his existence before one court of judgement becomes the contrary of his existence in the other, for what is at issue in the dispute between the two courts of judgement is the source from which man receives his being, the judgement and the word from which he lives, the judgement which provides his understanding of himself and the countenance which ultimately claims him and towards which his own face is ultimately turned, his back being turned towards the other. That is, the dispute is about what constitutes and determines his presence. If he is under the spell of the world, he is nothing before God, precisely because he supposes that he is something in the sight of God, whether it is through the exercise of religion, through open revolt against God, or through forgetting God. But if he listens to the word of God and accords it its due as the work of God which kills and brings to life in judgement and grace, he experiences in the judgement of the world the opposition which is the lot of those who, for the sake of God, try to do justice to the world as God's creation. Thus existence before God does not mean that existence before the world becomes valueless. The one adds to the other, for it is only through existence in the sight of God that a real distinction is made between the two *coram*-relationships, so that they are properly related to one another. For someone who takes a proper attitude to God through faith is thereby able to take a proper attitude to the world through love.

As a result of this insight into the fundamental significance of the *coram*-relationship, we can now understand how far we can speak of a duality with regard to personal existence without this leading to the dissolution of personal existence into a divided, schizophrenic consciousness. The word 'person' occurs in Luther in two unreconciled, if not contradictory, senses. We have already seen it distinguished from human works. There the person meant the unity and wholeness of man through his existence in the sight of God. The person in this sense is for Luther almost equivalent to the conscience. We next encounter the use of the word 'person' in the meaning of countenance, appearance or looks, that is, in a meaning which is associated with what is probably the original meaning of *persona* as a player's mask, and, derived from this, the role a person plays or the rank he fills. Here too, of course, man is considered in the wholeness of his manifestation and appearance, but not as the naked self which exists concealed in his heart— and therefore, as he is in his own sight, but not as he is in the sight of God. For man sees only what his eyes see, and sees even himself in this way, whereas God alone sees into the heart. Man is a person in the sense of a mask or a role, in what he is in the sight of the world, through his works, and in accordance with the function which he exercises. Behind this mask his naked self in the radical sense is concealed, and is clothed by it in the sight of the world.

This is the concept of the person referred to in the biblical expression 'to respect someone's person',[11] that is, to make a biased judgement on the basis of how someone is regarded by the world, and not to take him in his real existence as himself, but as it were in the clothing in which he presents himself and makes a particular impression. Thus it is said of God, that he does not respect the person of man. We men, on the other hand, are inclined to respect persons, and to make prejudiced and biased judgements; we allow ourselves to be blinded by appearances. But we must take care not to presume that we can judge by the same standards as God. Of course we ought not to be taken in by appearances. But this does not mean that we should hold in total contempt this mode of being a person, despise man in his functions and ranks, and fail to accord him his rights as such, evading his claim by thinking of him as it were in the weakness and nakedness of his inward undress, and attempting to root out what is concealed and drag it into the light. Rather, the word 'person', in the sense of a mask or role, points to man's existence in the world, a situation which cannot be avoided, and the right use of which ought not to be forgotten simply because it is misused through man's biased judgement and liability to be deceived. On the contrary, it is important to recognize the proper and necessary function of this mode of personal existence. But this is done not by seeking to inquire behind the outward appearance into the concealment of the heart. Instead we have to pay attention to the word of God which comes to us in personal existence of this kind, that is, in these offices and functions, to the gift which is imparted to us in them by God, to the divine commission to be which is to be observed in them, and to the will of God which makes its demands upon us in them.

We have already met this understanding of created being as a mask. Created beings are a mask not really and primarily because the existence of the human self is concealed behind them. This is also true, but it is a secondary aspect which ultimately does not concern us. They are a mask with regard to the word of God which lies behind them. To be a person in this sense means to carry out the task given one by God with regard to the world, to perform the service accorded to one, to fulfil, as the instrument of God, the work of God to which one is destined in the world, and even, by the command and in the place of God, to exercise authority and exert power and to say what has been entrusted to one.

Thus, properly speaking, there is no contradiction between the two concepts of the person. Both are concerned with the different ways in which man shares in the nature of reality as the word, and even, if he is aware of what this means, in the activity of the word of God in the world. The person as the existence of man in the sight of God is constituted by his encounter with the word of God, which is addressed to man's conscience and sets it free. The person as man's existence in the sight of the world is constituted by his being sustained and given a task by the word of God, which takes man into its service through his works.

However, the clarity of this distinction is obscured by two factors. The first is an inconsistency in Luther's linguistic usage which can easily give rise to confusion. The second is the difficulty which persists in spite of everything in the matter itself and which cannot be denied because the distinction has been asserted, but is the reason why the distinction has to be made. For it is not intended as a solution which will remove the problems once for all, but as a guide to the conscience which will enable it to face the difficulties as they arise in particular cases.

The two concepts of the person as we have elucidated them can be described either by a distinction between person and function—this ought to be quite clear from what we have just said; or as a distinction between two persons; or else as a distinction between two functions, in the sense that Christian existence as such, bearing witness through the word of faith, is also a function and a task. It is this that gives rise to the inconsistency of Luther's terminology.

We can see this in a number of passages in the exposition of the Sermon on the Mount. Thus on Matthew 5: 5, 'Blessed are the meek', we read: 'Here, however, we must first realize that Christ is not speaking of the authorities carrying out their function . . . but he is speaking only of individual persons, and of how each person should live on his own account with regard to others, apart from his function and authority as father and mother, and how each should live not as father and mother with regard to their children, nor carrying out their office of father and mother, but with regard to those who do not call them father or mother, such as neighbours and others. For I have often said elsewhere that one must clearly distinguish between the office and the person. He who is called Hans or Martin is a quite different man [cf. here the English term 'Christian name'!] from him who is called "Elector" or "Doctor" or "Preacher". For we here have as it were two different persons in one man, one in which we are created and born, and according to which we are all equal to one another, man, woman or child, young or old, etc. . . . But once we are born, God clothes and adorns you as another person, makes you a child, me a father, one a lord, another a servant, one a prince and another a citizen, and so forth. This is a divine person which we are given, since it carries out a divine office and goes adorned in the glory of that office, and is not called simply Hans or Klaus, but Prince of Saxony, or "father", or "lord". He says nothing of these here, but lets them carry out their office and their rule, as he has ordained it, but he is speaking instead of a mere individual natural person, and of what each person on his own account, as a human being, should do towards another.'[12]

Or on Matthew 5: 38 ff.: the command not to resist evil, he says: 'Now if someone should ask whether a Christian should go to law or defend himself, etc., I can answer straightforwardly and say: No. For a Christian is a person or being who has nothing to do with such worldly affairs and with the law . . .

There follows another question, whether a Christian, therefore, may be a man of the world and carry out the office and work of rule or of the law, so that the two persons or two offices should coincide in one person, who would simultaneously be a Christian and a prince, a judge, a lord, a knight or a maid, who are merely secular persons; for they belong to the secular rule. Here we say: Yes, for God himself has ordained and instituted this worldly rule and these distinctions, and has confirmed and praised them through his word. For without them this life could not be maintained, and we were all included in it, in being born in it before we became Christians, and therefore we must also remain in it, as long as we are on earth, but only with regard to our outward life and being . . . Thus we speak here of a Christian *in relatione* not as of a Christian, but as of one bound in his life to another person, whom he has below or above him, or even beside him, as lord, lady, wife, child, neighbour, etc., such that one has the obligation to defend, protect and guard the other when one can. Thus it would not be right in this context to teach people to turn the other cheek, and to throw the cloak after the coat.'[13]

As far as the linguistic aspect of this exposition is concerned, three observations must be made which cast considerable light on the matter.

Firstly, the origin of this conception in what we have shown to be Luther's approach to the *coram*-relationship is emphasized by the fact that he presents the distinction between the two persons as a distinction in the way in which they are addressed, in the names by which one and the same person is called.

Secondly, the gross misunderstanding which suggests that the distinction between the person as a Christian and the person in the world divides man into two separate spheres of life, one in which he is governed by the law of God and another in which he allows himself to be governed by the inherent law of the world, is refuted by the fact that Luther can exchange one attribute for another: the secular person, with regard to the task he carries out, is a 'divine person'; the person as a Christian, with regard to his nakedness in the sight of God, of which his birth and death are particularly characteristic, is a 'natural person'.

Finally, against the charge that a distinction is being made between a private sphere to which Christianity is restricted and a public sphere in which it is not practicable to be a Christian, it can be argued that in both respects it is a Christian who is being described and in both cases with regard to his attitude to his fellow-men. But the first case presents the Christian as it were carrying out the functions of the gospel, as a witness to faith, who on his own account takes seriously his self-commitment to his fellow-men, through the freedom from himself which he is given the courage to exercise by the Sermon on the Mount as the testimony of faith. In the second case, the Christian is presented carrying out the function of the law, as one who in certain respects is in bondage to his fellow-men and is obliged to act not for himself, but for others, with a particular function to carry out in maintaining the world in its provisional existence.

But we are now fully at grips with the real difficulties of the matter. It sometimes seems as though Luther regarded them as eliminated, for example when he writes: 'Thus both go perfectly well together, and you satisfy God's kingdom and the kingdom of the world at the same time, both outwardly and inwardly, at the same time suffering evil and wrong, and yet punishing evil and wrong, at the same time not resisting evil and yet resisting it. For in one case you are paying attention to yourself and your own affairs, and in the other to your neighbour and his affairs. For yourself and your own affairs you are clinging to the gospel, and suffering wrong as a true Christian, on your own account; with regard to others and their affairs, you cling to love and suffer no evil for your neighbour, which is something which the gospel does not forbid but actually commands elsewhere.'[14]

With regard to the many-sided conflict which there is no doubt is manifested here, the following indications should be noted:

First, the problems must always be traced back to the fundamental distinction between the gospel and the law, the righteousness of faith and the righteousness of works. That is why there should always be an absolute rejection of the false belief that there can be anything like a double moral standard. Both as a Christian person and as a secular person, man has to act on one and the same basis: love. The difference in the way love works in the two cases is due to a difference in the situation, in what has to be done for the sake of one's neighbour.

Secondly, the importance of faith for the secular person consists in the fact that the secular person is such in certainty and in truth, which cannot be the case without faith. This certainty sets man free to serve his neighbour without a calculating piety. It is in precisely this way that the fruits of the Holy Spirit are brought forth in unassuming worldly acts carried out in the service of one's neighbour.

Finally, if the distinction between the two persons is not to be misused and regarded as a distinction between two separate spheres of existence, but is to be constantly used as a guide to the conscience, then it enables man to guard conscientiously against answering the question about what he is commanded to do by conventional judgements and the prejudices which prevail in secular society, and to maintain a readiness to do what is unusual and extraordinary where it is presented to him as the truly reasonable thing to do, and also as the true commandment of love based on faith.

CHAPTER 13

FREEDOM AND BONDAGE

THE object of theology, according to Luther, is man who is guilty and lost and God who justifies and saves, that is, the knowledge of God and man in strict relation to what takes place between God and man. What cannot be fitted into the discipline of this single theme is an error and a poison in theology. By this standard one can tell not only whether what is said of man is theological, but also whether what is said of God is theological; for the latter is not assured by the mere fact of speaking about God.[1] Thus theology is concerned with the proper distinction between God and man, which asserts the proper mutual relationship between God and man.

This one object of theology keeps Luther's thought in a state of tension between contradictory assertions, as we have described from various points of view. This fundamental theological theme determines everything else, and we are now going to give an explicit exposition of it as a conclusion to our introduction to Luther's thought. Our next two chapters concern the freedom and the bondage of man and, finally, God hidden and revealed.

But we are in fact departing from the discipline of theological language laid down by Luther, by dividing the subject of theology in our final chapters, and speaking first only of man and then only of God. That the antithetical element is present in both themes in a fresh form, thus persisting to the very end, can be regarded as an indication of the degree to which the one object of theology asserts itself even here. For although we shall concentrate first upon man and then upon God, we shall do so in such a way that we shall speak of man *in the sight of God* and of God *with regard to man*. To express the meaning of 'in the sight of God', man will be regarded from the point of view of his freedom and bondage, and to express the meaning of 'with regard to man', God will be considered from the point of view of his concealment and revelation.

In all the previous antitheses we were able to perceive both the mutual conflict and mortal enmity and at the same time the mutual relationship of two distinct ideas, and the same is true in these last two cases. Here above all, as one would expect, we are faced with the difficult fact that freedom and bondage, or concealment and revelation, are not simply mutually exclusive or alternatives, but can co-exist in certain respects in spite of the presence of an exclusive element. The bondage of man cannot be considered as bringing an end to his freedom, nor can his freedom be considered as bringing an end to his bondage. Neither can the relationship between them be resolved into the parallel existence of partial freedom and partial bondage, but in one respect, and perhaps in more than one, we shall have to define man's freedom more closely as his bondage, and his bondage as his freedom. The same could be said of the revelation of God, that it is neither wholly nor partly the lifting of the concealment of God, but his revelation as revelation in concealment.

With regard to the theme which we are now going to discuss, we can say that no theologian—we may go even further and say no other thinker—has spoken in such compelling terms of the freedom of man on the one hand, and with such terrifying force of the bondage of man on the other, as Luther.

It is characteristic that the two works of Luther which deal with this theme are those which can most easily be described as a systematic presentation of his theology: the treatise 'On the Freedom of a Christian'[2] of 1520, and five years later, the great controversial work against Erasmus, *De servo arbitrio* ('That free will is nothing').[3]

Freedom is the very essence of salvation: 'A Christian is free and independent in every respect, a bondservant to none.'[4] Through Christ he is a king with absolute freedom, and what is far more, a priest who has the right and authority to appear before God.[5] 'By virtue of his kingship he exercises authority over all things, and by virtue of his priesthood he exercises power with God.'[6] When Luther goes on to assert the apparent opposite: 'A Christian is a dutiful servant in every respect, owing a duty to everyone',[7] he is by no means expressing the problem of the freedom and the bondage of man in its most extreme and paradoxical form. For the contrast between freedom and obligation to service, on which Luther bases his work 'On the Freedom of a Christian', only interprets in paradoxical terms the unity of both, and thus the nature of freedom. The freedom which a Christian has through faith is freedom to render the service of love. And it is only the service of love if it is carried out in freedom. 'Lo, that is how love and joy in God flow out of faith, and how love gives rise to a free, eager, and glad life of serving one's neighbour without reward.'[8]

This is the distinction between the time of the law and the time of grace: 'For as long as men kept the commandments of God not from free will and from love, but from servile fear or from a childish love, the commandment was only imposing an unbearable weight and burden upon them, and was impossible to fulfil, for God's commandments must be fulfilled voluntarily. And this is not possible for human nature, which is why it is sick and laid low under the law, and has become powerless to fulfil it . . . The other time is the time of grace and help, through which man is strengthened to keep God's will and commandments freely, from the pure love of God, and not to do it for the sake of its usefulness or for reward, nor to abandon it either through suffering or through death. And this is not the work of nature, but the work of grace.'[9]

This voluntary love is the fruit of the freedom revealed by the gospel, which is the essence of faith. But if the gospel, understood in its full profundity, is the revelation of freedom from the compulsion and curse of the law, in such a way that faith takes man, who is under the law, and places him above the law and outside the law (*supra legem* and *extra legem*[10]), so making him Lord over the law instead of a slave to the law, and if this, properly understood, applies to the law of God in its power to accuse and slay then the freedom of a Christian is, more than ever a freedom from all human ordinances. 'For this reason we hold, and desire to maintain without hindrance, that we are free of all papal and human teachings and commandments, and it should be a matter of our own will and pleasure whether we keep them or not.'[11] 'Thus as long as we are Christians we are free of such human commandments, as far as they touch our conscience. That is why we are obliged to risk our lives over it and not to abandon such freedom; for this would be to deny and condemn Christ, who commanded such freedom so firmly and strictly, and it is not in our power to change this freedom or give it up.'[12] Nevertheless; 'This Christian liberty, freedom and power must be understood in a purely spiritual sense . . . But spiritual freedom exists when the conscience remains free.'[13]

The course of the Reformation provided numerous opportunities to attack the misunderstanding and misuse of evangelical freedom. Luther attacked the forced introduction of new ordinances in the name of evangelical freedom during the transition to Protestant practice, on the grounds that it meant that consciences were being confused in a completely unevangelical way: 'As long as I . . . cannot pour faith into people's hearts, I neither am able nor ought to force or compel anyone to believe; for God alone does this, coming to dwell beforehand in the heart. That is why we should leave the word free and not add our work to it: we possess the *ius verbi*, but not the *executionem*. We have to preach the word, but the consequences should be left to God alone in his pleasure.'[14] 'Faith desires to be accepted freely, without constraint.'[15] Again, he opposed the direct derivation of political ordinances, such as the abolition of serfdom, from the freedom into which Christ has liberated us: 'This is to make Christian freedom purely carnal . . . For a serf can quite well be a Christian and possess Christian freedom.'[16] Again, he opposed the claim simply to be exercising the consequences of evangelical freedom made by those who wanted their Christianity to cost them nothing: 'Therefore we wish we had not preached to the people, nor would we willingly permit or allow them to enjoy anything of our freedom, but would like to let the Pope or his like be over them again, to compel them like a true tyrant. For such a mob, who will not obey the gospel, deserve nothing more than such a jailer, to be God's devil and executioner.'[17]

But the decisive assertion of the bondage of the human will forms a kind of counterpoint to this presentation of freedom as the essence of the gospel. Luther came to realize the radical bondage of the will, not in the face of the challenge of Erasmus as the advocate of the freedom of the will, but as soon as he comprehended the pure gospel. Thus as early as a disputation in

1516 he says: 'The will of man without grace is not free, but enslaved.'[18] A year later, in the *Disputatio contra scholasticam theologiam*, he says: 'It is not true that the free effort [of man] is able [to decide] on either of two opposed courses. Rather it is not free at all, but captive. It is not true that the will is by nature able to follow right guidance.'[19] 'Man cannot of his nature desire that God should be God; on the contrary, he desires that he himself might be God and that God might not be God.'[20] 'The best and infallible preparation and the sole disposition to grace is the eternal election and predestination of God.'[21] A year later, in the Heidelberg disputation, he says: 'To speak of free will after the fall is mere words. If it [this so-called free will] does what lies in its power it commits mortal sin.'[22]

This thesis was condemned, with others, as heretical in the papal bull of excommunication, but in his reply Luther did not merely confirm it, but made it even more radical. He said he had been wrong to qualify the statement concerning the freedom of the will by the reservation concerning grace which still remained to be imparted. He should have said, without qualification: 'Free will is in reality a fabrication, a mere turn of phrase without reality.' 'For no one has the power of himself even to think something good or evil, but everything ... is derived from absolute necessity.'[23] 'Men in their wretchedness are deceived by the inconstancy, or as the expression is, the contingency of human affairs; for they lower their foolish eyes to look upon mere things and on what is effected by things, and do not once lift their eyes up to look upon God, in order to recognize things that are above things, in God. For to us who look down into the depths, things appear arbitrary and fortuitous, but to those who look up, everything is necessary, for we live, act and suffer not as we will, but as he wills, and so does everything that exists. Free will, which is only apparent with regard to us and to temporal things, disappears in the sight of God.'[24] It was utterances such as these which provoked the opposition of Erasmus, when after long delay he saw himself compelled to attack Luther. Where free will was concerned, the humanist was in agreement with the scholastic tradition which he too criticized elsewhere.

It can be assumed immediately in the case of a thinker like Luther, who is so preoccupied with a single theme, that these two series of utterances, on freedom on the one hand, and on bondage on the other, are not simply parallel but contradictory assertions, without any inner relationship, but instead are inseparably associated. It is therefore clear that in order to speak adequately about freedom, the state of bondage must be properly related to it. This must not be done in such a way that what we say about the bondage of the human will as a condition of captivity and loss is merely the dark background which offsets more clearly what is said about salvation as man's translation into freedom. Instead, in certain respects at least, both must be accepted in conjunction with each other, so that to declare that *liberum arbitrium* is nothing is a necessary commentary on what freedom truly is. But this means that the purpose of discussing the bondage of the will is simply to be able to give a proper account of freedom. It is essential for an understanding of these difficult utterances of Luther concerning the bondage of the will, which are understandably so offensive and senseless to a superficial and impatient study, that one should constantly be aware that this relationship exists. The attestation that free will is nothing is ultimately meant to be recognized as the gospel, that is, as a testimony to the glorious freedom of the children of God. We might attempt to show the way out of the apparent contradiction by a slight change of terminology. Luther asserts the bondage of the *will* for the sake of the freedom of the *conscience*.

That we are dealing nevertheless with a complex of problems which has many aspects and needs to be clarified is shown by the following preliminary observations. That the human will is not free is no doubt in the first instance a statement about the will of sinful man, in accordance with John 8: 34: 'Everyone who commits sin is a slave to sin.' But Luther is not content with the statement that the human will is under the domination of sin, and to that extent is enslaved. He goes on to make general statements concerning the necessity of everything that takes place, and asserts the impotence and bondage of the human will in contrast to the free omnipotence of the divine will. For Luther says that 'free will is a divine name and is appropriate to no one except the divine majesty alone; for the latter can and does do everything it desires in heaven and on earth.'[25] To attribute the term 'free will' to man means no less than to attribute deity itself to him. Consequently this term ought to be reserved to God, and another expression used to refer to man.[26]

This co-existence of two ways of asserting the bondage of the will, which are apparently fundamentally different, makes the task of understanding Luther very difficult. It might be supposed—and this view has been held—that as far as the first aspect is concerned he was following the true tendency of his theology by dealing with the soteriological issue, the question of man's salvation, and was keeping within the sphere of sin and grace, whereas the introduction of the other aspect was a decline into metaphysical speculation and ran contrary to Luther's true intention. This would then be the origin of the principal problem with which Luther was involved; or at least, it was this that would have posed in a virtually hopeless form the problem of how this assertion of the bondage of the will could be reconciled with the necessity of appealing to the responsibility and so to the accountability and to the free will of man. In fact Luther appears to have involved himself in contradicting the freedom of choice which exists in practice as an indisputable object of our experience.

In order to find our bearings in what gives a first impression of vast confusion, let us begin with this last, unquestionably reasonable observation, which provides the strength and the ethical appeal of every defence of the freedom of the will. Luther himself has no intention of denying the situation which is experienced as the psychological freedom of the will, that I can choose between different possibilities of action. Least of all does he intend to deny the moral responsibility of man for his action. He can concede without question these obvious manifestations of the freedom of the will, because they fall outside the range of his discussion of free will. 'We are not disputing about nature, but about grace, and do not ask how we are constituted on earth, but how we are constituted in heaven before God. We know very well that man is appointed as lord over what is under him, which he has the right and the free will to use, so that these things are at his disposal and do as he wishes and intends. But we are asking whether he has free will towards God, so that he, God, obeys and does what man wills, or whether it is not rather God who has free will towards man, so that man wills and does what God wills, and cannot do anything except what God has willed and done.'[27]

We must be careful to note that a complete distinction between two separate spheres is not being made here. The picture that is being presented is somewhat as follows. Man can exercise his will with regard to things which are subject to man, and this includes, in a limited sense, the realm of morality, which we may describe as the sphere of activity of secular righteousness, where the concern is with works. But as soon as we turn to consider man in relation to God, it becomes meaningless to speak of free will. In relation to God it is impossible for man to be the subject of action, for here he can only be considered as one who receives, who is acted upon, who is subject to judgement, and who is accepted or rejected. But the being of man in the sight of God is not something extra and additional to the being of man in, and in the sight of, the world. Man's being in the sight of God defines the meaning of his being in the world, whether he admits this or not. Thus one may make the distinction that man has free will not with regard to what is over him, but only with regard to what is under him, and that this takes the form of the right to use, to do, or to set aside, according to his free choice, what lies within the sphere of his capabilities and possessions. But one must go on to add: 'Although this too is directed by the free will of God alone, in the way in which he pleases.'[28]

For that which we do, and everything that happens at all, appears to us to be something which could have been different, and is therefore fortuitous and freely chosen in any given case, is only the aspect of events which we see as long as we do not take God into account.[29] It is a mere illusion which only persists as long as things are not considered in the sight of God. This illusion of course is completely valid in so far as within certain limits it is justifiable, and can even be demanded of us, that we should as it were prescind from the question of God and pay attention simply to the things we encounter. 'Within certain limits' here means as far as it is a matter of mere works and not of the existence of man as a person; that is, as far as a conscience which is clear through faith gives the right and the freedom to do so. Thus it is a fact, though it sounds strange, that it is faith itself which, by acknowledging that free will is nothing, sets the conscience at liberty, and so makes it free to recognize the validity of the illusion of the freedom of the will within the limits imposed upon it. And it is faith, giving due place to God, which gives the freedom to ignore God in a way which is in accordance with the will of God and limited by it.

But we must not suppose that the apparent freedom of the will is consistently experienced. If we appeal to experience, we must not overlook the many examples of everyday language which testify to a presentiment of the predestination and fore-knowledge of God.[30] Moreover, we must bear in mind that 'free will' is a questionable concept. It can represent a tautology, in so far as it means nothing more than the 'will'. But the will is always committed, always determined by something. Consequently, the concept of 'free will' can also represent a contradiction in terms, in so far as it refers to a will which is not yet decided, but still has to come to a decision, so that it is not yet the will. Luther realizes that it is a completely abstract mode of thought to speak of an 'absolute' will, that is, the will completely isolated and undetermined.[31] The will is always already decided, involved and committed, and is not the natural will in the situation of absolute freedom of choice, the will considered in purely unhistorical terms. Consequently—and this is totally characteristic of Luther's mode of thought—the question of the *freedom* of the will is really the question of the *power* of the will. The will is only the free will to the extent that it is able to do what it wishes. 'You cannot know what the free will is if you do not know what the human will can do.'[32] And that is why free will is an attribute of God, because God's will is effective and is not hindered by anything, since it is in itself the proper and essential power of God.[33]

This makes it clear how far the question of man's free will is not merely one theme among others, but is the basic theme of theology. The point at issue between Erasmus and Luther does not lie in the first instance in the evaluation of the free will itself, but in the value of posing the question at all. For Erasmus this is fundamentally a superfluous, speculative and impious question. He reproached Luther not merely for what he says on the subject, but also for the very fact that he adopts such a firm attitude, whereas according to Erasmus the matter is something which is not made quite clear in the scriptures, and which it would therefore be best not to investigate any further. It is sufficient to assume the freedom of the will, to exert all one's forces, and for the rest to trust in God, whose nature is goodness. In opposition to this view, Luther declared in terms pregnant with significance: 'It is not impious, curious or superfluous, but more salutary and necessary than any other thing, for a Christian to know whether the will is of any effect or none in what concerns salvation. Indeed, you should realize that this is the point on which our disputation turns, the central issue of the whole argument. For our purpose is to investigate what the free will is capable of, where it is passive, and how it is related to the grace of God. If we do not know this, then we have no inkling of Christianity and are worse than all the heathen. Anyone who does not appreciate this must admit that he is not a Christian. And someone who condemns or despises it should realize that he is the worst enemy of Christians. For if I do not know what and how much I am able to do with regard to God, I will be equally uncertain and ignorant of what and how much God is able to do towards me, where it is in fact God who does absolutely everything. But if the works and the power of God are unknown to me, then I do not know God himself. But if I do not know God, then I cannot honour, praise, thank and serve God, since I do not know how much I must accord to myself and how much to God. That is why we must have an absolutely certain distinction between God's power and ours, and between God's work and ours, if we wish to live a devout life.'[34]

The question of what the will of man is capable of is only posed in radical terms when the question is raised of what the will is capable of with regard to God—and in man's practical situation this means what the will of man can do towards his salvation. Thus it is a question which touches the central issue, and is absolutely necessary to salvation. For the gospel, the Christian faith, and even God himself are denied if the freedom of the will is asserted as the power of man to choose his salvation for himself, instead of allowing God to be God in respect of the very basis of man's failure to possess salvation, which is his inability to alter the fundamental tendency of his will. Thus to hold and maintain that God does everything immutably and that one cannot resist his will, is the sole and highest comfort of the Christian. This is faith.

Luther made clear, in the most extreme terms, that there was no room here for a human will that still remained neutral. A decision had already been made in one sense or the other about the human will, so that the human will is determined in one of two directions. He compares the human will to a horse and a rider: 'When God sits upon it, then it desires to go and does go where God wills ... When Satan sits upon it, it desires to go and does go where Satan wills, and it has no choice as to which rider it will carry, nor can it seek him, but the riders themselves dispute its possession.'[35] The comparison with the rider and the horse was also used in scholastic theology to illustrate the problem of the freedom of the will, but there it was used to describe the co-operation between the natural power of the will and the supernatural and guiding power of the grace added to it, so that the horse was considered in some cases to be acting independently of the rider, or to be entirely dependent upon itself.

It would be a complete misunderstanding of Luther to accuse him here of falling into a metaphysical dualism and determinism. The appearance of dualism which arises from the co-existence and opposition between God and Satan disappears —although the problem becomes all the more urgent and acute as a result—if we realize that Satan is nothing more than the mask disguising the absence of God. We are faced here with the mystery of the fact that God himself can be either absent or present. This can be expressed more precisely, in a way which does justice to the omnipotence of God, by saying that God is present either as one who is absent or as one who is present. Setting aside for a moment the problems to which this gives rise, what is clear is that Luther's statements can only be interpreted in the sense of a metaphysical determinism if they are expounded in terms of the *coram*-relationship which determines his thought.[36] Here God's omnipotence does not destroy the human will altogether, but becomes the ultimate factor determining the human will in one direction or another, so permitting it to be the will in a concrete sense. But to conclude from this that everything then becomes a matter of indifference because it is subject to the arbitrary will of God, is to break out of the situation of being in the sight of God, which is formed by the word in preaching, and to regard the relationship between God and man from the detached attitude of an observer who is passing judgement. That everything that happens, happens necessarily and immutably from the point of view of the will of God, is not to be asserted as a theoretical statement, but only as a confession of faith in praise of God, as the utterance of one who acknowledges that he has no power over himself, but owes his being, including his will, to the will of God.

This gives us a profound insight into the difference between the way Luther speaks of man and of God, and that of the scholastic tradition. Scholasticism—and in this it is merely one representative of a theology which does not keep strictly to its theme, man who is guilty and lost and God who justifies and saves, and to the event between God and man which follows this pattern—builds up its theological statements about man on the basis of a definition of man assumed in advance and not derived from the event that takes place between God and man.[37] In its traditional form, this definition is that man is a rational animal, and implicit in this is that he is an animal who possesses free will. The structure of scholastic theology is such that it is not possible to shake this assumption, which is never questioned. It is the basis of all further argument, so that all theological statements depend upon it. This means that in spite of the doctrine of the creation, which is naturally associated with it, man is treated as in principle independent with regard to God, and is therefore considered with regard to God as one who acts and makes free decisions. The relationship between God and man is therefore reduced to a calculation of their respective powers, and grace to a supernatural restoration and exaltation of human nature. The doctrine of grace is therefore logically a doctrine about man who—naturally not without grace, but properly speaking through grace alone—realizes himself in his acts in the direction of his ultimate goal, blessedness. It is a way of considering God and man together which is very rational, but only carries conviction as long as God and man can each be regarded without question as entities in themselves, and their mutual relationship determined from this point.

But what is the situation if man is only able to speak of *God* at all in such a way that he, man, ceases to be a natural and unquestioned assumption of theology, concerning whose freedom there is no doubt? Who is God, if man cannot remain content with defining himself by comparison with the animals, but makes God the one from whom the whole determination of man's being, the whole definition of man is derived?

CHAPTER 14

GOD HIDDEN AND REVEALED

ALTHOUGH theology cannot abandon the theme of man to philosophy in order to concentrate upon God as its proper object, neither can it expect philosophy not to discuss God. Because theology must take into account what man is from the theological point of view and discuss the *homo theologicus*,[1] it is not enough for it to speak of God without further ado; it must also submit to critical examination the theological understanding of God, the *Deus theologicus*.[2]

Luther referred to the theology which discusses God in theological terms and therefore also discusses man in theological terms, as the theology of the cross, by contrast to the theology of glory, in which God and man are discussed in a pseudo-theological way. These terms, *theologia* or *theologus crucis* and *gloriae* were coined by Luther in 1518 in the course of the dispute over indulgences.[3] Although he did not make constant use of them as slogans to represent his theological outlook, but only took them up again on rare occasions,[4] they are a very accurate expression of his understanding of theology. He claims to characterize the basic principle of scholastic theology, based as it was on philosophy, as the *theologia gloriae*. Similarly, by the *theologia crucis* he does not mean a subsidiary theme or a special kind of theology, but the criterion and subject of all true theology: 'True theology and knowledge of God lies in the crucified Christ.'[5] It is true that the term 'theology of the cross' suggests a certain affinity with the mysticism of the Passion. And his polemic against the fatal and totally unspiritual concentration on the remission of punishment in the system of indulgences, in which he attempted to bring the dispute round to the fundamental issue, implies in particular an emphasis on the cross. Nevertheless, the term *theologia crucis* indicates more than a mere momentary concern or characteristic of the young Luther. The expression serves as an indication of the object of his constant concern, the fundamental orientation of theological thought.

The theology of the cross, he tells us, speaks of the crucified and hidden God.[6] Thus the characteristic of God as the *Deus theologicus* is that he is *Deus crucifixus* and *absconditus*. Luther developed this formula in allusion to the argument and language of 1 Cor. 1: 18 ff., where Paul describes his own language as the word of the crucified Christ, and of the hidden wisdom of God. Luther contrasts this *theologia crucis* with the knowledge of God obtained by the Gentiles, which is also described by allusion to Paul (Rom. 1: 20), and which was an attempt to perceive the invisible nature of God from the works of creation, through reason. By this method, the ascent from the visible to the invisible, one can only know the glorious God, the *Deus gloriosus*, in his metaphysical attributes as omnipresent and omnipotent, as the highest good and the highest object of *eros*. The invisibility of this glorious God, which belongs to the purely spiritual sphere, is therefore, not to be confused with the concealment of God shamefully crucified, who came forth in visible form, into the flesh, into history and into suffering. For the invisibility of the *Deus gloriosus* as perceived by reason is a glorification of the world. To know him in this way is a pretentious and deceiving wisdom, and the affirmation of man's endeavour to realize himself in his works in a way analogous to the divine principle of creation. By contrast, the concealment of the crucified God, which is an offence to reason, becomes for the believer the abrogation of all his own wisdom and righteousness, so that God can do his work.

The knowledge of God in his worldly and supernatural glory establishes a harmony between God and the world, and its determining principle is that of placing them on the same level and establishing a correspondence between them. On the other hand, the principle of the knowledge of God in the cross is that of contradiction. In spite of this, or in fact because of this, it is only the latter which does justice to reality. Alluding to Isa. 5: 20, Luther says that 'the theology of glory calls evil good and good evil: the theologian of the cross says what is true';[7] that is, he gives a true account of reality. He also gives a true account of what truth there is nevertheless in the knowledge of God in his glory and majesty. That wisdom is no more to be rejected as something evil than was the law. For things are not empty in themselves, but become empty and vain through vain men, who make a vain use of them. 'Without the theology of the cross man misuses the best things in the worst way.'[8] Thus the aim of the theology of the cross is in a pre-eminent sense 'practical', for its aim is a right use of reality.[9] It leads into experience, and is existential theology.

Thus true theology is 'practical', while speculative theology belongs in hell with the Devil.[10] But this does not imply a theology of works and a religious exaltation of man, but refers to the theology of faith. For it is a theology of the work and the word of God, a theology which is 'practised' in temptation, and in this way and for this reason alone it is a theology of certainty, in acute contrast to the moderate *theologia sceptica* of someone like Erasmus.[11] Luther once said at table that if he lived longer he would like to write a book about temptations,

for without them man could understand neither the holy
scripture, nor faith, nor the fear and love of God.[12] For the
only real understanding is that which endures when it is put
to the test, as Luther emphasized in similar terms on numerous
occasions: 'From the literal and historical point of view these
words are . . . easy to understand . . . but the confusion comes
when one has to test them and taste them and bring them into
life or experience; this is a real trial of the understanding and
can be very difficult . . .'[13]

Thus there is a knowledge of God through reason. How could
what is said about God concern all men without exception, and
have the nature of a strict obligation, if it did not touch on
something which is always present in man's humanity, spurring
him on, keeping him occupied, and questioning his existence?
But there is no question of the additional raising up and perfecting of the natural knowledge of God to the supernatural level
through revelation. Rather, faith is opposed to the wishful
thinking of reason, for the rational knowledge of God is a
challenge to seek God in the darkness. '. . . Reason can not
rightly accord him his deity nor attribute it to him as his own,
though it rightly belongs to him alone. It knows that God exists.
But who or what person it may be who is properly called God,
it does not know . . . Thus reason plays blindman's-buff with
God and makes vain errors and always misses the mark, calling
God what is not God, and not calling God what is God, which
it would not do if it did not know that God existed, or if it
did know what thing was God, or what God was. Thus it
rushes in and accords the name and the divine honour, and the
title, God, to what it thinks God is, and so never hits on the
true God, but always finds the Devil or its own darkness,
which the Devil rules. Thus there is a great difference between
knowing that a god exists, and knowing what or who God is.

The first is known to nature, and is written in every heart. The second is taught only by the Holy Spirit.'[14]

One example of such a rational knowledge of God is the speculative mystical theology of Neoplatonism, which seeks to penetrate to the inmost darkness, to hear the uncreated word, and to submerge itself in it.[15] Here the desire is to seek God in his divinity, God in his majesty, in total immediacy, naked man meeting naked God.[16] Luther knows from experience what this really means, if it does not remain mere speculation: this experience of God is hell.[17]

But the rational knowledge of God consists not merely of these high-flown speculations concerning God in his lofty majesty, but of all forms of religion or worldly wisdom without distinction. In all of them God is the God of the law.[18] For this is the fundamental attitude of man to God in nature; to make God calculable and at his own disposal, actively to encounter the danger which threatens from God and to force God into the role of one who sanctions what man does.[19]

'This is the highest principle of the Devil and the world from the very first: we do not wish to appear as evil-doers, but what we do must be sanctioned by God and all his prophets must approve it. If they do not do this, they must die. Down with Abel, long live Cain! This is to be our law. And this is in fact what happens.'[20]

Thus the knowledge of God in reason, carried to its logical conclusion, is nothing but atheism. For reason cannot resist the assault of the power and the paradox of evil in the world. 'Behold, God governs this corporeal world in outward matters in such a way that if one regards and follows the judgement of human reason, one is forced to say either that there is no God, or that God is unjust'; that is, that he himself is evil. This impression that God is evil, in Luther's view, has the force of something so terribly evident and there are so many arguments for it, that no reason and no light of nature can resist it.[21] But consequently, the feeble concept, completely avoiding reality, of the 'dear God', whose forgiveness is automatic,[22] amounts to the same thing. The rational, humanist piety of Erasmus reeks of Epicureanism and atheism.[23]

But in Luther's opinion the knowledge of God through reason dominates the theological thought of scholasticism, which came into being through the intrusion of the vocabulary of 'physics' into theology.[24] 'For physics flatters the natural reason, whereas the place of theology is far above the human understanding.'[25] By physics, of course, he does not mean natural science in the modern sense, although we can appreciate the situation which Luther has in mind by comparing it, *mutatis mutandis*, with the present-day problem of the alienation between theology and intellectual activity as a whole, as a result of the use of the forms of thought of natural science and the understanding of reality and truth which underlies them. Luther had in mind the *Physics* of Aristotle and the ontological terminology formed from it, of which scholasticism made use even in theology. Not least amongst these terms was the concept of nature itself, which means that in a thing which is real and active on the basis of its essence or inmost principle.

If we are guided by this concept of nature, and base our theology on what it affirms about the nature of God and the nature of man, we arrive at the following conceptual structure. God is regarded, by contrast and in relation to all being, as the sole original cause, *causa sui* and *causa prima*, and in such a way that God, in accordance with the teleological principle implied in the Aristotelian concept of causation, is the *principium* and *finis*, the origin and goal of his activity and his works. Although man as God's creature is naturally not his own cause, but is caused, yet from the point of view of his nature, he is the origin of his works. This expresses the idea that he is the image of God: like God, man is also the origin of his works, the source of contingent action, although this is so under the conditions of created being. In accordance with this, three factors are inseparably linked in this definition of human nature; that man possesses reason, that he possesses free will, and that he acts and, as one who acts, progresses and realizes himself in the direction of his goal.

This basic understanding of the nature of man gives rise to the necessity of interpreting theological statements in such a way that they fit this concept of nature. The decisive example of this is the doctrine of grace. Here the highest criterion is the preservation of man's free will. Grace is understood, if not as natural, at least as supernatural. That is, it is seen as a higher endowment of man directed towards his supernatural goal, and therefore as something which in the same way as his nature, which it perfects, makes him capable of leading an existence in accordance with grace, of putting grace into practice, and by virtue of the habitual grace he has received of carrying out meritorious works, which are worthy of the supernatural goal towards which he is moving. Naturally there are immense differences in the way this scheme is worked out, subtly developed and defended by different schools of thought. But its basic structure is such that the doctrine of grace is elaborated within a framework supplied by the understanding of man as nature.

As in the case of God, so the discussion of man begins with the consideration of man in himself. Of course from the first the relationship of God and the world and the relationship of man to God are implied, in the sense that God is regarded as uncreated being, and man as created being. Luther describes the substance of the relationship between God and man as the sole object of theology. Theology, he says, is concerned with man who is guilty and lost and God who justifies and saves. But it is interpreted by scholasticism in terms of the scheme of causation implied in creation. Scholastic thought only discusses it as a secondary theme on a previously assumed basis, in which God and man are already as it were 'fixed' both as what they are in themselves—although a distinction is made between their absolute and relative forms of being respectively—and also in their causal relationship, which is fundamentally free from contradiction. Not that there is not much that is correct in this. But this fixed affirmation of fundamental principles is made under the illusion that it is the assertion of neutral facts, as though theological thought could proceed by first ignoring the actual situation of man in the sight of God. And everything that follows is inescapably burdened by the fact that what takes place between God and man must first of all be made to fit this scheme of causation, and secondly adapted to this concept of the nature of man.

The concepts of *causa* and of *natura*, which are appropriate in their own sphere, are inappropriate as basic concepts in theology, which is concerned with the response of man in the sight of God and the word of God to man. Thus Luther feels that in scholasticism theology is deprived of its real seriousness and is a *theologia illusoria*, in which it has ceased to be a *theologia crucis*.[26] For as *causa sui*, God can ultimately be left in total isolation, if only it can be made possible to interpret his omnipotence and universal activity in such a way that neither the goodness of God nor the free will of man and his ability to carry out meritorious works are threatened. The only question is whether this basic tendency of scholasticism does not encourage a false religious security rather than reveal the certainty which makes it possible to endure in temptation. The closing passages of the ninety-five theses on the question of indulgences in 1517 have this theme in mind, and express what to Luther was a profound source of offence in scholastic theology as a whole: 'Away, then, with those prophets who say to Christ's people, "Peace, peace", where there is no peace. Hail, hail to all those prophets who say to Christ's people, "The cross, the cross", where there is no cross. Christians should be exhorted to be zealous to follow Christ, their Head, through penalties, deaths, and hells; and let them thus be more confident of entering heaven through many tribulations rather than through a false assurance of peace.'[27]

The knowledge of God which is given in Jesus Christ does not therefore constitute a particular item of doctrine which supplements a general knowledge of God, but is the beginning of all true knowledge of God and man. It is the complete opposite of speculation concerning God in his nakedness, God in his majesty, and points us towards God who came in the flesh and was therefore clothed in promises, who came close to us, imparted himself to us, and was thereby revealed; not towards the God who is wordless, and therefore renders us speechless in temptation, but towards the word of God, God proclaimed, God who bestows faith and gives assurance.

'You have often heard that in the holy scripture this guiding principle must be observed, that we must refrain from speculation concerning the majesty of God. The human body, let alone the mind, cannot tolerate such speculation. Thus the Pope, the Turks and the enthusiastic sects put Christ out of their sight and replace him by God the Father, and speak to him, pray to him and praise him, like the monks who think "I will act like this, and he will see it and be gracious because of my vow." Similarly, the Turks say, "If I have kept this rule, he will look on me [graciously]." Similarly, the Jews say, "If we have kept the law of Moses, God will preserve us." The sectary does the same, believing in the same way and carrying his cross. They all set aside the mediator. But Christian theology is a theology which teaches that God himself, to whom the sectaries, Turks and the Pope turn, should be excluded—we exclude him and replace him by the mediator. You must not climb up to God but begin where he began—in his mother's womb he became man—and deny yourself the spirit of speculation. If you wish to be certain in your conscience and beyond danger from the Devil, then you should know no God at all apart from this man, and depend upon this his humanity . . . In this matter, of how one should treat God and act towards God, forget speculation about his majesty. And in acting against sin and death, forget about God, because he cannot be tolerated here . . . Forget him and say, "We are dealing with a different matter here, for we are concerned with justification, and with how one finds God who justifies and accepts . . . Thus we must make sure when we are concerned with the theme of righteousness and grace, that whenever we have to do with death, sin and the law, as is the case for a Christian, we know of no God excepting only the incarnate and human God [*Deus incarnatus, Deus humanus*] . . . Paul . . . desires to teach Christian theology, which does not begin above in the utmost heights, like all other religions, but below in the profoundest depths . . . If you are concerned with your salvation, forget about all ideas of law, all philosophical doctrines, and hasten to the crib and to his mother's bosom and see him, an infant, a growing child, a dying man. Then you will be able to escape all fear and errors. This vision will keep you on the right way.'[28] He says the same in the briefest possible formula: 'To seek God outside Jesus is the Devil.'[29]

But this God, revealed and proclaimed, is himself, as the language of the *theologia crucis* calls it, the hidden God, hidden under his contrary. The understanding of revelation as revelation under a contrary was a determining factor in Luther's theological thought as early as the first lectures on the Psalms, and was maintained right up to the end. Let us give one single example, from his early period: 'If under the glory of the flesh God gave the glory of the Spirit, and under the riches of the flesh the riches of the Spirit, and under the graciousness and honour of the flesh gave the grace and honour of the Spirit, then the latter would rightly be described as profoundly concealed. But as it is, since he gives it under his contrary, and contradicts what is signified by the sign itself, it is not merely profoundly but far too profoundly concealed. For who could realize that someone who is visibly humbled, tempted, rejected, and slain, is at the same time and to the utmost degree inwardly exalted, comforted, accepted and brought to life, unless this was taught by the Spirit through faith?'[30] Though here, judged by the standard of Luther's more mature theology, there are still discordant notes, the decisive assertion is clear. Because the revelation of God takes place on the cross, everything depends upon the word and upon faith. The word and faith are the marks of the revelation which is concealed under its contrary.

The same approach, but in a purer and more carefully considered form, is found in *De servo arbitrio*: 'Faith has to do with things which are not seen [Heb. 11: 1]. Thus that there may be room for faith, everything which is believed must be concealed; but it cannot be more deeply concealed than under the contrary appearance, sensation and experience. Thus when God brings to life, he does it by killing; when he justifies, he does it by making guilty; when he exalts to heaven, he does it by leading to hell ... Thus he conceals his eternal goodness and mercy under eternal anger, his righteousness under unrighteousness.'[31]

The same conception is found again, this time in what is perhaps its most startling formulation: 'The outward appearance of grace is as though it were pure anger, so deeply is it concealed with two thick furs or skins, namely, that our resistance and the world condemn and avoid it as the plague and the wrath of God, so that the feeling we have within us is none other than that which Peter rightly describes, saying that the word alone shines on us like a light in a dark place [2 Peter 1: 19]. A dark place indeed. Thus God's faithfulness and truth must always first become a great lie, before it becomes the truth. For in the sight of the world it is known as heresy. Thus even to ourselves it always seems as though God wishes to abandon us and not keep his word, and that he is beginning to be a liar in our hearts. And finally, God cannot be God unless he first becomes a devil, and we cannot go to heaven unless we first go into hell, and cannot become the children of God, unless we first become the Devil's children ... But the world's lies in their turn cannot become lies unless they first become the truth, and the godless do not go down into hell, unless they have first been to heaven, and do not become the Devil's children unless they have first been the children of God.'[32] 'And finally, the Devil becomes and is no Devil, unless he has first been God ... We have spoken in extreme terms of this, and we must understand what is just as startling, that God's grace and truth, or his goodness and faithfulness, rule over us and demand our obedience ... For a little while I must accord divinity to the Devil, and consider our God to be the Devil. But this does not mean that the evening lasts for the whole day. Ultimately, his steadfast love and faithfulness are over us [Ps. 117: 2].'[33]

The concealment of revelation under its opposite is a theme that dominates everything which Luther has to say concerning the word and faith, justification and the new life, the Holy Spirit and the Church. At the same time, one must be on one's guard not to succumb to the emotional force of such utterances, or to resist it, without understanding the true reason for such a way of speaking, a reason which leads to much more than such paradoxical language, and which is not satisfied by the ecstasy of paradox.

In attempting to characterize Luther's mode of theological thought, in contrast to the peculiarities of scholastic thought which we have outlined above, we can repeat what we have previously stated at some length, that the basic determining factor in Luther's theological thought is not the relationship of casuality. The subjects of such a relationship are regarded from the point of view of their mutual correspondence, so that, for example, it is necessary to take great care that God as the *prima causa* is not allowed to become simply an immanent world principle, and that grace as an infused supernatural *habitus* is not allowed to become a principle of human action. Instead the fundamental determining factor of Luther's theological thought is the forensic relationship of existence in the sight of God, where it is possible to assert both that one cannot speak of God without speaking of his word and that one cannot speak of God without this taking place *in the sight of* God. This forensic relationship is characterized by contradiction and paradox, not of course in the form of rigid antitheses, but in the way revelation takes place between a contrary, the purpose of this being to create an appropriate response. Thus faith, which accords divinity to God, is the response to the word of God.

But the word of God is not taken seriously as such if it does not become, not merely as the law but in the proper sense as the gospel, our 'opponent', that is, the word which effects in us the opposite of what we are. As the word of the Creator it creates from nothing. As the word of the law, it destroys our own righteousness and self-assertion in the sight of God. As the word of the gospel it declares the sinner righteous. 'When the word of God comes, it runs contrary to our thought and desire.'[34] This means that God is only God where he is able to act as God; where God does what only God can do; where God carries out his work in his necessity, and therefore in his freedom.

If the *Deus theologicus* is, in this way, the God who works miracles, not merely here and there but in everything he does, then man in theology, the *homo theologicus*, is only properly defined when he is understood as the miraculous work of God, as the creature of God who is not abandoned by God in spite of his godlessness. 'In Romans 3: 28, "We hold that a man is justified by faith apart from works", Paul sums up the definition of man, that is, that man is justified by faith.'[35] Man is defined not by his *differentia specifica*, which distinguish him from other animals, but by the act of God, which in the process of justification distinguishes man from man himself, and makes the man of this life the material for his future life;[36] man is defined not in a doctrinal statement, but in an event which endures as long as this life lasts, and therefore as long as the process of the justification of the sinner lasts.

But the most astonishing feature of Luther's theological thought is that the distinction between the God of majesty and the crucified God, between the naked God and the incarnate God, between God himself, who remains withdrawn from us, and the word of God, to which we have to cling, did not mislead him into turning to one without being aware of the other, or into seizing hold of the one without knowing that he was seized by the other. Luther does not retreat into the kind of piety which venerates God in its own small corner, making him a personal and household idol and not daring to acknowledge him as Lord of the world. It would have been easy to have allowed the theology of the cross to become a quiet hole-and-corner piety such as this, venerating Jesus and living in his spirit, but not associating him with the God who is completely withdrawn from us, completely incomprehensible, who through his omnipotence does all things in his foreknowledge, and, since he is pure will, predetermines everything.

In his work 'The Bondage of the Will' Luther naturally entitled this omnipotent God who is withdrawn from us, without whom nothing happens that does happen and through whom everything happens according to his will, the *Deus absconditus*, the hidden God, by contrast to the God who is revealed and preached. This is an apparent contradiction to the terminology of the theology of the cross, in which it is the revealed, crucified God who is hidden under his contrary. Is there really a contradiction here? Not if it is recognized to be appropriate that the concealment within which the crucified is the revealed God, is a concealment desired and caused by God. The concealment itself is God, and the God who is revealed can only be believed in spite of God who is concealed and God only in spite of God; thus to be God in the strict sense, God must be *believed in*. The contradiction between the two statements, the one that the revealed God himself is the hidden God, and the other that the revealed God is distinguished from the hidden God, is resolved by the fact that in order that God may truly be God Luther maintains to the utmost degree the contradiction between God in Jesus Christ and the God of omnipotence and omniscience, between faith and experience. If it were not God who, even in the godless and in Satan, is ultimately at work because he is omnipotent,[37] he could not be taken seriously as God, and God would be a ridiculous God.[38]

But is the alternative merely between a ridiculous God and a fearful God, an impotent God and an incomprehensibly omnipotent God? Jesus, the crucified, allows us to believe in God as omnipotent in impotence, and only in this way makes God really God for us at all. For faith and God belong together.

Who can say, 'Now I have understood everything'? Luther's last note, written on a scrap of paper two days before his death says:

'No one can understand Virgil in the "Bucolics" and the "Georgics" unless he has been a shepherd or a farmer for five years.

'No one can understand Cicero in his letters—so I feel—unless he has spent forty years in a prominent office of state.

'No one should suppose that he has even an inkling of an understanding of the authors of holy scripture, unless he has governed the churches for a hundred years, together with the prophets. Thus John the Baptist, Christ and the apostles represent an immense miracle.' There follows a quotation from the Latin poet Statius: 'Do not lay hands upon the divine "Aeneid", but bow down and honour its tracks.' Then the note concludes with the last saying of Luther which we possess, which is as it were the legacy of the former mendicant monk, who knew more of the substance of theology than we do, and yet confesses: 'We are beggars. That is true.'[39]

THE WAY LUTHER
SPEAKS OF GOD

THERE is something challenging about the way Luther speaks of God. We cannot turn to his works without our own way of speaking about God faltering or falling silent or being brought into question, or without doubt being cast upon it. This implies that Luther's way of speaking of God expresses more than an ordinary degree of personal involvement, and therefore also involves us. All consideration of historical data in some respects involves the participation of the observer, so that the false ideal of a 'purely historical' consideration is neither possible nor desirable. In the same way, what has been said about God and handed down in tradition is even less capable of being dealt with by a 'purely historical consideration'. For to speak of God implies his essential presence, and this is true even of the statement 'God is dead', as can be seen from the way Nietzsche asserts the presence of the slain God: 'Do we still smell nothing of the divine putrefaction?'[1]

At a time when it has become exceedingly difficult to defend any attempt to speak about God, the decisiveness with which Luther spoke of God acts as a challenge—though he did not speak of him with an ill-considered facility, but with the utmost readiness to defend what he was doing, and with a certainty which seems completely alien to our problem of the vindication of any attempt to speak about God.

One might attempt to explain this on the basis of the change in basic assumptions which has taken place since then. Luther lived at a time—it might be argued—in which the word 'God' was still understandable without further discussion, and the claim it implied, together with the right to speak of God, was taken for granted. In spite of this, of course, or strictly speaking because of this, what was said of God was so much the subject of dispute that virtually all other disputed matters at that period were attracted by and drawn into the dispute about God, which took place in the denominational schisms and conflicts. All shared the assumption that the existence of God could be taken for granted, and besides this, there was a virtually undisputed recognition of the doctrine of the Trinity and of the Incarnation of the Son of God according to the testimony of the holy scripture and the Church. On this basis, in fact, a conflict arose which to this day cannot be regarded by Western Christianity as having been solved. Nevertheless, the situation has fundamentally changed, in that it is evident that the automatic assumption of the validity not only of the Christian idea of God, but of the idea of God as a whole, has finally and irrevocably ceased to be accepted.

It is true that proper distinctions must be made, in order to avoid a rough-and-ready argument on the basis of the automatic assumption of the existence of God at that period and the disappearance of such an assumption at the present day. But this does not alter the basic fact that not merely popular opinion but theology itself proceeded at that period from this automatic assumption, and as it were 'counted on it'. Scholasticism included the acceptance of the existence of God amongst the so-called *praeambula fidei*, that is, as something which was not in the strict sense the object of faith, because it was already evident to the apprehension of natural reason. Luther too was able to ascribe to all men either by nature, or by virtue of a universal tradition difficult to distinguish from nature, a knowledge of God, which was a knowledge of his existence, although not a knowledge of his will (he did not classify this knowledge of God in the dogmatic category of a *praeambulum fidei*). On the other hand, simultaneously with the virtual disappearance of the automatic assumption of the existence of God, modern Protestant theology from Schleiermacher to Karl Barth has made an increasingly radical attempt to eliminate any idea of a natural theology, although it has not adequately taken into account the consequences of so doing.

All the same, it is not possible to equate or even to confuse the automatic assumption of the existence of God, in however restricted a form, with the firm decisiveness of Luther's way of speaking about God. This forms a challenge to modern man, but did so to Erasmus as well, and is remarkable also by contrast with the scholastic tradition. This decisiveness is manifested in discussing matters which are not automatically self-evident, in so far as 'self-evident' is understood in the trivial sense of the knowledge of immediately obvious facts, which it would be superfluous and a mere waste of words to discuss. 'What is not self-evident', of which Luther speaks so decisively in his language about God, does not mean any arbitrary matter, but what can only be said of God, and therefore what can only be said because it comes from God, can only be understandable through him, and is, therefore, in a profound sense 'self'-evident because it provides in itself the only assurance of its truth. But this must be stated, confessed and asserted in *words*. It therefore requires to be spoken, and so appears in two aspects: it must be spoken with decisiveness, because it can only be *spoken*; and it needs to be spoken with *decisiveness*.

That Luther lays such an emphasis on the mode of speech and therefore on the situation that comes about in speech, follows from the substance of what is spoken. This cannot be derived from Luther's temperament or special charisma. We can ignore his person except in so far as it was given to him to realize with great force that one can only speak of God in form of a decisive assertion. Erasmus found Luther's categorical style a source of offence. Luther reproached him: 'It is not the way of a Christian heart to fail to delight in decisive assertions; rather, one must delight in them, or one is not a Christian ... Sceptics and academics are far from us Christians, but those are welcome to us, who, twice as obstinately as the Stoics themselves, present what they have to say with decisiveness. Tell me, how often did the apostle Paul insist on *plerophoria*, full assurance, that is, assertion with the utmost certainty, as firm as a rock to the conscience? ... Nothing is better known and more familiar to a Christian than decisive assertion. Do away with decisive assertions, and you have taken away Christianity ... The Holy Spirit is not a sceptic and has not written doubtful matters and mere opinions in our hearts, but decisive assertions which are more certain and sure than life itself and all experience.'[2]

These utterances concerning the appropriate way to speak of God naturally go much further than the mere assertion of God's existence. On the one hand they extend to the whole of Christian doctrine, and on the other hand they recognize that human existence is drawn into it and is involved in it. But it would not be accurate to say of Luther that he developed the basic assertion of the existence of God in these two directions. What seem to be two different issues which are drawn together are in fact a single point. Nothing would be said of God, if the whole of Christian doctrine and man also were not already involved. But the reason for this is that what is at issue in Christian doctrine and also in human existence is nothing other than the basic assertion of the existence of God.

The way Luther speaks of God—and this explains his decisiveness—has both an all-embracing and inclusive tendency, and also a radical and exclusive tendency. The latter, as is well known, finds its expression in the so-called *particula exclusiva*, the word 'alone', which is found in his formulation of the decisive points of his theology, and always has the same purpose of giving pointed utterance to a true theological understanding: 'God alone', 'Christ alone', 'the scripture alone', 'the word alone', 'faith alone'. Of course when the exclusive particle is used in this way its meaning must be precisely elucidated. An unthinking and emotional profession of faith, or an uncomprehending and reckless assertion would be quite out of place in this mode of theological thought. What must be realized is that in spite of the different ways in which it is applied, the recurrent word 'alone' expresses a fundamental theological understanding: that whenever anything is said about God, it must be made fully evident that it is God who is being discussed. But if God is to be spoken of at all, then it is necessary for God's sake to rely on God alone, on Christ alone, on the scripture alone, on the word alone, and on faith alone; that is, one must exclude everything which prevents God from being God, and which gives an opportunity of speaking of theological matters in an untheological or pseudo-theological way.

But this exclusive tendency, which concentrates everything upon a single issue, is not modified and compensated by an opposed tendency to an all-inclusive comprehensiveness; this would be meaningless. For the point of the exclusive particle itself is to discuss everything in a single light, rather than isolating individual aspects. No less characteristic of Luther's theological thought than the term 'alone' is the apparently contradictory, but, if properly understood, closely associated term 'at the same time', which is likewise used in various ways, and is best known in the formula, 'righteous and a sinner at the same time'. One could term it the *particula inclusiva*, which does not weaken the sense of the *particula exclusiva*, but clarifies it and makes it more precise.

It will scarcely be disputed that the use of the particle 'alone' expresses the distinctive nature and also the decisiveness of Luther's way of speaking about God. Proceeding from this, however, his power of drawing everything together into a single theme is also a characteristic of his way of speaking of God. Luther does not allow the content of Christian doctrine to be fragmented into a profusion which is coherent only in a positivist and historical sense. It is foolish to deny, as is often done, that he possesses the power of systematic thought. But he displays it not in the summarizing and harmonizing architectural structure of a system of doctrine, nor in the speculative derivation of numerous lines of thought from a single principle, but rather by a critical and a liberating demonstration that God is God indeed, in the language of the biblical tradition. It is a complete misunderstanding of the concentration of Luther's theological thought on the doctrine of justification to regard it as the arbitrary choice of a partial aspect of doctrine, to which he wilfully adds a special emphasis of his own. According to Luther it points to the way in which God can be made God indeed in the whole of Christian doctrine. For the whole of Christian doctrine consists not of a profusion which forms a supplement to the doctrine of God itself, but of the doctrine of God and nothing more. Christian doctrine is a guide to the right way to speak of God.

But from this it is obvious that to the extent that it is God who is being spoken of, man is also involved whenever this takes place and does not have to be brought in later. Similarly, what is said of God does not have to be applied later to man. Thus what is said of God is addressed to man. For how could it be possible to speak of God if what was said were not the direct concern of man? But if what is said of God possesses certainty, then it brings certainty with it when it is addressed to someone. This is not a formal aspect which is additional to the concept of what is said of God, nor is it merely one partial aspect, which is present in so far as God has to do with man. For Luther certainty is the essence of God's being with man and therefore of man's being with God. In the presence of God, and there alone, there is no uncertainty. But uncertainty is man's sin, and certainty is salvation.

We began by observing the decisive way in which Luther spoke of God. From this we were able to see the vast extent of what he has to say of God; and at the same time we saw this whole vast extent gathered together into a single point. This justified the hope of seeing the essence of Luther's theology in what he says of God, and moreover, of being able to apprehend what he says of God from a single point of view. Finally, if in this way we have attained to the very heart of all Luther says about God, he can help us, in spite of our different situation, to answer the problem which faces us at present, of how to vindicate any attempt to speak of God. When he was a theological student, only twenty-five years old, Luther expressed the view in a letter that the only theology which was of any value was that which penetrated the kernel of the nut and the germ of the wheat and the marrow of the bones.[3]

By beginning with the decisive way in which Luther speaks of God, we have in fact already arrived at the kernel of the nut. All that is necessary is a more precise and penetrating statement, to give us as it were the basic formula from which it is possible to understand and expound how the attempt to speak of God can be vindicated. This basic formula is as follows: *God and faith belong together.* This follows from the whole structure of Luther's theology, and does not require a detailed demonstration. We shall nevertheless give an example of it from a particular text, which because of its original purpose is of particular importance, and must be regarded as having been formulated with great care. We can use it as the starting-point of our development of this basic formula. For our further inquiry into the way Luther speaks of God will consist of nothing other than the further consideration of this basic formula; and of how far the fact that God and faith belong together enables us to understand what God is.

The text is found in the 'Greater Catechism' at the beginning of the exposition of the first commandment: ' "You shall have no other gods." That is, you shall regard me alone as your God. What does this mean, and how is one to understand it? What does it mean to have a god, or what is God? Answer: A god is that on which one should rely for everything good, and with which one can take refuge in every need. Thus to have a god is nothing other than to trust and to believe in him from the heart—or, as I have often said, that only trust and faith in the heart make both God and a false god. If your faith and trust is right, then your God is right as well, and again, where the belief is false and wrong, then the right God is absent too. For the two belong together, faith and God. So that to which you give up and hand over your heart is truly your God.'⁴

We will admit at once how dangerous this text is. While our first approach, to the decisive way in which Luther speaks of God, gave us the impression that he is very remote from the spirit of the present day, in this passage he seems strangely close to us. One could almost imagine that one was listening to Ludwig Feuerbach, who taught that God was the projection and product, or even the essence of man; a theology transformed and swallowed up in anthropology! This apparent similarity is confirmed by a demonstrable connection between the two. Feuerbach, who was a theologian himself at first, was thoroughly well-acquainted with Luther's works, and, as a supplement to his work "The Nature of Christianity" (*Wesen des Christentums*), published in 1844 a study of 'The Nature of Faith According to Luther'. Not that he simply obliterated the difference: 'No religious doctrine is more consciously and deliberately contrary to human understanding, thought and feeling, than that of Luther. No other seems more firmly to reject the basic idea of "The Nature of Christianity", and no other provides such evidence of the origin of what it contains outside and above man; for how could he arrive of himself at a doctrine which degrades and humbles man to the utmost degree, and which in the sight of God at least, that is before the highest and therefore the only decisive court of appeal, denies him all honour, all merit, all virtue, all will-power, all value and trustworthiness, all reason and understanding whatsoever? This is how it seems; but what seems to be is not necessarily the case.'⁵ Feuerbach implies that in his very opposition to Luther he can appeal to Luther himself, and to the real consequences of his basic ideas.

Theologians have been horrified at the thesis of Feuerbach, that the mystery of theology is anthropology. In the desire to defend theology against the destructive tendencies of modern psychology and historicism, they have turned to their task anew, and this has meant a change from an anthropocentric to a theocentric theology. Karl Barth in particular has led the struggle against even the most disguised tendency on the part of theology to turn to anthropology—quite rightly, in so far as it really represents the abandonment of the true theme of theology in the sense of the exclusive 'alone' of the Reformation. Certainly, under the influence of Feuerbach's interpretation of Luther, Barth became suspicious of Luther[6] and came to believe it necessary to seek the methodological foundation of his dogmatic theology not in Luther but in Anselm of Canterbury, in order to restore an objective basis to theology.

It has been necessary at least to hint at the heated dispute in which we become involved if we attempt to go deeper into the meaning of what Luther says about God, under the guidance of his statement that 'faith and God belong together.' We cannot embark at length upon a dialogue with Feuerbach and Barth. We must restrict ourselves to a mere outline of what is contained in this conjunction of God and faith, and there are three guiding principles which will provide our starting-point. What God is can be made clear by interpreting this basic formula in the light of the phrases 'God alone', 'through faith alone', and 'through the word alone'.

1. The very passage in which Luther gives the most precise definition of what he means by 'God alone', in his exposition of the first commandment, is that which contains his suspicious association between God and faith. At a point where everything should be concentrated upon authority and uncondi-

tional obedience, Luther, regardless of the fact that the word 'God' is something which he is supposed to be able to take for granted, stresses the question of *understanding*: 'What does this mean, and how is one to understand it? What does it mean to have a god, or what is God?' It seems immediately suspicious that he should combine the question of the meaning of 'to have a god' and that of the being of God, and should attempt to answer both simultaneously. Surely it is necessary to affirm what God *is* before it is possible to say what it means to *have* him? Surely the being of God must be laid down and clarified before dealing with the question of 'letting God be God'? Surely it is the fundamental definition of the nature of God that nothing precedes him, that nothing imposes any conditions upon him, that he alone is the origin of all things, and that, as is expressed by the technical term 'aseity', he derives his being from himself?

It would be nonsense to try and impute to Luther the denial or watering-down of this idea, and to interpret the phrase 'that only trust and faith in the heart make both God and a false God' in such a sense that man becomes the creator and God the creature. But the idea of the aseity, the underived existence of God is not sufficient in itself to maintain with the utmost rigour that to be God and to be the creator are identical, and to be man and to be a creature are identical. The implications of the idea have not been fully considered as long as one fails to take into account the fact that man himself is involved in thinking and uttering this idea. This does not mean that it is justifiable to jump to the conclusion that this implies the dependence of God upon man, in such a way that the assertion of the aseity of God would be a logical contradiction. For the very aim and purpose of the idea of aseity is to define the position of the creature and of man. Without this specific application there would be nothing left of the idea of aseity. The emphasis on the independence of God from man is addressed to man.

The objection to such metaphysical statements about the nature of God is not so much to what they say, but rather to what they conceal as the result of a deficient doctrine of the understanding, an unsound hermeneutic theory. The objection lies in the significance for *what* is said of the fact that it is *said*. No account is taken of the fact that the metaphysical theorist is not suspended in a no-man's-land between God and the world. He is himself affected by what he thinks, and addresses what he says to his fellow-men, and therefore he ought to give consideration to the significance of the assertion of God's aseity on the concrete process of its utterance. The aseity of God thought out in abstract terms is in fact self-contradictory, because it is dependent on the abstract independence and individuality of man, who carries out the process of abstraction. Ignoring the question of whether metaphysics suffers in any essential respect from this short-sighted theory of the understanding, it ought at least to be clear that the question 'What is God?' is not being conducted along false lines, but in the only adequate way, when God is spoken of and understood as the absolute concern of man and is considered with regard to the way in which he is the absolute concern of man.

Thus we are concerned not with a proof of God's existence, something which at least in the conventional sense is directly contradictory to the divinity of God, but with a demonstration of the reason why man is addressed whenever anything is said about God. The purpose is not to *derive* the being of God from the being of man, but to *direct* man towards the situation in which he can understand what is said of God. This situation is not one which is essentially alien to his nature—in which case it would be a baseless fantasy to speak of God—but is a situation which decisively affects him, and in which he already finds himself.

The word 'faith' refers to this basic human situation. It would be an inadequate if not a misleading explanation of the statement that faith and God belong together, to say that because God is invisible and beyond experience we have to make do with faith, as a substitute as it were. For this would fail to explain what obligation or right there is to do this at all, and in what situation faith, understood as a substitute for knowledge, can be regarded as something necessary.

If one examines this problem, it becomes clear that it is possible to understand how far faith brings knowledge with it, not in the bad sense of uncertain conjecture or a mere probable opinion but as a rock-like certainty, only on the basis of the situation in which man is driven to seek certainty. Luther says simply: 'In every need'. Thus the nature of faith is that of a knowledge which brings help, salvation, courage, hope and relief in need. Accordingly, what is said of God tells man that he is obliged to wait and hope, that he is concerned with what still lies beyond him, outside his control, so that man is always reaching out beyond himself and is drawn outside himself and beyond his own control. He cannot avoid this sallying out beyond himself, this attempt to make uncertainty certain, which Luther calls hanging his heart on something; he must have something to rely on, to trust and to believe. This situation always exists. Consequently, it is the basic human situation, although the degree to which it is palpable and obvious varies greatly. We shall not analyse it in detail, but we must warn against one or two misunderstandings which readily arise.

It can appear as though God is now made a substitute for our power, just as it was suggested before that faith might be seen as a substitute for our knowledge. But it must be noted that the emphasis is not on flight *from* need, but on a refuge *in* need, not upon a change in circumstances, but on a changed attitude to the circumstances, not on the affirmation that the saving action has taken effect, but on certainty with regard to an effect which is still to come and is still awaited. Nevertheless, the suspicion still lingers that this is a theology which only brings in God to satisfy a human need. But one must be cautious in advancing this objection. It would be a dangerous theology which was *not* orientated towards human need and therefore towards the aspect of necessity.

Of course everything here depends upon the proper understanding of what is absolutely necessary and therefore on the apprehension of what true faith and trust is. Only a superficial view can suppose that it is possible to escape the question of truth by approaching the matter from the point of view of human need. Luther gives offence by seeming to stand the relationship between faith and God upon its head: 'If faith and trust are right, then your God is right as well, and again, where the belief is false and wrong, then the right God is absent too.' But it must be pointed out that it is in purity of faith, that is, in the radical degree to which the situation of faith is maintained, that it can be seen whether God is taken seriously as God, or whether he is furtively avoided and replaced by idols of man's own making. In his lectures on the Epistle to the Romans Luther says of the love of God that it is exclusively directed towards the one God alone, and not towards his gifts. Thus its place is where there is nothing visible or accessible to experience, either inwardly or outwardly, in which one can place one's trust, or which one can love or fear; but it is drawn beyond everything else to the invisible and incomprehensible God, beyond experience, and hidden in the innermost darkness.[7] Here, though still with borrowings from the language of mysticism, the meaning of the way in which faith and God belong together is clearly set out. It is no accident that the context of what is said of God is one in which there is only a hair's breadth distinction between it and every form of idolatry. To let God be God, that is to believe rightly, means not to make gods for oneself in any way, but above all to allow oneself to be deprived of deity and brought to nothing, so that one is hurled outside oneself and the whole creation into nothingness, and one is certain of having fallen into the hands of God.[8] That faith and God belong together is the theology of the cross, a theology not based on human wishes, but upon the will of God.

2. We have spent some time in discussing the text from the 'Greater Catechism' with reference to our first guiding principle, 'God alone'. That God and faith belong together is in no sense contrary to the principle of 'God alone', but is what actually makes it possible. For only to faith is God alone of value, and God is God in that he desires nothing but faith. Thus the second guiding principle, 'by faith alone', is already implied in the first. But it must be evaluated on its own if we are to make any progress with the question, 'What is God?' For until we come to this principle, the answer is largely a negative one: God takes away the power of false gods as faith takes away the power of superstition. And just as faith is a trust which reaches out into the darkness, so God is the presence, affirmed in spite of every experience of his absence, of the one being who is worthy of faith, never disappoints, never fails,

and deserves total reliance. But what kind of knowledge of God is implied by faith in the strict sense?

In Luther's longer series of lectures on the Epistle to the Galatians we read: 'See what faith is—something incomparable and of immeasurable power, that is, to give honour to God. It does not do something for God; but because it believes, faith accords wisdom, goodness and omnipotence to God, and imputes everything divine to him. Faith is the creator of deity, not in person, but in us. Apart from faith, God loses his righteousness, glory, riches, etc., and there is no majesty or deity where there is no faith. You see what great righteousness faith is ... God demands only that I make him God. If he possesses his deity pure and unspotted, then he has everything that I can accord him. This is the wisdom beyond all wisdom, religion beyond all religion. This is what makes the highest majesty, which faith bestows upon God. That is why faith justifies; for it pays what it owes, and whoever does this is righteous.'[9] This again is put in a very bold and paradoxical way. Yet is it not in fact paradoxical that man should be called to honour God, and to give him what God alone has of himself, that is, to give God what is divine? But what is called faith creates the divine in man, which man accords to God. The creative power of faith—Luther terms it, with unsurpassed boldness, *creatrix divinitatis*—means nothing other than that faith is not the work of man, but the work of God, or as Luther says in a play on words, not a *facere Deo* (something done for God) but *facere Deum* (making God). But this means nothing less than to let God act, to let God be God, to do justice to God through faith alone. If one takes God seriously, one cannot attain to God by an action, but through faith alone, or shall we say, by delighting in God. The only adequate way to speak of God is in praising him, not in the sense of a particular literary form, but as the basic definition of all proper speech about God.

Then why does Luther adopt such paradoxical turns of phrase? Not because he confuses delight in God with delight in paradox; but because to speak of God is to speak of something that happens, of the way in which God establishes himself as God, and finds faith. One cannot as it were first speak of God in himself, disregarding the actual situation of the way God is dishonoured, even in religion itself, and excluding the question of how God obtains his rights. In this world, in fact, God is humiliated and insulted, seeks his honour only by calling for faith, and desires to be honoured through faith alone. What is at issue is not the description of passive attributes, such as what God is in himself, what man is in himself, and how they are related. What is said of God is concerned with something that happens, of which what is said itself forms part. This is the key to the understanding of Luther's work *De servo arbitrio* ('The Bondage of the Will'), which could equally be called *De Deo*. Because God is being spoken of, so must man be spoken of. For self-knowledge and the knowledge of God form a unity, and the reason for this is that they are both concerned with an inseparable association which consists of something that *happens*. To know God means to know what God can and does do, not his power and his potentialities, but his power as it is actually at work in everything that exists, an omnipotence that is active.[10] But if man has to know, for the sake of his salvation and his certainty, what he is capable of with regard to his salvation, then he evidently knows neither what he is capable of, nor what God is, until he knows for certain that he can *do nothing* towards his salvation. And that very inability permits him to be certain of salvation, which is based upon the act of God alone. One can have no inkling of God, if one has not a clear understanding of the problem of the bondage of the will in matters of salvation. To engage in a dialogue with God on the basis of the will is godless. Thus it is necessary for salvation to be able to distinguish between the action of God and the action of man, not in order to weigh one against the other as co-operating forces, but to make a fundamental distinction between them. By contrast with man, God is an unlimited force, whereas by contrast with God, man cannot be considered as one who acts, however much action may be demanded from him in the sight of God towards the world. Man's understanding of himself in relation to God only does justice to God if man regards himself as one who has been made what he is, as one who is subject to God's will, has received all he has as a gift, and is therefore a creature, righteous not by works, but through faith alone.[11] Only when man lays claim to freedom of action before God is man radically enslaved; by understanding himself as the work of God, that is through faith, he becomes free, participating, as one who belongs to God, in the freedom of God.

3. We turn now to the question of what takes place in the conjunction of God and faith, how God can be honoured, and how faith can come about. The answer we receive from Luther is, *through the word alone*. This answer provokes numerous questions. We shall reduce them to three fundamental objections to the way Luther speaks of God, which must now be raised and considered as the conclusion of our study. Is not the word too little? How far does the course of history matter? What is the place of our fellow-men?

The first objection is, *is the word not too little?* 'Through the word alone' forms a strict parallel to 'by faith alone'.[12] In both these principles Luther is radically opposed to scholastic theology and Roman Catholic doctrine, which in fact allege here that 'the word alone' is 'too little', that a mere 'verbal revelation' is replacing a 'revelation of reality', to quote the slogans of modern controversial theology,[13] and that mere faith takes the place of perfection through a real change in man. Thomas Aquinas based the precedence of love amongst the so-called theological virtues, faith, love and hope, on the assertion that, like hope, faith also implied a separation from its object, that is, from God, whereas love united one with the beloved.[14] This shows with great clarity the difference between the denominations. By contrast to an understanding of God, the aim of which is the perfection of nature until it is super-natural, Luther's view is that in fact the overriding action which derives from God can take place in a way appropriate to God and to faith through the word alone. In this way the basis of salvation remains strictly outside man as a promise which is believed. Indeed, man himself is drawn out of himself towards the word of Christ. The word must guarantee that faith is *extra nos*; this is essential if what is said of God is to be certain. Luther says: 'Our theology is certain, for it places us outside ourselves.'[15] The word makes it possible to distinguish between God and man and to maintain this distinction. To desire more than the word alone would result in having less. For what God gives to man for his salvation can be imparted essentially and effectively only through the word. 'One thing and that alone is needful for life, for righteousness and for Christian freedom. That is the holy word of God, the gospel of Christ ... We should regard it as certain and irreversible: the soul can do without everything except the word of God, without which nothing at all is of any use to us. But whoever possesses the word is rich and needs nothing, for it is the word of life, of truth, of light, of peace, of righteousness, of salvation, of joy, of freedom, of wisdom, of power, of grace, of glory and of everything good, in an inestimable way ... But since these promises of God are holy, true, righteous, free and peaceable words, and are full of pure goodness, it comes about that the soul which clings to them with firm faith is so united, or even absorbed by them, that it does not merely partake in them, but becomes sated and drunk with all their power ... As the word is, so it makes the soul.'[16]

The second question is, *how far does the course of history matter?* Luther's way of speaking of God can be suspected of implying a radical retreat into the inner life and spiritualization, which, if it does not abandon the relationship between God and the world, God and history and God and living reality, does not seem to take adequate account of them. One ought not to be too hasty in qualifying this impression, which is caused by the fact that what Luther says of God is concentrated to an extraordinary degree upon the conscience. 'Conscience', of course, does not mean what it means in the usual but question-able interpretation of the conscience as the essence of the normative contents of the consciousness and of the autonomous faculties of judgement, that is, the presence of the decisive norm and appeal within man himself. Rather, what Luther understands by 'conscience' is the reliance of man upon the word, in the sense that he is always, and not merely in some particular respect but in his very person, claimed, commanded, questioned, and subjected to judgement, so that in one way or another he is always a determined, listening and receiving conscience; either confused or arrogant in an imaginary freedom, which means his bondage to the powers of this world; or assured and comforted in obedient attention to God, which is true freedom with regard to the world. This understanding of the conscience is decisive for the understanding of what Luther says of God. For it makes clear that the sole aim of the apparent retreat into the inner life and spiritualization, is to locate what is said of God at the point where a universal event in the strictest sense takes place, and God and the world, and God and Satan, struggle with one another like two riders struggling to possess their mount.[17] Thus the concentration on the conscience is a concentration upon the process in which the most powerful and most strictly opposed powers that exist are at work, a process which, precisely because it is centred upon the hidden heart of man, gives rise to the most powerful consequences in his outward and visible life.

It is therefore essential to Luther's way of speaking of God, concentrating as it does upon faith alone and the word alone, not to understand God as something which exists in a remote place, outside and beyond the world, and which has nothing to do with the everyday experience of the world. On the contrary: if the word is to be believed, and faith is to be brought about by the word, then God and the world must be thought of simultaneously and together in such a way that there can sometimes be a suspicion of pantheist or even atheist language. With an amazing freedom Luther subjected theological argument in naïve theistic terms to a ruthless criticism, condemning it as rationalism disguised as devotion. Thus he says of the conception of heaven: 'The deity does not come down from heaven, like someone from a mountain, but is in heaven and remains in heaven, but at the same time is upon earth and remains upon earth ... Is there any need to discuss this at length? Surely the kingdom of heaven is upon earth. The angels are both in heaven and upon earth at once. Christians are both in the kingdom of God and upon earth, in the sense in which "on earth" is understood, as they say, *mathematice* or *localiter* ...

Ah, they speak childishly and foolishly about heaven, making a place for Christ up above in heaven, like the stork makes a nest upon a tree, and they do not know themselves what they are saying.'[18] Or again, with regard to the concept of God's omnipresence: '. . . as though God were a great and vast being who filled the world and extended beyond it, as when a sack is full of straw, and the straw sticks out at the top and the bottom.'[19] Luther portrayed the omnipresence and omnipotence of God with such perception, that in the way he speaks of God it is impossible to ignore the reality of the world. 'Thus he [God] must himself be in every creature at its very heart and in every way, all about, through and through, above and below, before and behind, so that there can be nothing more present or more deep-rooted in all creatures than God himself with his power . . . Indeed, who knows what it is that is called God? He is above the body, above the mind, above everything that one can say, or hear or think: How can such a being at the same time be wholly and entirely present in every body, creature and being everywhere, and again be bound to be and able to be nowhere, outside and above every creature and being; for our faith and the scripture testify both things of God. Here reason must give up at once and say, "Alas, there is certainly no such thing, and there must be no such thing!" '[20] 'God is not an extended, long, broad, thick, high, or deep being . . . but a supernatural and inscrutable being, who at the same time is wholly and entirely in every grain of corn, and yet is in and above and outside every creature. Thus there is no need for any fence to be built round him . . . for a body is far too great for the deity, and many thousands of deities could be contained in it, and yet it is far too small, for not a single deity could find room in it. Nothing is so small that God is not smaller, and nothing is so large that God is not larger, nothing is so short that God is not shorter, nothing is so long that God is not longer, nothing is so wide that God is not wider, nothing is so narrow that God is not narrower, and so on; he is an ineffable being above and beyond everything that one can name or think.'[21]

This presence of God in the world, which goes far beyond the conventional alternative between transcendence and immanence, and which it shows to be a completely mistaken approach to the question, is also true of history. God's omnipotence is the power at work in everything, and without it nothing would exist and nothing would happen. The rigour with which Luther maintains this idea sometimes suggests the horrible conception that God is the motor in a gigantic machine which it would be impossible to stop, even if the men were cleared away from it and carried out to die, unless one blasphemously desired God to cease to be God.[22] It is not Luther's intention to lose sight of the difficult problems that arise here. For the sake of God and of faith he does not wish to conceal them nor to leave it to the blasphemers to stir them up.

For in truth, if God is seen in his naked majesty and encountered in his concealment, which is the same thing, and the attempt is made to understand him as God, God presents the same fearful countenance which reality ultimately displays if one encounters it without God's word and without faith, and tries to think about it. The result is unrelieved despair, idolatry or atheism. But these are not fundamentally different alternatives. Luther can do no more than warn against undertaking speculation about God in his majesty, in his concealment. It is necessary to speak of God from below, beginning in the depths with the fact that the word of God became flesh, became history, and gave the power to carry out the act of preaching; that is, the starting-point must be Jesus, the crucified.[24] Of course to turn away from the hidden God and to turn towards the revealed God does not mean that the concealment of God is no longer the concern of faith. For revelation itself is concealed beneath its contrary, beneath the cross.[25] Faith is only faith because it is exposed to the forces of temptation. Consequently, it is necessary to speak of the *Deus absconditus*, in order that the revealed God may be taken seriously as God in his revelation.[26]

The last question, that of *the place of our fellow-men in what is said of God*, arises from the idea that the thought of Luther is preoccupied with a religious individualism which is concerned only with the blessedness of the individual. It is suggested that it is to this that the doctrine of justification owes its central place in Luther's theology. To answer this objection, it would be necessary to go on to consider Luther's ethics and his doctrine of the Church. We shall limit ourselves, however, to one fundamental point. Luther's ethics and his doctrine of the Church—in so far as one can use these academic classifications at all, since Luther always sees all aspects as they are involved with each other—are not as it were complementary to what he says about God, but can only be understood in their proper sense as ways of speaking about God. But it then becomes obvious, with regard to both points, how a concentration upon the word and faith which is apparently orientated entirely towards the individual also includes our fellow-men in its scope. The word which creates faith, the word of the gospel, deals with the law which accuses and slays, and therefore it deals with man under the pressure of his existence in the world, the decisive and determining aspect of which is his involvement with his fellow-men. The basic experience of man is that a demand is always being made upon him, and that he is constantly aware of having failed, and the claim which the gospel makes upon man is a response to this, a response to the voice of the law. Consequently, the expression 'in every need' in the 'Greater Catechism' is primarily exemplified in man's unfulfilled common humanity, the disappointments he has suffered and caused, and his inability to overcome hatred, to arouse trust, or to love creatively. It is the need brought about by his failure to be what he really ought to be as God's creature: the image of God who has shared our humanity. If the essence of the gospel is that God shares our humanity, then faith can do nothing other than be effective in love. Faith is really no less than the courage to love on the basis of love received in faith, the freedom to love on the basis of the liberating promise of love.

But on no account must the distinction between faith and love laid down here be obscured. Because, as Luther says, faith is the doer and love the deed,[27] everything depends upon the source of the doer's life. Consequently the relationship between faith and love corresponds to the relationship between doctrine and life. Life is usually given precedence over doctrine, but instead Luther gives the pre-eminence to doctrine, precisely for the sake of the life created and desired by God. Doctrine is heaven, life is the earth.[28] For doctrine, the word of God, is, to put it briefly, the bread of life.

Thus with regard to the Church, our humanity is not displayed in the first instance in the manifestations of the common life of the Church, but in the fundamental event which makes the Church into the Church, the word of faith, which takes place between one person and another, and reveals its divinity by making men human. The community of the Church, which is based upon what takes place in the word, is an indication that true community ultimately lives entirely by the word and by faith. For what takes place in the true word is love. Thus the word of God, by making faith possible, also makes love possible; for—this is the source and the conclusion of all that is said about God—God is love, or as Luther, who was horrified at Erasmus's frigid, ice-cold way of speaking about God,[29] said with the full assurance of ultimate certainty: 'A glowing furnace full of love'.[30]

NOTES

Chapter 1: Luther's linguistic innovation

1. 30, 3; 386, 14–17 (1531).
2. 30, 3; 386, 17–387, 1 (1531).
3. 30, 3; 385, 17–386, 3 (1531).
4. 30, 3; 522, 2–8 (1532).
5. On the following passages cf. WA, Br 1; 404, No. 179, 15–18 (22. 5. 1519); 407, No. 181, 9 f. (24. 5. 1519); 408, No. 182, 11 ff. (30. 5. 1519); WA, Br 2; 96, No. 283, 8 f. (1. 5. 1520) 98, No. 284, 15 f. (5. 5. 1520). Further references in K. Aland, 'Die Theologische Fakultät Wittenberg und ihre Stellung im Gesamtzusammenhang der Leucorea während des 16. Jahrhunderts', in *450 Jahre Martin-Luther-Universität Halle-Wittenberg* I (1952), 155 ff., esp. 169 f.
6. WA, Br 1; 99, No. 41, 8–13 (18. 5. 1517). Bonn Ed. (2nd Ed.) 6; 5, 7–12.
7. WA, Br 1; 170, No. 74, 33–38 (9. 5. 1518).
8. Cf. esp. H. Stephan, *Luther in den Wandlungen seiner Kirche* (1907; 2nd ed., 1951); A. Herte, *Das katholische Lutherbild im Bann der Luther-kommentare des Cochläus I–III* (1943); E. W. Zeeden, *Martin Luther und die Reformation im Urteil des deutschen Luthertums. Studien zum Selbst-verständnis des lutherischen Protestantismus von Luthers Tode bis zum Beginn der Goethezeit I. II* (1950–52); H. Bornkamm, *Luther im Spiegel der deutschen Geistesgeschichte. Mit ausgewählten Texten von Lessing bis zur Gegenwart* (1955).
9. The letter itself is lost, but the statement can be reconstructed from a letter of Ulrich Zasius to Zwingli on 13th November 1519 (*Corpus Reformatorum* 93; 222, 11 f.) and a letter of Zwingli to Oswald Myconius on 4th January 1520 (*Corpus Reformatorum* 94; 250, 11).
10. On this expression cf. below, pp. 27ff.
11. Cf. 40, 1; 526, 2–527, 9 (1531).

Notes

Chapter 2: Luther's person

1. E. Fuchs, *Gesammelte Aufsätze* I (1959), 281 ff.; *Gesammelte Aufsätze* II (1960), 424 ff.
2. Letter to Knebel, 22. 8. 1817 (No. 7848). *Goethes Werke*, Weimar (1887 ff.), IV, 28; 227, 23–28. Cf. also H. Bornkamm, *Luther im Spiegel der deutschen Geistesgeschichte*, 1955, 134.
3. F. G. Klopstock, *Die deutsche Gelehrtenrepublik*, Pt. I, 1774, 170. Cf. also H. Stephan, *Luther in den Wandlungen seiner Kirche*, 2nd ed., 1951, 53.
4. *Fragmente. Von der neuern römischen Literatur*, 1767. *Sämtliche Werke*, ed. by B. Suphan 1, 372. Cf. also H. Bornkamm, op. cit., 123.
5. Fr. Schlegel, *Geschichte der alten und neuen Literatur*, 1812. *Sämtliche Werke* 2, 178 f. Cf. also H. Bornkamm, op. cit., 163 f.
6. 15; 37, 4–6. 17–20. 38, 7–15 (1524); Bonn Ed. 2; 450, 31–34. 451, 7–10. 25–34.
7. 10, 3; 214, 15 f. (1522).
8. 8; 685, 4–15 (1522); Bonn Ed. 2; 308, 5–17.
9. WA, TR 1; 16, 13 No. 46 (1531).
10. G. E. Lessing, *Briefe an den Herrn P. betr. Fall Lemnius*, 1753. In: *Sämtliche Schriften*, ed. by K. Lachmann, 3rd ed., 1886–1924, V, 43 f. Cf. also H. Bornkamm, op. cit., 118.
11. E. Grossmann, *Beiträge zur psychologischen Analyse der Reformatoren Luther und Calvin*, 1958, 20.
12. 47; 90, 35 (1538).
13. 33; 106, 26–30 (1531).
14. 8; 573, 30–574, 10 (1521); Bonn Ed. 2; 189, 9–24.
15. 1; 557, 33–558, 15 (1518); Bonn Ed. 1; 57, 5–33.
16. 54; 185, 14–186, 16 (1545); Bonn Ed. 4; 427, 14–428, 10.

Chapter 3: Luther's words

1. 30, 2; 573, 7 f. 10–16. 573, 18–574, 6 (1530); Bonn Ed. 4; 171, 22 f. 25–32. 34–40.
2. WA, Br 1; 72, No. 28, 4–13 (26. 10. 1516).
3. 32; 4, 16 ff. (1530).
4. 30, 2; 340, 13–341, 3 (1530); Bonn Ed. 4; 135, 18–24.
5. 27; 251, 16 (1528).
6. 10, 1, 1; 728, 9–21 (1522).
7. 50; 657, 2 f. (1539). 54; 179, 13 f. (1545); Bonn Ed. 4; 421, 15 f.
8. 50; 658, 2–4 (1539).

9. 1; 154–220: 'The Seven Penitential Psalms with a commentary in German'.

10. 9; 1–115 (on Augustine, Peter Lombard, Tauler, etc.). Other material has so far only appeared in a separate edition: *Luthers Randbemerkungen zu Gabriel Biels Collectorium in quattuor libros sententiarum und zu dessen Sacri canonis missae expositio*, ed. by H. Degering, 1933.

11. 3 and 4; 1–526. Fascicules of a new edition of the first lectures on the Psalms began to appear in 1963, provided with an exhaustive apparatus: 55, 1 (Glosses) and 55, 2 (Scholia).

12. 56.

13. 57.

14. 56; 274, 14 (1515); Bonn Ed. (2nd Ed.) 5; 242, 11.

15. 18; 610, 5 (1525); Bonn Ed. 3; 103, 40 f.

16. 2; 436–618.

17. 5; 1–673.

18. 39, 1; 334–584 (1537–1540).

19. In WA, DB 3 and 4.

20. 30, 2; 636, 16–20 (1530); Bonn Ed. 4; 183, 24–28.

21. Cf. nn. 16 and 17.

22. 51; 561, 9–12 (1541); Bonn Ed. 4; 373, 10–13.

23. 51; 469, 17–26. 29 f. (1541); Bonn Ed. 4; 322, 14–323, 2. 5 f.

24. Cf. n. 9.

25. 1; 247–256 (1518). 2; 57–65 (1519). 2; 74–130 (1519). 6; 11–19 (1519). 6; 20–22 (1519). 7; 194–229 (1520); Bonn Ed. 2; 38–59.

26. 2; 131–142 (1519); Bonn Ed. 1; 154–160.

27. 2; 680–697 (1519); Bonn Ed. 1; 161–173.

28. 2; 738–758 (1519); Bonn Ed. 196–212. 6; 349–378 (1520); Bonn Ed. 1; 299–322.

29. 2; 724–737 (1519); Bonn Ed. 1; 185–195.

30. 2; 709–723 (1519); Bonn Ed. 1; 174–184.

31. 6; 61–75 (1520); Bonn Ed. 1; 213–226.

32. 2; 162–171 (1519).

33. 6; 1–8 (1519). 6; 33–60 (1520).

34. 6; 196–276 (1520); Bonn Ed. 1; 227–298.

35. 7; 12–38 (1520); Bonn Ed. 2; 1–27.

36. 30, 1.

37. 35.

38. H. Dannenbauer, *Luther als religiöser Volksschriftsteller*, 1930, 30.

39. 30, 2; 637, 19–22 (1530); Bonn Ed. 4; 184, 25–28.

Notes

Chapter 4: Luther's actions

1. In Enea Silvio Piccolomini, *De ritu, situ, moribus et conditione Theu-toniae descriptio*. Translated into German in *Das Buch der Reformation*, ed. by K. Kaulfuss-Diesch, 1917, 21 f.
2. 1; 627, 27–31 (1518); Bonn Ed. 1; 145, 36–146, 4.
3. 6; 404, 11 f. (1520); Bonn Ed. 1; 363, 33 f.; cf. Eccles. 3: 7.
4. 6; 404, 14 f. (1520); Bonn Ed. 1; 364, 3 f.
5. 6; 405, 27–31 (1520); Bonn Ed. 1; 365, 12–16.
6. Cf. esp. 6; 204, 25–32 (1520); Bonn Ed. 1; 229, 27–34.
7. 6; 406, 7–11. 13–18 (1520); Bonn Ed. 1; 365, 29–33, 35–41; Woolf, I, 111 f.
8. 8; 682, 12–16. 23 f. 682, 31–683, 17 (1522); Bonn Ed. 2; 305, 17–21. 29. 305, 37–306, 21.
9. WA, Br 2; 455 f., No. 455, 75–94 (5. 3. 1522); Bonn Ed. (2nd Ed.) 6; 105, 1-20.
10. 10, 3; 18, 8–19, 7. 11–13 (1522); Bonn Ed. 7; 369, 25–370, 1. 5–7.
11. vv. 1226–1228, 1236 f.
12. 40, 2; 46, 5 ff. 51, 1 ff. 8 ff. (1531). 40, 1; 39, 10 f. 48, 10 ff. (1531) 194 f. Cf. below, pp. 171 f.
13. 40, 1; 645, 4–6 (1531).
14. 40, 1; 181, 8 f. (1531).
15. 40, 1; 182, 1–5 (1531).
16. 4; 9, 18 f. (1513/15).
17. *Virtus* (virtue) was, as a consequence of the use of Aristotelian psychology and ethics, a basic concept in the scholastic doctrine of grace, which took the form of a doctrine of supernatural, so-called 'theological' virtues. As early as the first lectures on the Psalms, following the linguistic usage of the Vulgate in the Psalms, Luther took the word *virtus* as strictly applying to God, that is, as the power through which God is mighty in faith, so that man can call God his *virtus*. E.g. 3; 117, 6 f. (1513/15). Cf. also below and also pp. 90 ff., 152 ff.
18. WA, Br 2; 135, No. 309, 22–29 (9. 7. 1520).
19. WA, Br 2; 210 f., No. 351, 20–24 (4. 11. 1520).
20. WA, Br 2; 242, No. 365, 9–11. 16–21 (29. 12. 1520).
21. 6; 484–573; Bonn Ed. 1; 426–512.

Chapter 5: Philosophy and theology

1. WA, Br 1; 17, No. 5, 40–44 (17. 3. 1509).
2. 56; 371, 17–27 (1515/16).

3. S. th. I q. 1 a. 8 ad 2.
4. 9; 43, 5 (1510/11).
5. 9; 23, 7 (ca. 1509).
6. 9; 27, 22–24 (ca. 1509).
7. WA, Br 1; 171, No. 74, 72 f. (9. 5. 1518).
8. WA, Br 1; 170, No. 74, 38–40 (9. 5. 1518).
9. WA, Br 1; 150, No. 61, 41–43 (22. 2. 1518).
10. 3; 176, 3–14 (1513/15); Bonn Ed. (2nd Ed.) 5; 107, 12–25.
11. 3; 419, 25–420, 1 (1513/15); Bonn Ed. (2nd Ed.) 5; 136, 10–26.
12. 56; 371, 2–372, 25 (1515/16).
13. 1; 226, 14–18. 26–28 (1517); Bonn Ed. (2nd Ed.) 5; 323, 21–24. 324, 8–10.
14. E.g. 1; 226, 8 (1517).
15. 39, 1; 174–180 (1536).
16. 39, 1; 174, 9 f. (1536).
17. 40, 1; 361, 8 f. (1531).

Chapter 6: The letter and the Spirit

1. Cf. above, pp. 76 ff.
2. E.g. 30, 2; 300, 4–6 (1530).
3. Cf. above, p. 86.
4. E.g. 1; 507, 34 f.
5. Cf. above, pp. 39 ff.
6. 3; 12, 2–4 (1513/15). Now also: 55, 1, 1; 4, 25–27.
7. 3; 255, 41–256, 38 (1513/15); Bonn Ed. (2nd Ed.) 5; 112, 32–113, 37.
8. 3; 258, 8 f. (1513/15).
9. Ps. 119: 125.
10. 4; 365, 5–14 (1513/15); Bonn Ed. (2nd Ed.) 5; 204, 11–21.
11. 3; 12, 32–35 (1513/15). Now also: 55, 1, 1; 6, 30–34; Bonn Ed. (2nd Ed.) 5; 46, 27 f. 47, 25–28.
12. 4; 439, 20 f. (1513/15).
13. 4; 82, 19–24 (1513/15); Bonn Ed. (2nd Ed.) 5; 181, 3–9.
14. 3; 150, 27 (1513/15).
15. 4; 450, 39–451, 27 (1513/15).
16. 4; 272, 22–24 (1513/15).
17. 4; 376, 13–16 (1513/15).
18. 5; 27, 8 (1519).
19. 18; 181, 30–36 (1525).
20. 50; 245, 1–18; 246, 20–29 (1538); Bonn Ed. 4; 316; 5–16; 317, 3–9.

Notes

Chapter 7: The law and the gospel

1. 3; 12, 2 f. (1513/15). Cf. above, p. 98.
2. 7; 502, 34 f. (1521).
3. 40, 1; 207, 17 f. ([1531] 1535).
4. 36; 9, 6–8; 10, 2–5 (1532).
5. 39, 1; 361, 1–4 (1537).
6. 2; 453, 2–6 (1519).
7. 40, 1; 41, 2–44, 2 (1531).

Chapter 8: The twofold use of the law

1. 12; 260, 9–21 (1523).
2. 10, 1, 1; 17, 7–12 (1522).
3. 10, 1, 1; 627, 1–3 (1522).
4. 18; 653, 30 (1525); Bonn Ed. 3; 142, 13.
5. 18; 605, 32–34 (1525); Bonn Ed. 3; 100, 31–33.
6. 1; 183, 39–184, 10 (1517).
7. 39, 1; 361, 30 (1537).
8. 39, 1; 477, 7 (1538).
9. 39, 1; 353, 37 f. (1538).
10. 40, 1; 603, 5–11 (1531).
11. E.g. 40, 1; 519, 11–520, 10 (1531).

Chapter 9: Person and work

1. 1; 355, 4 f. (1518); Bonn Ed. (2nd Ed.) 5; 379, 24 f.
2. S. th. I q. 1 a. 8 ad q. 2 2 a. 2 ad 1.
3. 39, 1; 175, 9 f. (1536).
4. 18; 164, 25–27 (1525).
5. 40, 1; 361, 7–9 (1531).
6. 'Contradictory' here and in the passage that follows is not used in the conventional sense of the word of the contradiction arising from the affirmation and negation of one and the same statement, but in the historical sense of conflicting powers and claims.
7. 40, 2; 18, 4 f. (1531).
8. 39, 1; 47, 23 f. (1535).
9. 40, 1; 208, 5 ff. (1531).
10. 39, 2; 22, 1 f. (1539).
11. 40, 1; 526, 2 f. 8 f. (1531).
12. 40, 1; 527, 7–9 (1531).

13. 4; 3, 28. 32 f. (1513/15).
14. 56; 3, 13 f. 4, 11 (1515/16).
15. 56; 268, 4–7 (1515/16).
16. WA, Br 1; 70, No. 27, 29–32 (19. 10. 1516); Bonn Ed. (2nd Ed.) 6; 2, 27–30.

Chapter 10: Faith and love

1. 17, 2; 97, 7–11 (1525).
2. 17, 2; 98, 5 (1525).
3. 10, 1, 1; 100, 8–101, 2 (1522).
4. 12; 559, 20–31 (1523).
5. 4; 362, 35–363, 2 (1513/15).
6. 4; 319, 8–10 (1513/15).
7. 4; 350, 15 f. (1513/15); Bonn Ed. (2nd Ed.) 5; 201, 26 f.
8. 4; 342, 11–13 (1513/15).
9. 56; 441, 15 f. (1515/16); Bonn Ed. (2nd Ed.) 5; 280, 13–15.
10. 56; 442, 15–21 (1515/16); Bonn Ed. (2nd Ed.), 5; 281, 1–7.
11. 56, 264, 16–21 (1515/16). Instead of *gemitu cordis, voce* operis, *opere corporis,* I read: *gemitu cordis, voce* oris, *opere corporis.* I owe this illuminating conjecture to Dr. R. Schwarz, Tübingen.
12. 39, 1; 83, 16 f. (1536).
13. 39, 1; 252, 8–12 (1537).
14. 39, 1; 521, 5–522, 3 (1539).
15. 39, 1: 176, 5–177, 14 (1536).
16. Cf. above pp. 159 f.
17. WA, DB 7; 10, 10, 9–15 (1522).
18. WA, DB 7; 10, 6–9 (1522).
19. 40, 1; 282, 3–6 (1531).
20. 40, 1; 285, 5–7 (1531).
21. 6; 204, 25 f. 31 f. (1520); Bonn Ed. 1; 229, 27 f. 33 f.
22. 6; 205, 6–13 (1520); Bonn Ed. 1; 230, 1–8.
23. 6; 207, 26–30 (1520); Bonn Ed. 1; 232, 21–25.
24. 6; 206, 8–13 (1520); Bonn Ed. 1; 231, 3–8.
25. 6; 217, 12–15 (1520); Bonn Ed. 1; 242, 7–11.
26. 6; 206, 33–36 (1520); Bonn Ed. 1; 231, 29–32.
27. 7; 21, 1–4 (1520); Bonn Ed. 2; 11, 6–9. Cf. below, pp. 212. Woolf, I, 357.
28. Cf. above, pp. 68 f.
29. 40, 1; 200, 10–201 (1531).
30. 40, 2; 46, 5–8 (1531).

31. 40, 2; 51, 1–3 51, 8–52, 2 (1531).
32. 39, 1; 282, 16 (1537).
33. 40, 1; 589, 8 (1531).

Chapter 11: The kingdom of Christ and the kingdom of the world

1. 40, 1; 596, 1–11 (1531).
2. 51; 239, 22–30 (1534/35).
3. 6; 407, 10–15. 17–19. 22 f. 408, 8–11 (1520); Bonn Ed. 1; 366, 30–35. 366, 37–367, 1. 4. 30–33; Woolf I, 113 f.
4. 6; 408, 17–25 (1521); Bonn Ed. 1; 367, 39–368, 8.
5. 11; 249, 24–27. 33–35 (1523); Bonn Ed. 2; 364, 33–37. 365, 4–7.
6. 11; 251, 1 f. (1523); Bonn Ed. 2; 366, 7 f.
7. 11; 249, 36–250, 7 (1523); Bonn Ed. 2; 365, 7–15.
8. 11; 251, 2–18 (1523); Bonn Ed. 2; 366, 8–24.
9. 11; 251, 35–252, 3 (1523); Bonn Ed. 2; 367, 5–10.
10. 27; 417, 13–418, 4 (1528).
11. 51; 242, 1–8. 15–19 (1534/35).
12. 11; 267, 30–268, 14 (1523); Bonn Ed. 2; 382, 21–36.
13. 51; 217, 10–12 (1534/35).
14. 51; 239, 39 ff. (1534/35).
15. 11; 271, 35–272, 3 (1523); Bonn Ed. 2; 386, 13–17.
16. 11; 257, 19–23. 257, 32–258, 3 (1523); Bonn Ed. 2; 372, 21–25. 372, 36–373, 3.
17. 52; 26, 21–27 (1544).
18. 32; 467, 15 (1530/32).
19. 32; 467, 18–20 (1530/32).
20. 32; 467, 22–25 (1530/32).
21. 51; 240, 27–26 (1534/35).

Chapter 12: Man as a Christian and man in the world

1. 4; 511, 11–13 (1513/15).
2. 4; 483, 7 f. (1513/15).
3. 3; 435, 37–39 (1513/15).
4. 56; 232, 34–233, 19 (1515/16).
5. 10, 2; 294, 21–23. 27–29 (1522); Bonn Ed. 2; 351, 18–21. 26–28.
6. 30, 1; 308, 19–22 (1529).
7. 40, 1; 174, 3 (1531).
8. 40, 1; 176, 1–8 (1531).
9. 40, 1; 175, 3–6 (1531).

10. 5; 163, 28 f. (1519).
11. E.g. Gal. 2: 6.
12. 32; 316, 6–7. 10–29 (1530/32).
13. 32; 389, 36–390, 1. 390, 8–18. 33–38 (1530/32).
14. 11; 255, 12–21 (1523); Bonn Ed. 2; 370, 16–25.

Chapter 13: Freedom and bondage

1. 40, 2; 327, 11–329, 2 (1532). Cf. also the printed version: 327, 17–328, 35 (1538).
2. In two versions: the German version, 7; 12–38; Bonn Ed. 2; 1–27, and the revised and extended Latin version, 7; 39–73.
3. 18; 551–787; Bonn Ed. 3; 94–293.
4. 7; 21, 1 f. (1520); Bonn Ed. 2; 11, 6 f.; Woolf, I, 357.
5. 7; 57, 24–26 (1520).
6. 7; 28, 14–16 (1520); Bonn Ed. 2; 18, 10 f.; Woolf, I, 366.
7. 7; 21, 3 f. (1520); Bonn Ed. 2; 11, 8 f.; Woolf, I, 357.
8. 7; 36, 3 f. (1520); Bonn Ed. 2; 25, 17–19; Woolf, I, 376.
9. 1; 699, 5–10. 18–22 (1518).
10. E.g. 40, 1; 42, 11. 47, 1. 204, 6 etc. (1531).
11. 10, 2; 15, 15–18 (1522); Bonn Ed. 2; 314, 37–315, 1.
12. 10, 2; 18, 15–20 (1522); Bonn Ed. 2; 317, 8–13.
13. 10, 2; 15, 24–27 (1522); Bonn Ed. 2; 315, 8–12.
14. 10, 3; 15, 6–12 (1522); Bonn Ed. 7; 368, 14–20.
15. 10, 3; 18, 11 f. (1522); Bonn Ed. 7; 369, 28 f.
16. 18; 326, 15. 327, 2 f. (1525); Bonn Ed. 3; 64, 35. 65, 5 f.
17. 30, 1; 234, 21–26 (1529).
18. 1; 147, 38 (1516); Bonn Ed. (2nd Ed.) 5; 316, 11.
19. 1; 224, 15–18 (1517); Bonn Ed. (2nd Ed.) 5; 321, 3–6.
20. 1; 225, 1 f. (1517); Bonn Ed. (2nd Ed.) 5; 321; 24 f.
21. 1; 225, 27 f. (1517); Bonn Ed. (2nd Ed.) 5; 322, 23 f.
22. 1; 354, 5 f. (1518); Bonn Ed. (2nd Ed.) 5; 378, 21 f.
23. 7; 146, 4–8 (1520).
24. 7; 146, 27–33 (1520).
25. 18; 636, 28–30 (1525); Bonn Ed. 3; 127, 30–32.
26. 18; 636, 30–637, 4 (1525); Bonn Ed. 3; 127, 32–40.
27. 18; 781, 6–13 (1525); Bonn Ed. 3; 285, 25–33.
28. 18; 638, 8 f. (1525); Bonn Ed. 3; 129, 4 f.
29. 18; 615, 31–33 (1525); Bonn Ed. 3; 108, 30–33.
30. Cf. 18; 617, 24–618, 18 (1525); Bonn Ed. 3; 110, 1–24.
31. Cf. 18; 669, 20–26 (1525); Bonn Ed. 3; 159, 4–11.

32. 18; 614, 39 f. (1525); Bonn Ed. 3; 107, 31 f.
33. 18; 615, 33 f. (1525); Bonn Ed. 3; 108, 33 f.
34. 18; 614, 1–16 (1525); Bonn Ed. 3; 106, 25–107, 3.
35. 18; 635, 18–22 (1525); Bonn Ed. 3; 126, 23–28.
36. Cf. above pp. 193 ff.
37. On the following passage cf. 39, 1; 175, 1–177, 14 (1536).

Chapter 14: God hidden and revealed

1. 39, 1; 176, 24 (1536).
2. 40, 2; 327, 11 (1532). 327, 37 (1538).
3. 1; 354, 17 ff. (1518); Bonn Ed. (2nd Ed.) 5; 379, 1 ff. 1; 361, 31 ff. (1518); Bonn Ed. (2nd Ed.) 5; 388, 4 ff. 1; 613, 21 ff. (1518); Bonn Ed. 1; 128, 29 ff.
4. E.g. 40, 3; 193, 6 f. (1532/33).
5. 1; 362, 18 f. (1518); Bonn Ed. (2nd Ed.) 5; 388, 29 f.
6. 1; 613, 23 f. (1518); Bonn Ed. 1; 128, 32 f.
7. 1; 354, 21 f. (1518); Bonn Ed. (2nd Ed.) 5; 379, 5 f.
8. 1; 354, 27 f. (1518); Bonn Ed. (2nd Ed.) 5; 379, 11 f.
9. Cf. 40, 3; 193, 6 ff. (1532/33).
10. WA, TR 1; 72, 16–21 No. 153 (1531/32); Bonn Ed. 8; 25, 14–20.
11. Cf. 18; 613, 24 (1525); Bonn Ed. 3; 106, 24.
12. WA, TR 4; 490, 24–26, No. 4777 (1530 ff.).
13. 49; 257, 39 f. 258, 17–19 (1542).
14. 19; 206, 31–33. 207, 3–13 (1526).
15. Cf. 56; 299, 27 ff. (1515/16); Bonn Ed. (2nd Ed.) 5; 248, 8 ff. 6; 562, 8 ff. (1520); Bonn Ed. 1; 499, 17 ff.
16. Cf. 40, 2; 330, 1 f. (1532).
17. Cf. 1; 557, 33 ff. (1518); Bonn Ed. 1; 57, 5 ff. Cf. above pp. 38 ff.
18. Cf. 40, 1; 603, 5 ff. (1531).
19. Cf. 40, 1; 34, 11 ff. (1531).
20. 40, 1; 34, 22–26 (1531).
21. 18; 784, 36–39. 785, 12–14 (1525); Bonn Ed. 3; 290, 7–10. 27–29.
22. 18, 611, 4 (1525); Bonn Ed. 3; 104, 26 f.
23. 18; 605, 27 ff. 611, 7 (1525); Bonn Ed. 3; 100, 25 ff. 104, 31.
24. 39, 1; 229, 22–24 (1537).
25. 39, 1; 229, 2–5 (1537).
26. 1; 613, 21–23 (1518); Bonn Ed. 1; 128, 29–32.
27. 1; 238, 14–21 (1517); Bonn Ed. 1; 9, 16–23; Woolf, I, 42–43.
28. 40, 1; 75, 9–77, 9. 78, 3–6. 79, 7–80, 1 (1531). Cf. 40, 2; 392, 3 ff. (1532).

Notes

29. 40, 3; 337, 11 (1532/33).
30. 4; 82, 14–21 (1513/15).
31. 18; 633, 7–15 (1525); Bonn Ed. 3; 124, 16–26.
32. 31, 1; 249, 16–250, 1 (1530).
33. 31, 1; 250, 24 f. 28 f. 35–37 (1530).
34. 56; 423, 19 f. (1515/16).
35. 39, 1; 176, 33–35 (1536).
36. 39, 1; 177, 3 f. (1536).
37. 18; 710, 1 ff. (1525); Bonn Ed. 3; 204, 32 ff.
38. 18; 718, 15–20 (1525); Bonn Ed. 3; 213, 35–41.
39. 48; 241, 2 ff. (16. 2. 1546).

The way Luther speaks of God

1. Fröhliche Wissenschaft, p. 125.
2. 18; 603, 10–12. 22–24. 28 f. 605, 32–34 (1525); Bonn Ed. 3; 97, 31–33. 98, 6–9. 13–15. 100, 31–33.
3. WA, Br 1; 17, No. 5, 43 f. (17. 3. 1509). Cf. above, pp. 76 f.
4. 30, 1; 132, 32–133, 8 (1529); Bonn Ed. 4; 4, 21–32.
5. Feuerbachs Sämtliche Werke, ed. by W. Bolin, and Fr. Jodl, VII (1903), 311.
6. K. Barth, 'Ludwig Feuerbach' (1926). In: K. Barth, Die Theologie und die Kirche, 1928, 212–239, esp. 230 f.
7. 56; 306, 26–307, 15 (1515/16); Bonn Ed. (2nd Ed.) 5; 250, 10–30.
8. 5; 167, 38–168, 7 (1519/21).
9. 40, 1; 360, 2–361, 1 (1531).
10. 18; 718, 28–31 (1525); Bonn Ed. 3; 214, 11–14.
11. 18; 614, 1–26 (1525); Bonn Ed. 3; 106, 25–107, 15.
12. E.g. 6; 516, 30–32 (1520); Bonn Ed. 1; 448, 8–11.
13. W. H. van de Pol, Das reformatorische Christentum im phänomenologischer Betrachtung, 1956, 259 ff. Cf. my article 'Worthafte und sakramentale Existenz. Ein Beitrag zum Unterschied zwischen den Konfessionen', in Im Lichte der Reformation. Jahrbuch des Evangelischen Bundes VI, 1963, 5–29, esp. 13 ff. Reprinted in my book Wort Gottes und Tradition. Studien zu einer Hermeneutik der Konfessionen, 1964, 197–216; an English translation appears under the title 'Word and Sacrament' in The Word of God and Tradition, Collins, London, and Fortress Press, Philadelphia, 1968, 206–224.
14. S. th. 1, II q. 66 a. 6.
15. 40, 1; 589, 8 (1531). Cf. above, p. 174.
16. 7; 50, 33–51, 3. 53, 15–18. 26 f. (1520).

17. 18; 635, 17–22 (1525); Bonn Ed. 3; 126, 23–28. Cf. above pp. 222 f.
18. 26; 421, 16–422, 10 (1528); Bonn Ed. 3; 445, 32–446, 5.
19. 26; 339, 27–29 (1528); Bonn Ed. 3; 404, 20–22.
20. 23; 135, 3–6. 137, 25–31 (1527).
21. 26; 339, 33–340, 2 (1528); Bonn Ed. 3; 404, 26–38.
22. 18; 712, 19–24 (1525); Bonn Ed. 3; 207, 26–32.
23. E.g. 40, 1; 75, 9–80, 2 (1531).
24. 18; 689, 18–25 (1525); Bonn Ed. 3; 182, 8–17.
25. E.g. 18; 633, 7–23 (1525); Bonn Ed. 3; 124, 16–37.
26. 18; 685, 3–686, 13 (1525); Bonn Ed. 3; 177, 12–178, 25.
27. 17, 2; 98, 25 (1525). Cf. above p. 159.
28. 40, 2; 51, 8 f. (1531). Cf. above pp. 172.
29. 18; 611, 5 (1525); Bonn Ed. 3; 104, 27 f.
30. 36; 425, 13 (1532).

INDEX

Index

Index

Law (contd.),
double significance of, 125-40
fulfilled in the gospel, 134
and the gospel, 110-24, 142, 147
and Christian preaching, 116-18
distinction between, 111-18, 120-4
and justification, 137-9
man's knowledge of, 135, 136
negation of Christ, 144
Stoic doctrine, 136
theological use of, 142
time of, 147
Law of nature, 126-7, 128-9
Law of obligation (moral law), 127-8
and freedom of choice, 127-9
Leipzig: disputation in, 72
Life: doctrine and, 172
Lombard, Peter, 49
'Look, to': meaning and ambiguity, 194-6
Love, 68, 167
in Christian and secular actions, 208
the deed, 159
and faith, 68, 159-74, 266-7
and freedom, 212-13
Luther: antithesis in his thought, 24, 25
attitude to criticism, 54
Catholic interpretation, 30
coarseness, 53-4
disputations, 47, 51
evaluation of his inherited traditions, 22-4
excommunication and outlawry, 65, 72
German writings, 55

and human authority, 30-1
ignorance concerning, 19-20
and indulgences, 74
Latin writings, 48
lectures, 47, 48, 49-51
letters, 56-7
linguistic innovation, 27-30
person and theology, 32-3
personality, 33-4
and philosophy, 78, 141
preaching, 44, 45, 52
reasons for entering monastery, 34-6
and the Reformation, 60-75
Reformation experience, 39-41
and sacramental doctrine, 74
and salvation, 37-9
and scriptural interpretation, 49-52, 96-9
sermons, 46-7, 52-3
student, 15-16
study and understanding of, 22-4
style, 29
Table Talk, 57
temptations, 37-9
theological studies, 36-7
and theology, 93, 96-9
preferred to philosophy, 77
translation, 51-2, 58
university professorship, 15, 16-19, 76-7
on university reform, 19
vocation, 17
volume of work, 43-4
way of speaking of God, 242-67
and the word alone, 63-8
and the word of God, 44-6
writings, 46-57
circulation, 57-8

284